COLLINS

GLASGOW
STREETFINDER
COLOUR ATLAS

Contents

HarperCollins*Publishers*

Published by Collins
An imprint of HarperCollins*Publishers*
77-85 Fulham Palace Road, Hammersmith, London W6 8JB

The HarperCollins website address is:
www.**fire**and**water**.com

Copyright © HarperCollins*Publishers* Ltd 2000
Mapping © Bartholomew Ltd 1985, 1987, 1989, 1992, 1993, 1995, 1997, 2000

Collins® is a registered trademark of HarperCollins*Publishers* Limited

Bartholomew website address is: www.bartholomewmaps.com

Based upon the Ordnance Survey Mapping with the permission of The Controller of Her Majesty's
Stationery Office © Crown copyright 399302

The contents of this publication are believed correct at the time of printing. Nevertheless, the publisher
can accept no responsibility for errors or omissions, changes in the detail given, or for any expense or
loss thereby caused.

The representation of a road, track or footpath is no evidence of a right of way.

Printed in Hong Kong   ISBN 0 00 448998 5   MI 10245   ANN

e-mail: roadcheck@harpercollins.co.uk

Key to map symbols

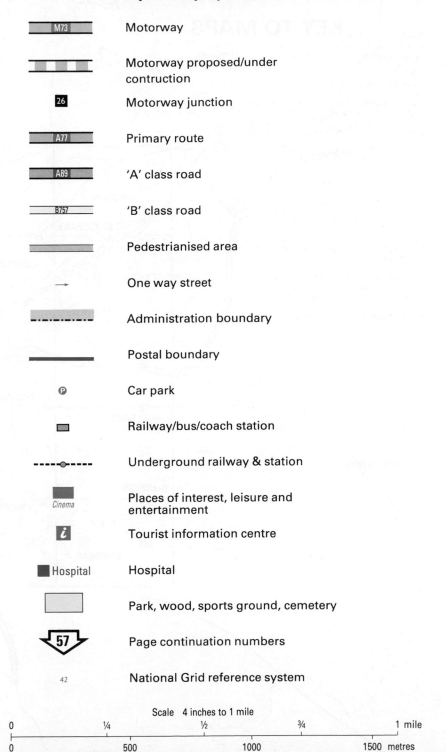

M73	Motorway
	Motorway proposed/under contruction
26	Motorway junction
A77	Primary route
A89	'A' class road
B757	'B' class road
	Pedestrianised area
→	One way street
	Administration boundary
	Postal boundary
Ⓟ	Car park
	Railway/bus/coach station
	Underground railway & station
Cinema	Places of interest, leisure and entertainment
i	Tourist information centre
Hospital	Hospital
	Park, wood, sports ground, cemetery
57	Page continuation numbers
42	National Grid reference system

Scale   4 inches to 1 mile

0   ¼   ½   ¾   1 mile

0   500   1000   1500 metres

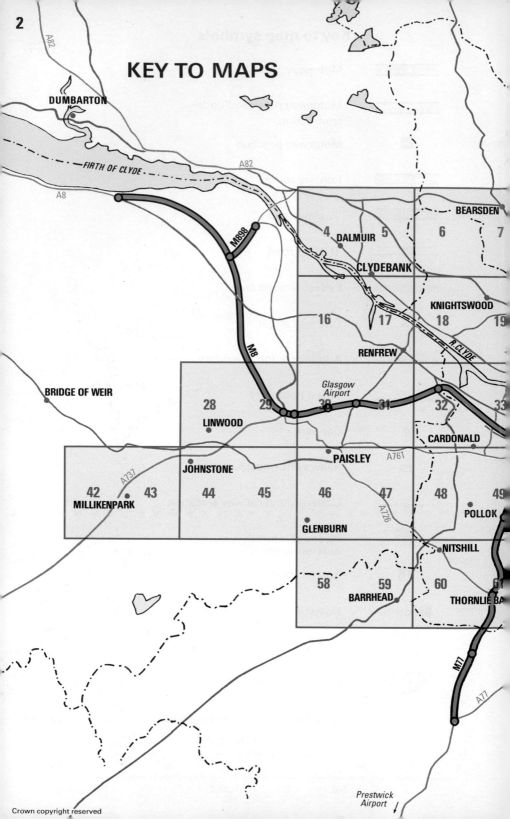

KEY TO MAPS

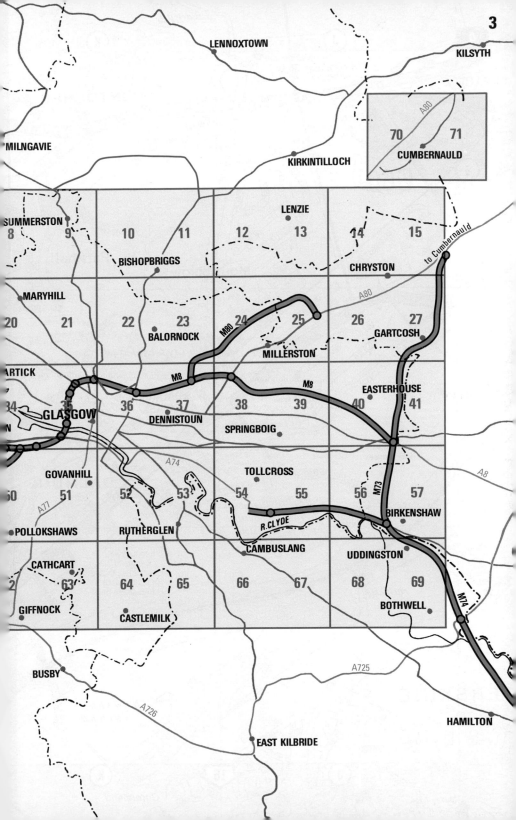

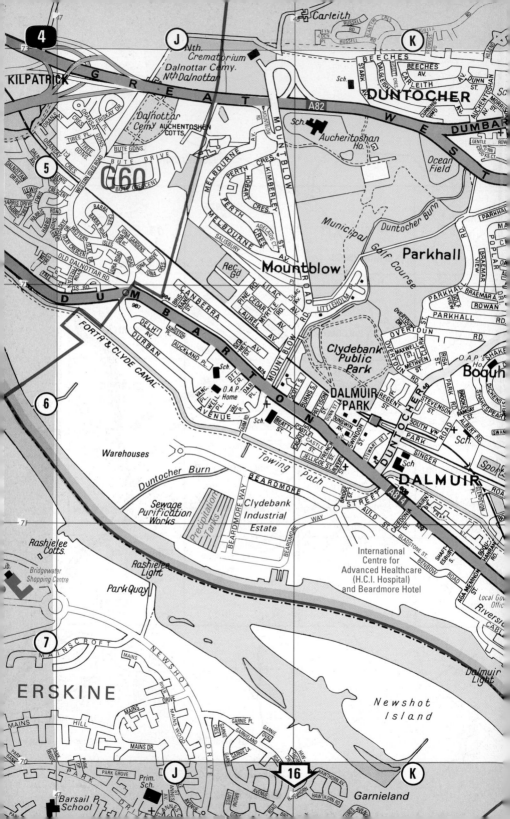

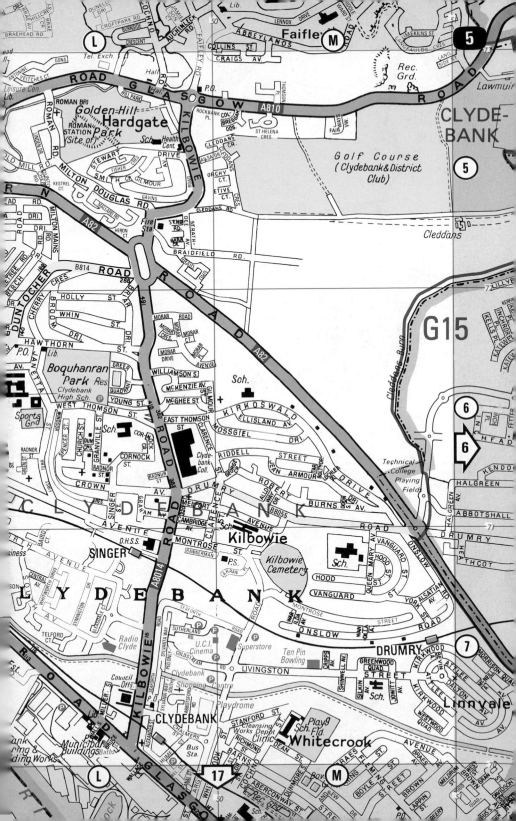

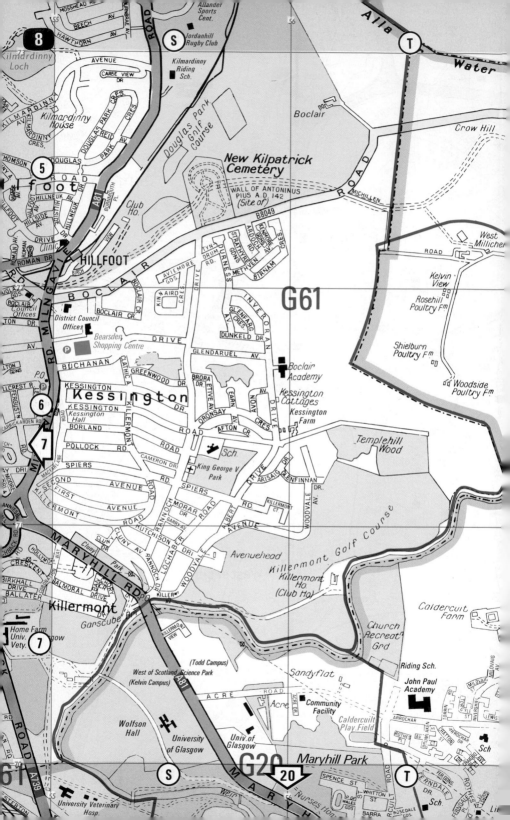

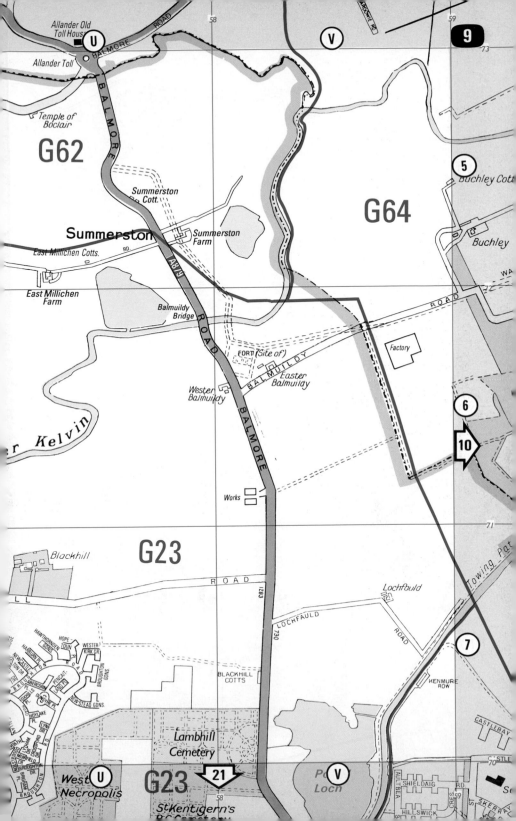

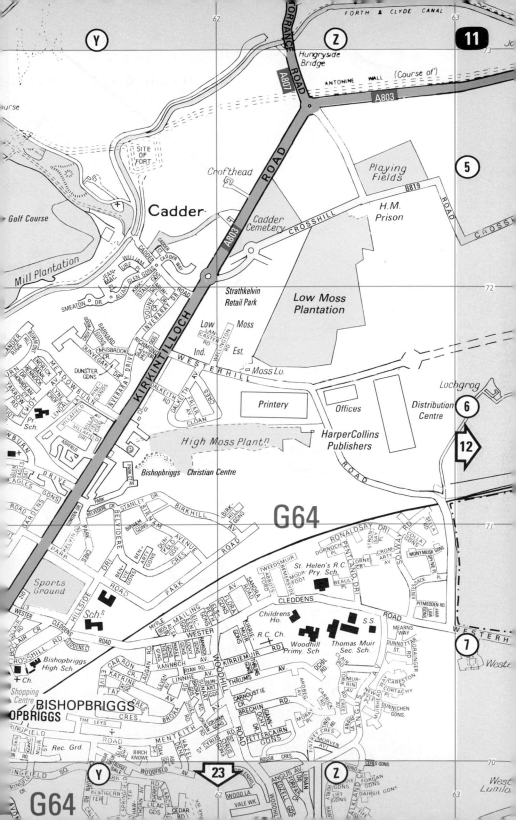

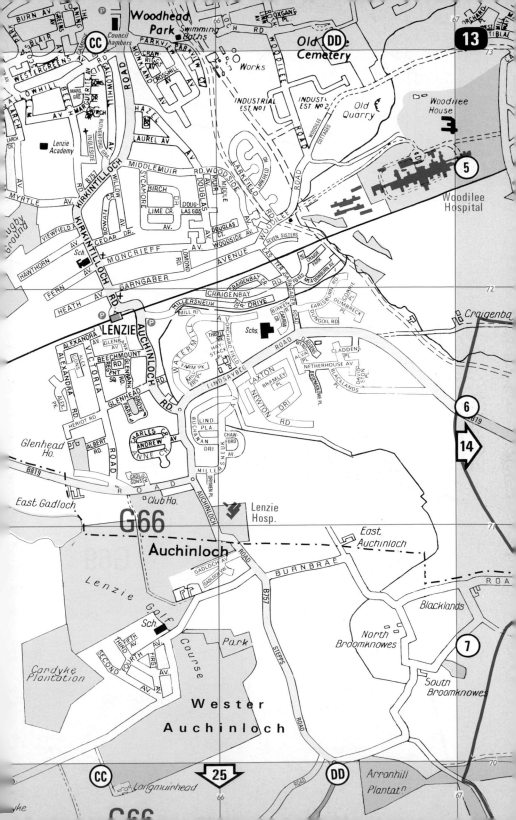

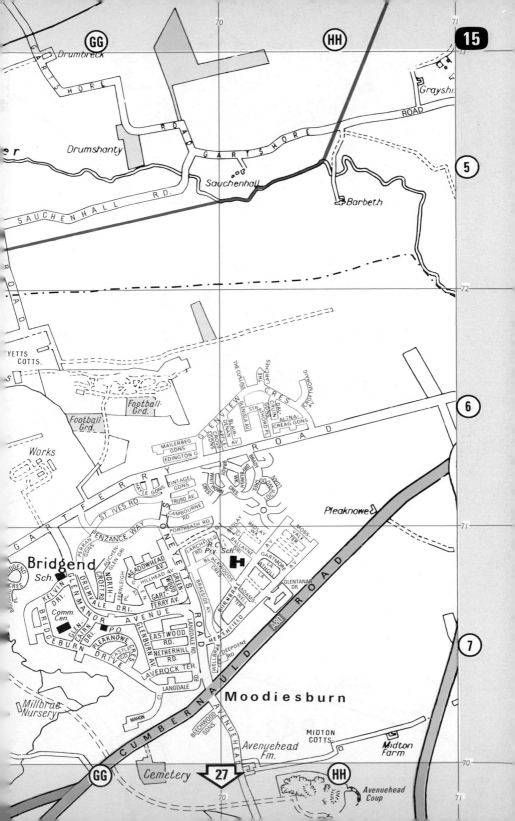

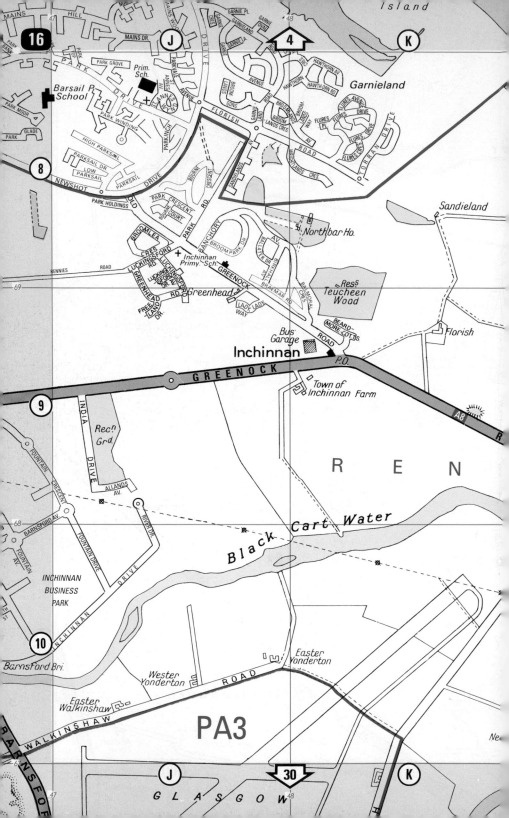

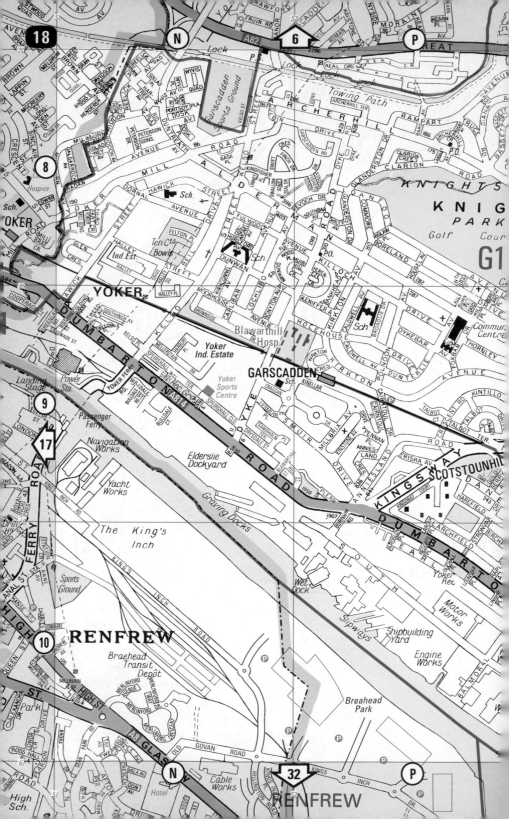

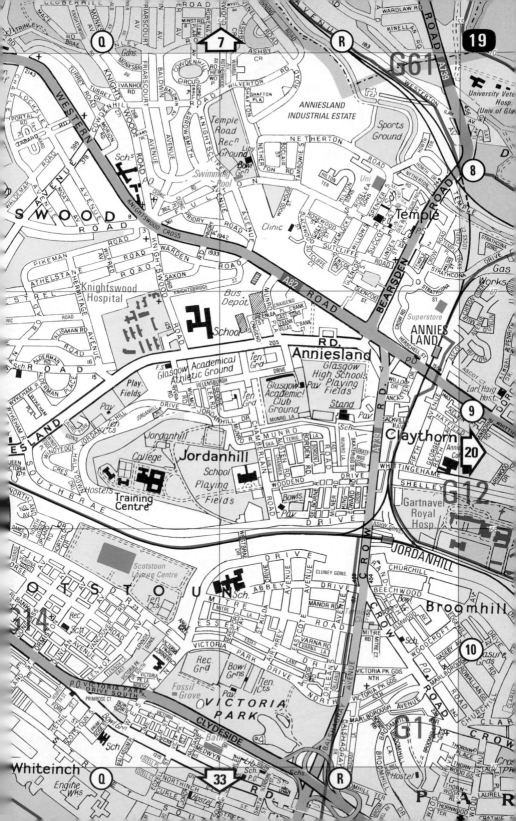

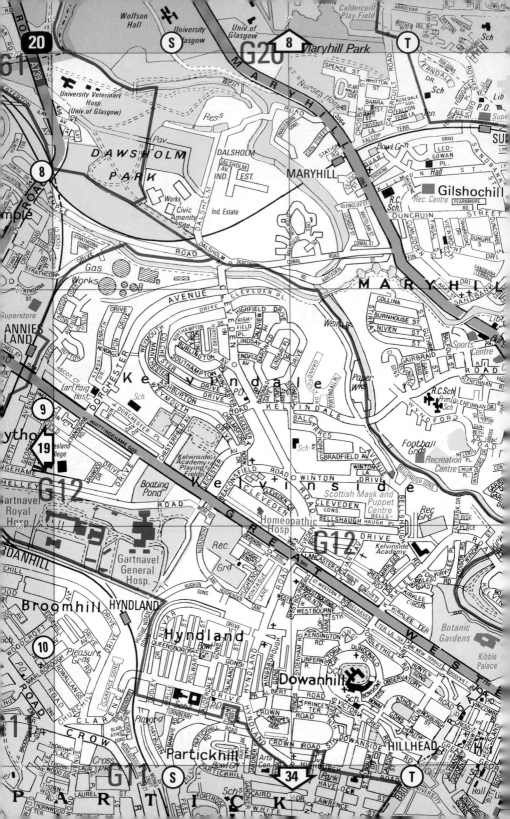

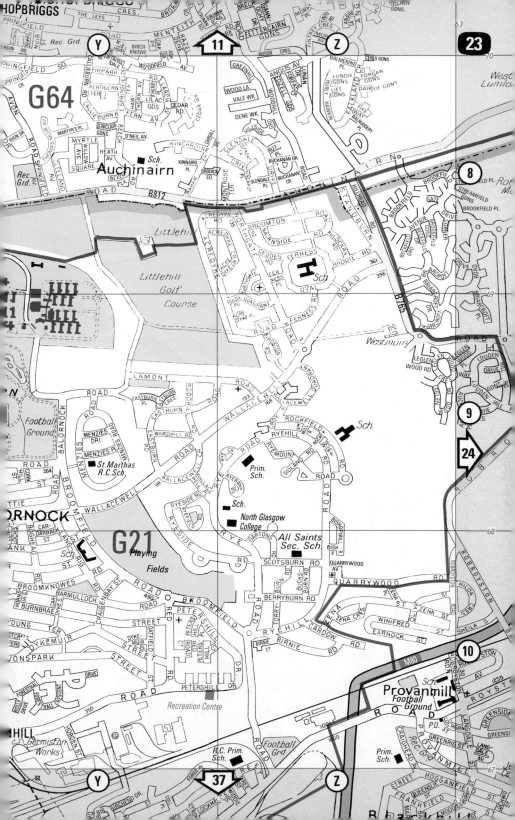

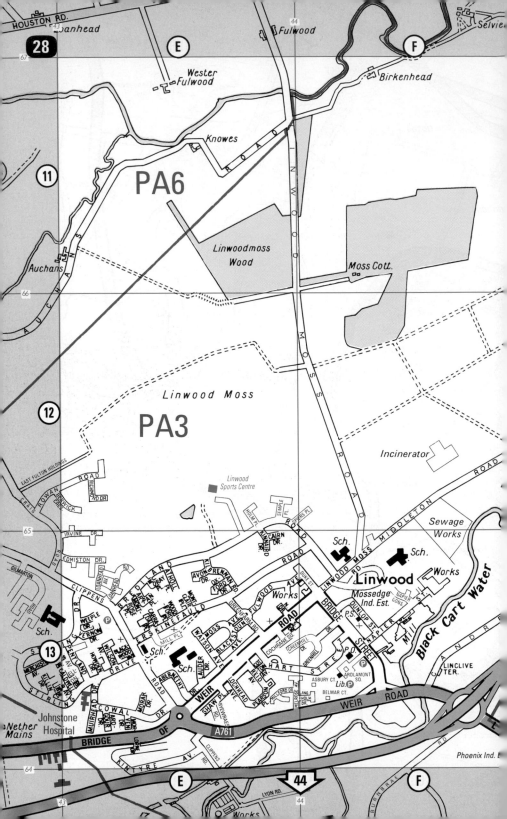

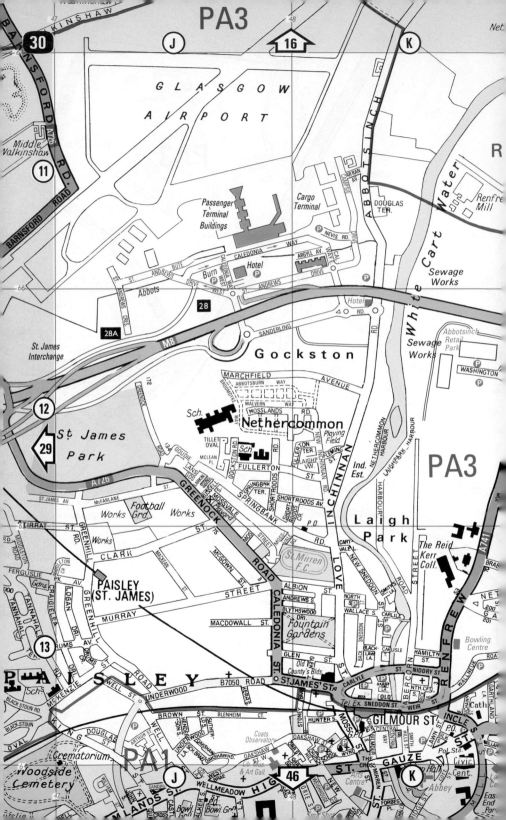

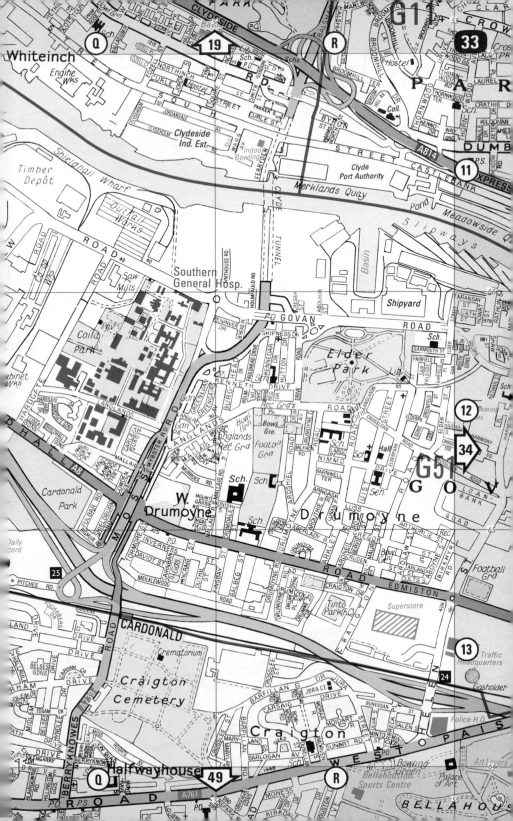

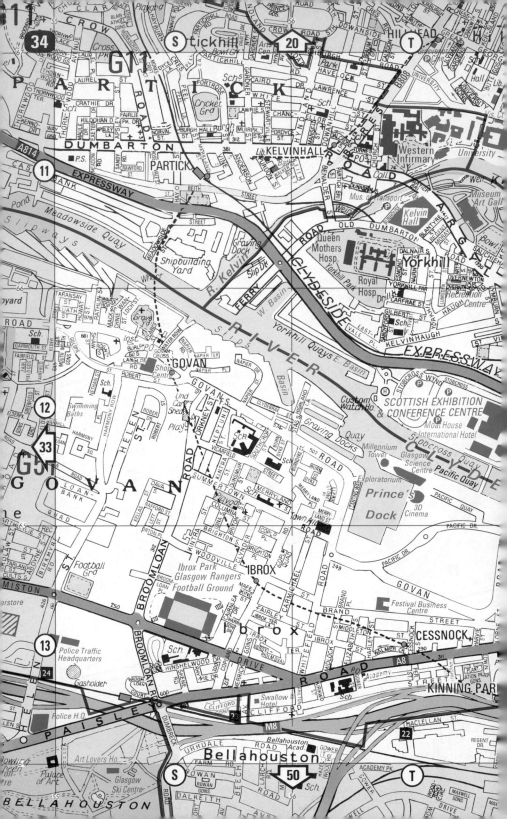

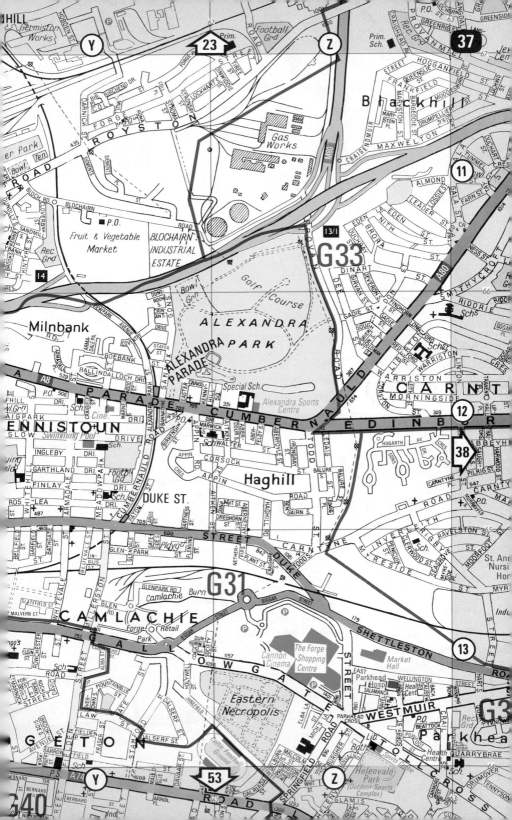

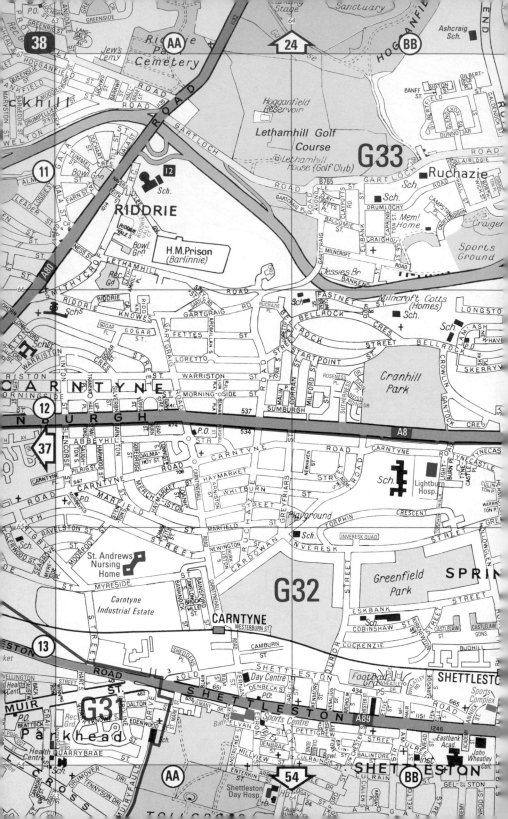

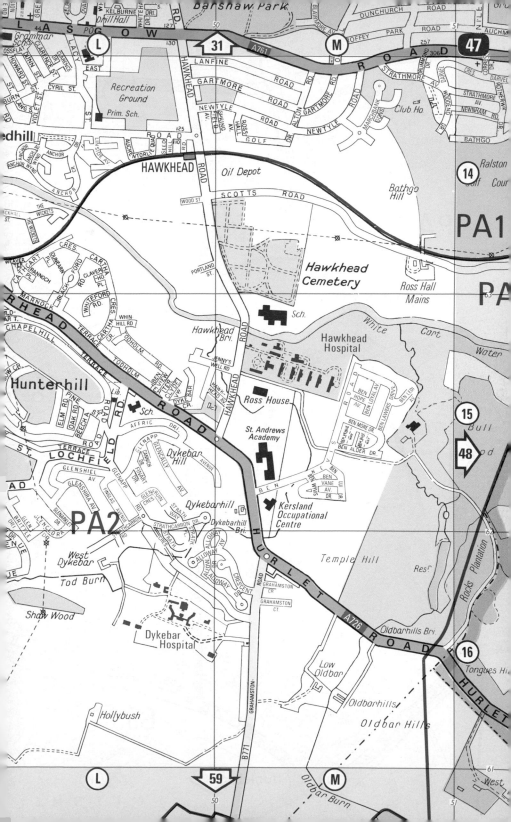

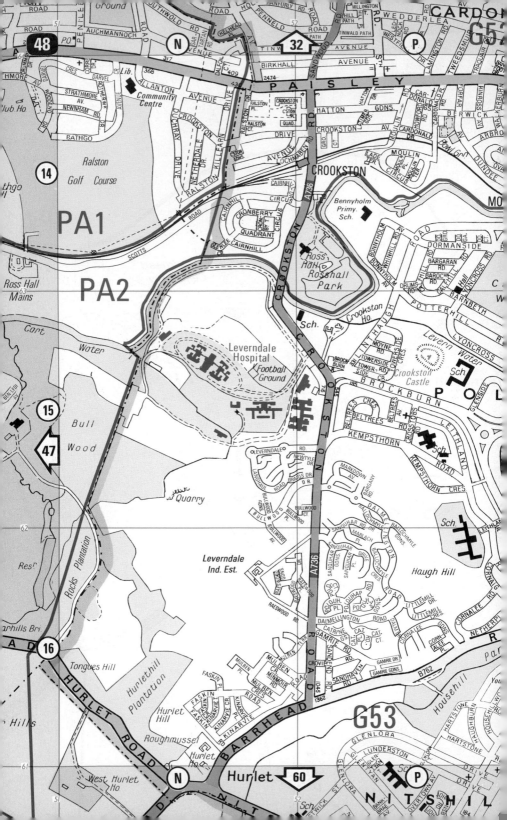

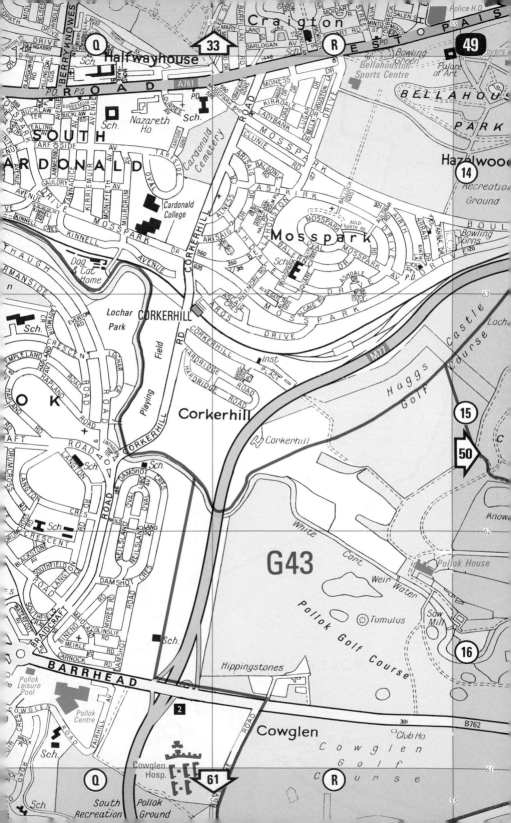

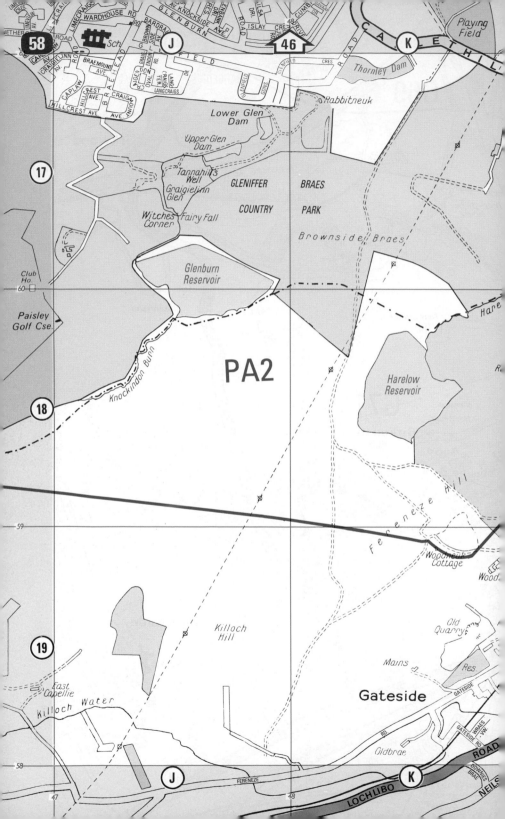

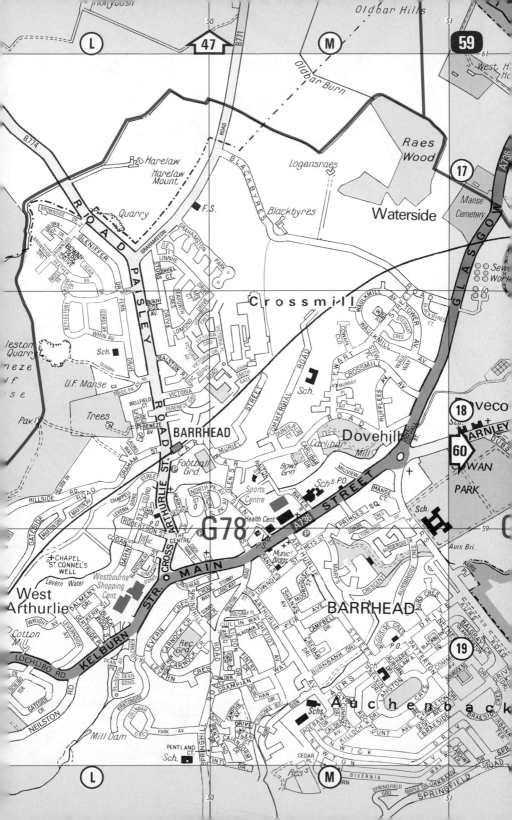

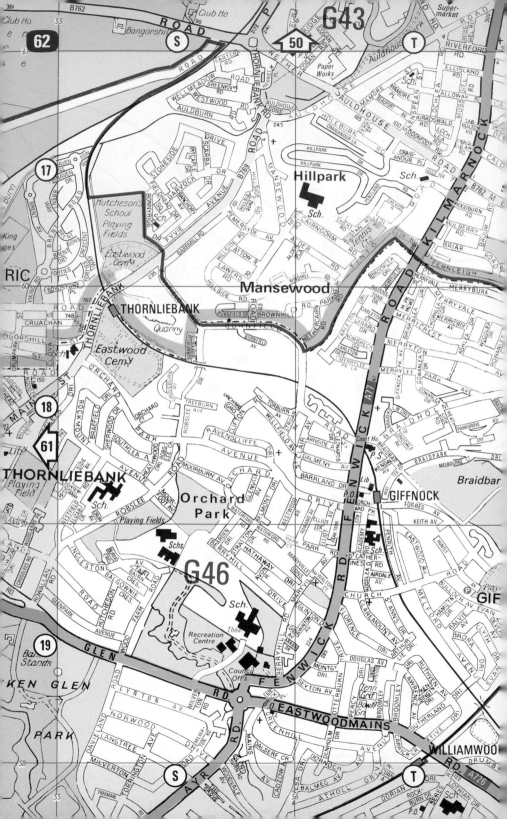

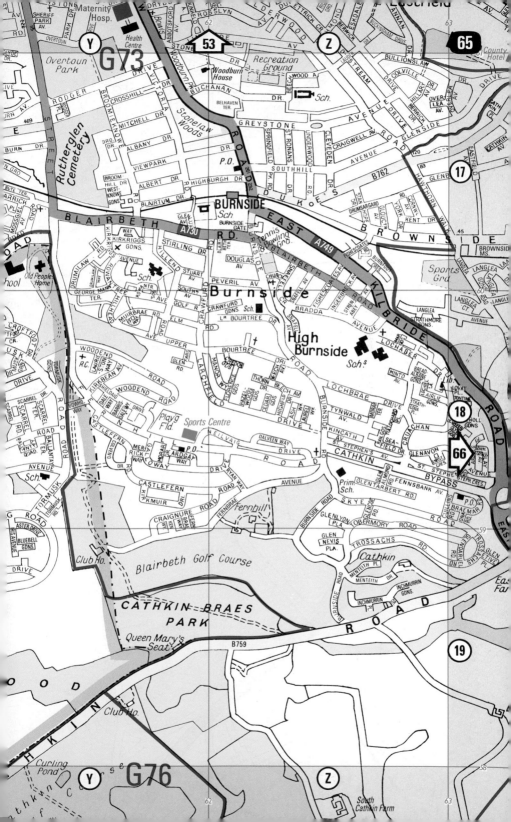

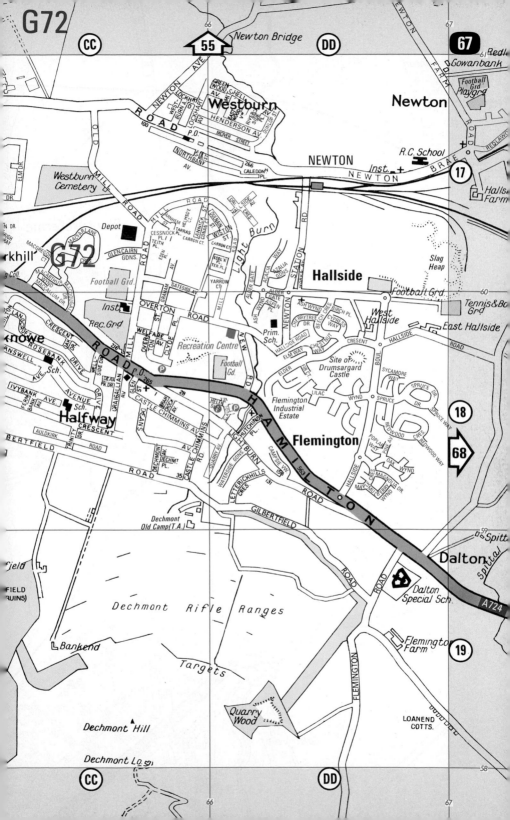

Glasgow

Information

Contents

The City of Glasgow began life as a makeshift hamlet of huts huddled round a 6thC church, built by St. Mungo on the banks of a little salmon river - the Clyde. It was called Gleschow, meaning 'beloved green place' in Celtic. The cathedral was founded in 1136; the university, the second oldest in Scotland, was established in the 15thC; and in 1454 the flourishing medieval city wedged between the cathedral and the river was made a Royal burgh. The city's commercial prosperity dates from the 17thC when the lucrative tobacco, sugar and cotton trade with the New World flourished. The River Clyde, Glasgow's gateway to the Americas, was dredged, deepened and widened in the 18thC to make it navigable to the city's heart.

By the 19thC, Glasgow was the greatest shipbuilding centre in the world. From the 1820s onwards, it grew in leaps and bounds westwards along a steep ridge of land running parallel with the river. The hillside became encased in an undulating grid of streets and squares. Gradually the individualism, expressed in one-off set pieces characteristic of the 18thC and early 19thC, gave way to a remarkable coherent series of terraced squares and crescents of epic proportions - making Glasgow one of the finest of Victorian cities. But the price paid for such rapid industrialisation, the tremendous social problems manifest in the squalor of some of the worst of 19thC slums, was high. Today the city is still the commercial and industrial capital of the West of Scotland. The most notorious of the slums have been cleared but the new buildings lack that sparkling clenchfisted Glaswegian character of the 19thC. Ironically, this character was partially destroyed when the slums were cleared for it wasn't the architecture that had failed, only the bureaucrats, who designated such areas as working class ghettos.

Districts
Little remains of medieval Glasgow, which stood on the wedge of land squeezed between the cathedral and the River Clyde. Its business centre was The Cross, a space formed by the junction of several streets - the tall, square Tolbooth Steeple, 1626, in the middle. Opposite is Trongate, an arch astride a footpath, complete with tower and steeple salvaged from 17thC St. Mary's Church - destroyed by fire in 1793. The centre of 20thC Glasgow is George Square, a tree-lined piazza planned in 1781 and pinned down by more than a dozen statues including an 80 foot high Doric column built in 1837 to carry a statue of Sir Walter Scott. Buildings of interest: the monumental neo-Baroque City Chambers 1883-88 which takes up the east side and the Merchants' House 1874, on the west. To the south of the square, in a huddle of narrow streets, is the old Merchant City. Of interest here is the elegant Trades House, 85 Glassford Street, built by Robert Adam in 1794. An elegant Ionic portico stands on a rusticated ground storey flanked by domed towers. Hutcheson's Hospital, 158 Ingram Street, is an handsome Italianate building designed by David Hamilton in 1805. Nearby is Stirling's Library, originally an 18thC private residence, it became the Royal Exchange in 1827 when the Corinthian portico was added. To the north west is Kelvingrove, Victorian Glasgow at its best. Built around a steep saddle of land, landscaped by Paxton in 1850 and lined along its edge with handsome terraces.

Last but not least are the banks of the River Clyde. From Clyde Walkway on the north bank you can see: the Suspension Bridge of 1871 with its pylons in the form of triumphal arches; 17thC Merchants' Steeple; the Gothic Revival St. Andrew's R.C. Cathedral of 1816; the church, built 1739, in nearby St. Andrew's Square is a typical copy of London's St. Martin-in-the-Fields.

City of Glasgow Local Information Guide

Useful Information

Area of City 79 sq. miles (approx)

Population (Glasgow City)
1998 619,680

Electricity
240 volts A.C.

Emergency Services
Police, Fire and Ambulance. Dial 999
on any telephone.

Licensing Hours
Public Houses
City Centre
Daily except Sundays 11 a.m.-12 midnight
Sundays 12.30 p.m.-12 midnight

Restaurants, Hotels and Public Houses
with catering facililities; same as above
but can be extended for drinks with
meals.

Information Bureau

Tourist Information Centres:
11 George Square, Glasgow, G2 1DY
0141 204 4400

Town Hall, 9a Gilmour Street,
Paisley, PA1 1DD
0141 889 0711

Glasgow International Airport (Abbotsinch),
Paisley, PA3 2ST
0141 848 4440

7a Clyde Square, Greenock, PA15 1NB
01475 722007

Help & Advice

British Telecom Scotland (Glasgow Area)
Westergate Chambers,
11 Hope Street, Glasgow, G2 6AB.
All Enquiries 0141 220 1234
FREEFONE 0800 309 409

Chamber of Commerce
30 George Square, G2 1EQ.
0141 204 2121

Citizens Advice Bureau
48 Albion Street, Glasgow, G1 1LH
0141 552 5556

119 Main Street,
Bridgeton, Glasgow, G40 1QD
0141 554 0336

27 Dougrie Drive, Castlemilk,
Glasgow, G45 9AD
0141 634 0338/9

139 Main Street (Town Hall),
Rutherglen, G73 2JJ
0141 647 5100

216 Main Street, Barrhead, G78 1SN
0141 881 2032

1145 Maryhill Road, Glasgow, G20 9AZ
0141 946 6373

4 Shandwick Square, Easterhouse,
Glasgow, G34 9DS
0141 771 2328

Drumchapel, 49 Dunkenny Square,
G15 8NE
0141 944 2612

1361-1363 Gallowgate
Parkhead
G31 4DN
0141 554 0004

Consumer Advice Centre
Nye Bevan House,
20 India Street,
Glasgow, G2 4PF
0141 287 6681

Customs and Excise
21 India Street, G2 4PZ
0141 221 3828

Enable
(Organisation for people with learning disabilities)
6th Floor
7 Buchanan Street
Glasgow, G1 3HL
0141 226 4541

H.M. Immigration Office
Public Enquiry Office
Dumbarton Court,
Admin Block D, Argyll Avenue, Glasgow
International Airport, Paisley, PA3 2TD
0141 887 2255

Housing Aid and Advice
Shelter, 53 St. Vincent Crescent,
Glasgow, G3 8NQ
0141 221 8995

Lost Property
Trains - There is a railway switchboard
number that will put you through to Lost
Property (whichever station).
0141 335 3276

Buses - Office of bus company
Elsewhere in City - Strathclyde Police.
Lost Property Department,
173 Pitt Street, G2 4JS
0141 532 2000

**Registrar of Births, Deaths and
Marriages**
1 Martha Street, G1 1JJ
0141 287 7652

Marriages only:
22 Park Circus, G3 6BE
0141 287 8350
Hours: Monday 9.15 a.m. - 5.00p.m.
Tuesday to Friday 9.15 a.m. - 4.00 p.m.

Births must be registered within twenty
one days, deaths within eights days and
marriages within three days. The
Registrar should be consulted at least
one month before intended date of
marriage.

Children First
c/o SCET, 74 Victoria Crescent Road,
Glasgow, G12 9JN
0141 334 2547

**RNID - Royal National Institute for
the Deaf**
9 Clairmont Gardens, Glasgow, G3 7LW
0141 332 0343

Samaritans
210 West George Street, Glasgow,
G2 2PQ
0141 248 4488

Shopmobility
To book a free battery powered
wheelcahir or scooter, or to request a
guide at the Sauchiehall, Saint Enoch and
Buchanan Galleries Shopping Centres.
0141 332 6486

**Society for the Prevention of
Cruelty to Animals**
Central Control Telephone Number:
0131 339 0111

Media

British Broadcasting Corporation
Queen Margaret Drive, G12 8DG
0141 339 8844

Scottish Television
Cowcaddens, G2 3PR
0141 300 3000

Morning Daily Newspapers
Daily Record
40 Anderston Quay, G3 8DA.
0141 248 7000

The Herald
195 Albion Street, G1 1QP
0141 552 6255

Scottish Daily Express
Park House, Park Circus Place,
G3 6AF
0141 332 9600

The Scotsman
Regent Court, 70 West Regent Street
G2 2QZ
0141 236 6410

Evening Daily Newspapers
Evening Times
195 Albion Street, G1 1QP
0141 552 6255

Sunday Newspapers
Scottish Sunday Express
Park House, Park Circus Place, G3 6AF
0141 332 9600

Sunday Mail
40 Anderston Quay, G3 8DA
0141 248 7000

Sunday Post
144 Port Dundas Road, G4 0HZ
0141 332 9933

Parking

Car Parking in the central area of Glasgow is controlled. Parking meters are used extensively and signs indicating restrictions are displayed at kerbsides and on entry to the central area. Traffic Wardens are on duty.

Multi-Storey Car Parks (Open 24 Hours)
Cadogan Square, G2: Cambridge Street, G2: Charing Cross, G2: Concert Square, G1: George Street, G1: Mitchell Street, G1: Oswald Street (for Central Station), G1: Sauchiehall Centre, G2:
St. Enochs Shopping Centre, G1 (not 24 Hours)

Surface Car Parks
Anderston Centre, G2: Cathedral Street, G1: Charlotte Street, G1: Dundasvale, G4: Dunlop Street, G1: Great Dovehill, G1: High Street, G1: Ingram Street, G1: King Street, G1: Little Dovehill, G1: Lilybank Gardens, G1: Moir Street, G1: Newton Street, G2: St. Andrew's Lane, G1: Spoutmouth, G1: Washington Street, G1

Post Offices

Head Post Office
47 St. Vincent Street, Glasgow G2 5QX
0141 204 3688
Open Monday to Friday 8.30a.m. - 5.45p.m. Saturdays 9 a.m. - 5.30 p.m.

Branch Offices
228 Hope Street, Glasgow G2 3PN
0141 332 4598
Open Monday - Thursday
8.30a.m. - 5.30p.m.
Friday - 9.00a.m. - 5.30p.m.
Saturday - 8.30a.m. - 5.30p.m.

87-91 Bothwell Street, Glasgow G2 7AA
0141 221 0666
Open Monday - Friday
9.00a.m.-5.30p.m.

Taxis

Glasgow has over 1400 traditional London type taxis, all licensed by the Glasgow District Council and all fitted with meters sealed and approved by the Council. A fare card stating the current tariff is displayed in a prominent position within each taxi. At the time of publishing a three mile journey costs approximately £5. The total price of each journey is shown on the meter and is calculated by distance or time or a combination of both.Fares are normally reviewed annually by the council. Each taxi can carry a maximum of five passengers.

The major taxi companies in the city offer City tours at fixed prices, listing the places of interest to be visited, leaflets are available at all major hotel reception areas. Tours vary from 1 to 3 hours and in price between £15 and £45. A tour "Glasgow by Night" is also available.

Any passenger wishing to travel to a destination outside the Glasgow District Boundary should ascertain from the driver the fare to be charged or the method of calculating the fare PRIOR to making the journey.

Complaints
Any complaints regarding the conduct of a taxi driver should be addressed to the Taxi Enforcement Officer, City Building Department, 73 Hawthorn Street, Glasgow G22 6HY.
0141 287 3326

Local Government

East Dunbartonshire
PO Box 4, Tom Johnston House, Civic Way, Kirkintilloch, G66 4TJ
0141 578 8000

East Renfrewshire
Council Offices, Eastwood Park, Rouken Glen Road, Giffnock G46 6UG
0141 577 3000

Glasgow City
City Chambers, George Square, Glasgow G2 1DU
0141 287 2000

North Lanarkshire
Civic Centre, Motherwell, ML1 1TW
01698 302222

Renfrewshire
Cotton Street, Paisley, PA1 1BU
0141 842 5000

South Lanarkshire
Council Offices, Almada Street, Hamilton ML3 0AA
01698 454444

West Dunbartonshire
Council Offices
Garshake Road
Dumbarton
G82 3PU
01389 737000

Glasgow Cathedral is a perfect example of pre-Reformation Gothic architecture. Begun in 1238, it has a magnificent choir and handsome nave with shallow projecting transepts. On a windy hill to the east is the Necropolis, a cemetery with a spiky skyline of Victoriana consisting of pillars, temples and obelisks, dominated by an 1825 Doric column carrying the statue of John Knox. Other churches of interest: Landsdowne Church built by J. Honeyman in 1863; St. George's Tron Church by William Stark 1807; Caledonian Road Church, a temple and tower atop a storey-high base, designed by Alexander Thomson in 1857; a similar design is to be found at the United Presbyterian Church, St. Vincent Street, 1858, but on a more highly articulated ground storey; Queen's Cross Church 1897 is an amalgam of Art Nouveau and Gothic Revival by the brilliant Charles Rennie Mackintosh.

Churches within the central area of Glasgow are:

Church of Scotland
Glasgow Cathedral
Castle Street, G4
Renfield St. Stephen's Church
262 Bath Street, G2
St. George's Tron Church
165 Buchanan Street, G1
St. Columba Church (Gaelic)
300 St. Vincent Street, G3

Baptist
Adelaide Place Church
209 Bath Street, G2

Episcopal Church in Scotland
Cathedral Church of St. Mary
300 Great Western Road

First Church of Christ Scientist
Berkeley Street, G3

Free Church of Scotland
265 St. Vincent Street, G2

German Speaking Congregation
Services held at 7 Hughenden Terrace, G12

Greek Orthodox Cathedral
St. Luke's, 27 Dundonald Road, G12

Islamic Centre
Glasgow Central Mosque, Mosque Avenue, G5

Jewish Orthodox Synagogue
Garnethill, 29 Garnet Street, G3

Methodist
Woodlands Church
229 Woodlands Road, G3

Roman Catholic
St. Andrew's Cathedral
190 Clyde Street, G1
St. Aloysius' Church
25 Rose Street, G3

Unitarian Church
72 Berkeley Street, G3

United Free
Candlish Wynd
62 Daisy Street, G42

Buildings & Shops

Interesting Buildings

Victorian Glasgow was extremely eclectic architecturally. Good examples of the Greek Revival style are Royal College of Physicians 1845, by W.H. Playfair and the Custom House 1840, by G.L. Taylor. The Queen's Room 1857, by Charles Wilson, is a handsome temple used now as a Christian Science church. The Gothic style is seen at its most exotic in the Stock Exchange 1877, by J. Burnet. The new Victorian materials and techniques with glass, wrought and cast iron were also ably demonstrated in the buildings of the time. Typical are: Gardener's Stores 1856, by J. Baird; the Buck's Head, Argyle Street, an amalgam of glass and cast iron; and the Egyptian Halls of 1873, in Union Street, which has a masonry framework. Both are by Alexander Thomson. The Templeton Carpet Factory 1889, Glasgow Green, by William Leiper, is a Venetian Gothic building complete with battlemented parapet.

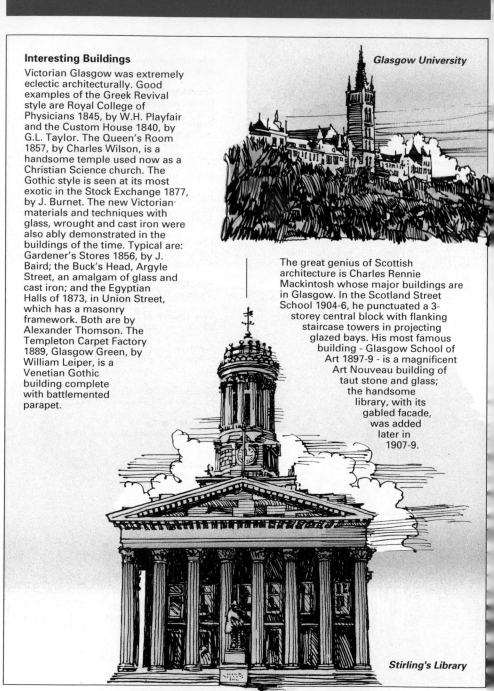

Glasgow University

The great genius of Scottish architecture is Charles Rennie Mackintosh whose major buildings are in Glasgow. In the Scotland Street School 1904-6, he punctuated a 3-storey central block with flanking staircase towers in projecting glazed bays. His most famous building - Glasgow School of Art 1897-9 - is a magnificent Art Nouveau building of taut stone and glass; the handsome library, with its gabled facade, was added later in 1907-9.

Stirling's Library

Galleries & museums

Scotland's largest tourist attraction, The
Burrell Collection, is situated in Pollok
Country Park, Haggs Road and has
more than 8,000 objects, housed in an
award winning gallery. The Museum
and Art Gallery, Kelvingrove Park,
Argyle Street, a palatial sandstone
building with glazed central court, has
one of the best municipal collections in
Britain; superb Flemish, Dutch and
French paintings, drawings, prints, also
ceramics, silver, costumes and armour,
as well as a natural history section.
The McLellan Galleries in Sauchiehall
Street provide an important venue for
touring and temporary art
exhibitions. Provand's Lordship
c1471, in Castle Street, is
Glasgow's oldest house and now a
museum of 17th-18thC furniture
and household articles (Please note;
Provand's Lordship will be closed
for major structural repairs,
throughout 1999/2000). Pollok House,
Pollok Country Park, a handsome
house designed by William Adam in
1752, has paintings by William Blake
and a notable collection of Spanish
paintings, including works by El Greco.
The Museum of Transport, housed in
Kelvin Hall, Bunhouse Road, has a
magnificent collection of trams, cars,
ships models, bicycles, horse-drawn
carriages and 7 steam locos. The
People's Palace, Glasgow Green built 1898
with a huge glazed Winter Garden, has a
lively illustrated history of the city. But the
oldest museum in Glasgow is the
Hunterian Museum, University of
Glasgow, University Avenue, opened in
1807, it has a fascinating collection of
manuscripts, early painted books, as
well as some fine archaeological and
geological exhibits.

Streets & shopping

The Oxford Street of Glasgow is
Sauchiehall (meaning 'willow meadow')
Street. This together with Buchanan
Street, The Buchanan Galleries Shopping
Centre, Argyle Street, Princes Square
and St. Enoch Centre form the main
shopping area. Here you will find the
department stores, boutiques and

Old Sheriff Court

general shops. All three streets are largely
pedestrianised, but the most
exhilarating is undoubtedly Buchanan
Street. Of particular interest is the
spatially elegant Argyll Arcade 1828,
the Venetian Gothic-style Stock
Exchange 1877, the picturesque Dutch
gabled Buchanan Street Bank building
1896 and the Glasgow Royal Concert
Hall (opened 1990). In Glasgow Green
is The Barras, the city's famous street
market, formed by the junction of
London Road and Kent Street. The
Market is open weekends.

*Museum & Art
Gallery Kelvingrove*

Entertainment

As Scotland's commercial and industrial capital, Glasgow offers a good choice of leisure activities. The city now has many theatres where productions ranging from serious drama to pantomime, pop and musicals are performed. The Theatre Royal, Hope Street is Scotland's only opera house and has been completely restored to its full Victorian splendour. The Royal Scottish National Orchestra gives classical music concerts at the Glasgow Royal Concert Hall between October and April and is the venue for the proms in June. Cinemas are still thriving in Glasgow, as are the many public houses, some of which provide meals and live entertainment. In the city centre and Byres Road, West End, there is a fair number of restaurants where traditional home cooking, as well as international cuisines, can be sampled. More night life can be found at the city's discos and dance halls.

Outdoors, apart from the many parks and nature trails, there is Calderpark Zoological Gardens, situated 6 miles from the centre between Mount Vernon and Uddingston. Here you may see white rhinos, black panthers and iguanas among many species. Departing from Anderston Quay, you can also cruise down the Clyde in 'P.S. Waverley' - the last sea-going paddle- steamer in the world.

Cinemas

ABC Cinema, 380 Clarkston Road
0141 633 2123
Glasgow Film Theatre
12 Rose Street
0141 332 6535
Grosvenor Cinema
Ashton Lane
0141 339 4298
Kelburne Cinema
(Manager), Glasgow Road, Paisley
PA1 3BD.
Odeon Film Centre
56 Renfield Street 0141 332 8701
UCG
The Forge Shopping Centre
1221 Gallowgate,
G31 4EB
0141 556 4282

Halls

City Halls, Candleriggs, G1
Couper Institute
86 Clarkston Road, G44
Langside Hall, 5 Langside Avenue, G41
Partick Burgh Hall, 9 Burgh Hall Street, G11
Woodside Hall, Glenfarg Street, G20

More information about the above G.C.C. halls contact,
Cultural and Leisure Services, 1st Floor, 32 Albion Srteet, Glasgow,
G1 5LH
0141 287 5008

Glasgow Royal Concert Hall
2 Sauchiehall Street, G2 3NY
0141 333 9123
Henry Wood Hall, 73 Claremont Street, Glasgow, G3 7JB
0141 225 3555

Theatres

Arches Theatre
30 Midland Street G1 4PR
0141 221 9736
Citizens' Theatre
119 Gorbals Street G5 9DS
0141 429 0022
King's Theatre
297 Bath Street, G2 4JN
0141 287 5022
Mitchell Theatre and Moir Hall
Granville Street G3 7DR
0141 287 4855
New Athenaeum Theatre
100 Renfrew Street G2 3DB
0141 332 5057
Pavilion Theatre
121 Renfield Street G2 3AX
0141 332 1846
Theatre Royal
282 Hope Street G2 3QA
0141 332 9000
Tramway
25 Albert Drive G41 2PE
0141 422 2023
Tron Theatre
63 Trongate, Glasgow G1 5HB
0141 552 4267

The Ticket Centre
Candleriggs, G1 1NQ
Glasgow's Central Box Office for Centre for Contemporary Arts, Citizens' Theatre, City Hall at Candleriggs, Cottier Theatre, King's Theatre, Mitchell Theatre, Tron Theatre, Scottish Exhibition Centre and Glasgow Royal Concert Hall.
Counter Service and telephone lines open:
Mon.- Sat. 9.00a.m. - 9.00 p.m. Sun. 10.00a.m. - 5.00 p.m.
0141 287 5511

Weather

The City of Glasgow is on the same latitude as the City of Moscow, but because of its close proximity to the warm Atlantic Shores, and the prevailing westerly winds, it enjoys a more moderate climate. Summers are generally cool and winters mostly mild, this gives Glasgow fairly consistent summer and winter temperatures. Despite considerable cloud the City is sheltered by hills to the south-west and north and the average rainfall for Glasgow is usually less than 40 inches per year. The following table shows the approximate average figures for sunshine, rainfall and temperatures to be expected in Glasgow throughout the year.

Weather Forecasts
For the Glasgow Area including Loch Lomond and the Clyde Coast:
Weatherline 0891 232 791 (Recording)
The Glasgow Weather Centre (Meteorological Office), St. Vincent Street, G2 5QD
0141 248 3451

Month	Hours of Sunshine	Inches of Rainfall	Temperature °C		
			Ave. Max.	Ave. Min.	High/Low
January	36	3.8	5.5	0.8	-18
February	62	2.8	6.3	0.8	-15
March	94	2.4	8.8	2.2	21
April	147	2.4	11.9	3.9	22
May	185	2.7	15.1	6.2	26
June	181	2.4	17.9	9.3	30
July	159	2.9	18.6	10.8	29
August	143	3.5	18.5	10.6	31
September	106	4.1	16.3	9.1	-4
October	76	4.1	13.0	6.8	-8
November	47	3.7	8.7	3.3	-11
December	30	4.2	6.5	1.9	-12

Sport & Recreation

For both spectator and participant, football is Glasgow's favourite sport. Both Celtic and Rangers, Scotland's most famous rival teams, have their grounds within the City. Glasgow houses Scotland's national football stadium at Hampden Park.

Badminton

Scottish Badminton Union's Cockburn Centre, 40 Bogmoor Place, G51 4TQ.
0141 445 1218

Bowling Greens

There are greens in all the main Parks. Information about clubs from the Scottish Bowling Association: 50 Wellington Street, G2 6EF.
0141 221 8999

Cricket Grounds

Huntershill Crowhill Road, Bishopbriggs, G64
Pollok Dawholm, 2060 Pollokshaws Road, G43.
West of Scotland Peel Street, G11.

Football Grounds

Broadwood (Clyde F.C.) Cumbernauld, G68
Celtic Park (Celtic F.C.) 95 Kerrydale Street, G40 3RE
Firhill Park (Partick Thistle F.C.) Firhill Road, G20 7AL
Hampden Park (Queen's Park F.C.) Somerville Drive, G42 9BA
Ibrox Stadium (Rangers F.C.) Edmiston Drive, G51 2XD
St. Mirren Park (St. Mirren F.C.) Love Street, Paisley, PA3 2EJ

Golf Courses

9 holes
Alexandra Park, Sannox Gardens, G31
Cambuslang, Westburn Drive, Cambuslang G72
King's Park, Carmunnock Road, Croftfoot, G44
Knightswood, Lincoln Avenue,G13
Ruchill, Brassey Street, G20

18 holes
Barshaw, Glasgow Road, Paisley, PA1
Douglaston, Strathblane Road,Milngavie, G62 (Five miles from Glasgow).
Elderslie, Main Road, Elderslie, PA5
Lethamhill, Cumbernauld Road, G33
Littlehill, Auchinairn Road, G74
Linn Park, Simshill Road, G44
Pollok, Barrhead Road, Pollokshaws, G43

Putting Greens
There are putting greens in some of the main parks.

Pitch & Putt
Courses at Bellahouston Park, Queen's Park and several others.

Rugby Grounds

Auldhouse (Hutchesons'/Aloysians) Thornliebank
Cartha Queens Park Haggs Road, G41
Garscube Estate Switchback Road, Maryhill, Glasgow, G61
Hughenden (Hillhead High School) Hughenden Road, G12.
New Anniesland (Glasgow Acad.) Helensburgh Drive, G13.
Old Anniesland (Glasgow High School F.P. & Kelvinside Academicals) Crow Road, G11.

Sports Centres

Barrhead, Main Street, Barrhead G78 1SW
0141 881 1900
Bellahouston 31 Bellahouston Drive, G52 1HH.
0141 427 5454
Burnhill 60 Toryglen Road, Rutherglen, G73 2JH.
0141 643 0327
Crownpoint Crownpoint Road, Bridgeton, G40 1HH.
0141 554 8274
Linwood, Brediland Road, Linwood PA3 3RA.
01505 329 461
Springburn Key Street, Springburn, G21 1LY.
0141 557 5878
Tryst, Tryst Walk, Cumbernauld G67 1EW.
01236 728138

Swimming Pools

Drumchapel, 199 Drumry Road East, G15 8NS.
0141 944 5812
Easterhouse, Bogbain Road, G34 9OU. 0141 771 7978
Elderslie, 3 Stoddard Square, Elderslie. PA5 9AS
01505 328133
Lagoon Leisure Centre, Mill St., Paisley PA1 1LZ.
0141 889 4000
North Woodside, Braid Square, G4 9YB. 0141 332 8102
Pollok Leisure Pool, Cowglen Road, G53. 0141 881 3313
Renfrew Victory Baths, Inchinnan Road, Renfrew PA4 8ND.
0141 886 2088
Scotstoun Leisure Centre 72 Danes Drive, Scotstoun, G14 9HO. 0141 959 4000
Tollcross Park Leisure Centre Wellshot Road, Tollcross G32 7QR 0141 763 1222

Tennis

There are courts in some of the main parks. Information about clubs from the Secretary of the West of Scotland Lawn Tennis Association: Mr J Stevenson 01505 814337.

Strathclyde Further Education

Anniesland College
Hatfield Drive, Glasgow, G12 0YE
0141 357 3969

Ayr College
Dam Park, Ayr, KA8 0EU
01292 265184

Bell College of Technology
Almada Street, Hamilton, Lanarkshire,
ML3 0JB
01698 283100

**Cardonald College of Further
Education**
690 Mosspark Drive, Glasgow, G52 3AY
0141 272 3333

Central College of Commerce
300 Cathedral Street, Glasgow, G1 2TA
0141 552 3941

Clydebank College
Kilbowie Road, Clydebank,
Dunbartonshire, G81 2AA
0141 952 7771

Coatbridge College
Kildonan Street, Coatbridge,
Lanarkshire, ML5 3LS
01236 422316

Cumbernauld College
Town Centre, Cumbernauld, Glasgow,
G67 1HU
01236 731811

Glasgow Caledonian University
70 Cowcaddens Road, Glasgow, G4 0BA
0141 331 3000

**Glasgow College of Building and
Printing**
60 North Hanover Street, Glasgow,
G1 2BP
0141 332 9969

**Glasgow College of Food
Technology**
230 Cathedral Street, Glasgow, G1 2TG
0141 552 3751

Glasgow College of Nautical Studies
21 Thistle Street, Glasgow, G5 9XB
0141 565 2500

James Watt College
Finnart Street, Greenock, Renfrewshire,
PA16 8HF
01475 724433

John Wheatley College
1346 Shettleston Road, Glasgow,
G32 9AT
0141 778 2426

Kilmarnock College
Holehouse Road, Kilmarnock, Ayrshire,
KA3 7AT
01563 523501

Langside College
50 Prospecthill Road, Glasgow, G42 9LB
0141 649 4991

Motherwell College
Dalzell Drive, Motherwell, Lanarkshire,
ML1 2DD
01698 232323

North Glasgow College
110 Flemington Street, Glasgow,
G21 4BX
0141 558 9001

Reid Kerr Gollege, The
Renfrew Road, Paisley, Renfrewshire,
PA3 4DR
0141 581 2222

South Lanarkshire College
Hamilton Road, Cambuslang, Glasgow,
G72 7BS
0141 641 6600

Stow College
43 Shamrock Street, Glasgow, G4 9LD
0141 332 1786

University of Glasgow
University Avenue, Glasgow, G12 8QQ
0141 339 8855

University of Paisley
High St, Paisley, PA1 2BE
0141 848 3000

University of Strathclyde
16 Richmond Street, Glasgow, G1 1XQ
0141 552 4400

Parks & Gardens

There are over 70 public parks within the city. The most famous is Glasgow Green. Abutting the north bank of the River Clyde, it was acquired in 1662. Of interest are the Winter Gardens attached to the People's Palace. Kelvingrove Park is an 85-acre park laid out by Sir Joseph Paxton in 1852. On the south side of the city is the 148-acre Queen's Park, Victoria Road, established 1857-94. Also of interest: Rouken Glen, Thornliebank, with a spectacular waterfall, walled garden, nature trail and boating facilities; Victoria Park, Victoria Park Drive, with its famous Fossil Grove, flower gardens and yachting pond. In Great Western Road are the Botanic Gardens. Founded in 1817, the gardens' 42 acres are crammed with natural attractions, including the celebrated Kibble Palace glasshouse with its fabulous tree ferns, exotic plants and white marble Victorian statues.

Alexandra
671 Alexandra Parade, G31.

Barshaw
Glasgow Road, Paisley.

Bellahouston
Dumbreck Road, G51.

Botanic Gardens
730 Great Western Road, G12.

Hogganfield
Cumbernauld Road, G33.

Glasgow Green
Greendyke Street, G40.

Kelvingrove
Sauchiehall Street, G3.

King's
325 Carmunnock Road, G44.

Linn
Clarkston Road at Netherlee Road, G44.

Pollok Country Park
Pollokshaws Road, G43

Queen's
Victoria Road, G42.

Rouken Glen
Rouken Glen Road, G46.

Springburn
Broomfield Road, G21.

Tollcross
461 Tollcross Road, G32.

Victoria
Victoria Park Drive North, G14.

Kibble Palace

The City of Glasgow has one of the most advanced, fully integrated public transport systems in the whole of Europe. The Strathclyde Transport network consists of: the local railway network, the local bus services and the fully modernised Glasgow Underground, with links to Glasgow International Airport and the Steamer and Car Ferry Services.
For information contact:
Strathclyde Transport Travel Centre
Buchanan Bus Station, Killermont Street, G2 0141 332 7133
Open everyday 6.30 a.m. - 9.30 p.m.
Telephone enquiries everyday 7.00 a.m. - 9.30 p.m.

For City services, ferry services, local train services. Free timetables are available.

Bus Services and Tours
Long Distance Coach Service
Citylink 0990 505050
National Express 0990 808080
Scottish Citylink Coaches Ltd and National Express provide express services to London and most parts of Scotland including Campbeltown, Tarbert, Ardrishaig, Inverary, Oban, Fort William, Skye, Stirling, Perth, Dundee, Arbroath, Montrose, Aberdeen, Aviemore, Inverness and Edinburgh.

Local Bus Services
A comprehensive network of local bus services is provided by a variety of operators within the City of Glasgow and also direct to the following destinations:
Airdrie, Ardrossan, Ayr, Balfron, Barrhead, Bearsden, Beith, Bellshill, Bishopbriggs, Bishopton, Blantyre, Bo'ness, Caldercruix, Cambuslang, Campsie Glen, Carluke, Clydebank, Coatbridge, Cumbernauld, Denny, Drymen, Dunfermline, Duntocher, Eaglesham, East Kilbride, Erskine, Falkirk, Glenrothes, Grangemouth, Hamilton, Irvine, Johnstone, Kilbarchan, Kilbirnie, Killearn, Kilmarnock, Kilsyth, Kirkintilloch, Kirkcaldy, Lanark, Largs, Larkhall, Lennoxtown, Lochwinnoch, Motherwell, Milngavie, Newton Mearns, Old Kilpatrick, Paisley, Prestwick, Renfrew, Saltcoats, Shotts, Stirling, Strathblane, Strathaven, Uddingston, Wishaw.

These services depart from City Centre bus stops or from Buchanan Bus Station. 0141 332 7133

Coach Hire and Day, Half Day and Extended Tours
Scottish Citylink Coaches Ltd
Private hire and seasonal tours
0990 505050

Haldane's of Cathcart
12, Delvin Road, Cathcart, G44 3AA
Private hire and tours
0141 637 2234

First Glasgow
4 Glencryan Road, South Carbrain, Cumbernauld, G67 2UL.
Private hire and seasonal tour
01236 782491

Railway Services
National Rail Passenger enquiries:
0345 484 950
ScotRail enquiries: 0345 550 033

ScotRail trains serve over 170 stations in Glasgow and Strathclyde (see map). ScotRail services operate to most destinations in Scotland.
East Coast Ltd., West Coast Ltd. and Cross Country Trains Ltd. operate services to England.

Glasgow Queen Street Station
for services to Cumbernauld, Edinburgh, Falkirk, Stirling, Perth, Dundee, Arbroath, Montrose, Aberdeen, Pitlochry, Aviemore, Inverness, Durnbarton, Balloch, Helensburgh, Oban, Fort William, Mallaig, Coatbridge, Airdrie.

Glasgow Central Station
for services to Gourock (ferry connection to Dunoon), Greenock, Wemyss Bay (ferry connection to Rothesay), Paisley, Johnstone, Largs, Ardrossan (ferry connection to Brodick), Irvine, Ayr, Girvan, Stranraer, East Kilbride, Kilmarnock, Dumfries, Motherwell, Hamilton, Lanark, Carlisle, Shotts, Edinburgh, Berwick, Newcastle.
London and destinations on West and East Coast Main Lines.

Strathclyde Transport

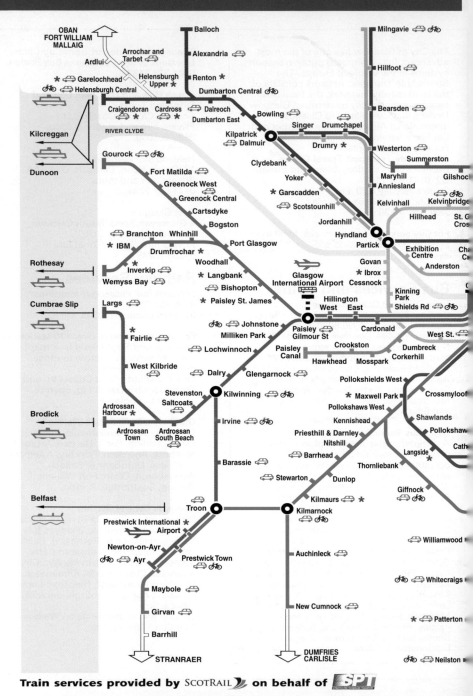

OBAN
FORT WILLIAM
MALLAIG

Arrochar and Tarbet

Ardlui

Garelochhead

Helensburgh Central

Helensburgh Upper

Kilcreggan

Dunoon

Gourock

Fort Matilda

Greenock West

Greenock Central

Cartsdyke

Bogston

Branchton Whinhill

IBM

Drumfrochar

Woodhall

Rothesay

Inverkip

Langbank

Wemyss Bay

Bishopton

Paisley St. James

Largs

Johnstone

Fairlie

Milliken Park

Lochwinnoch

West Kilbride

Dalry

Glengarnock

Stevenston

Saltcoats

Ardrossan Harbour

Kilwinning

Ardrossan Town

Ardrossan South Beach

Irvine

Brodick

Barassie

Stewarton

Dunlop

Belfast

Troon

Kilmaurs

Prestwick International Airport

Newton-on-Ayr

Ayr

Prestwick Town

Kilmarnock

Auchinleck

Maybole

Girvan

Barrhill

STRANRAER

New Cumnock

DUMFRIES
CARLISLE

Balloch

Alexandria

Renton

Dumbarton Central

Bowling

Singer Drumchapel

Dumbarton East

Kilpatrick

Dalmuir

Craigendoran Cardross Dalreoch

RIVER CLYDE

Clydebank

Yoker

Drumry

Garscadden

Scotstounhill

Jordanhill

Port Glasgow

Hyndland

Partick

Glasgow International Airport

Govan

Ibrox

Cessnock

Hillington
West   East

Paisley Gilmour St

Cardonald

Crookston

Paisley Canal

Hawkhead Mosspark

Pollokshields West

Maxwell Park

Pollokshaws West

Kennishead

Priesthill & Darnley

Nitshill

Barrhead

Thornliebank

Giffnock

Kilmaurs

Milngavie

Hillfoot

Bearsden

Westerton

Summerston

Maryhill

Anniesland

Kelvinhall

Hillhead

Kelvinbridge

St. G
Cros

Exhibition Centre

Anderston

Kinning Park

Shields Rd

West St.

Dumbreck

Corkerhill

Crossmyloof

Shawlands

Pollokshaw

Langside

Cath

Williamwood

Whitecraigs

Patterton

Neilston

Train services provided by SCOTRAIL on behalf of SPT

86

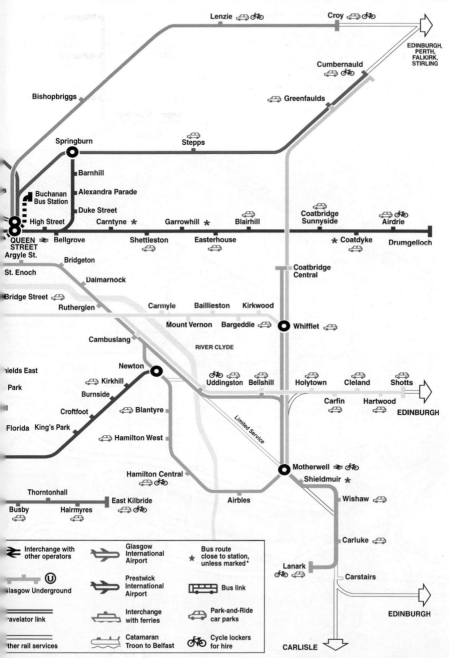

Lenzie

Croy

EDINBURGH,
PERTH,
FALKIRK,
STIRLING

Cumbernauld

Bishopbriggs

Greenfaulds

Springburn

Stepps

Barnhill

Buchanan
Bus Station

Alexandra Parade

Duke Street

High Street

Carntyne ★

Garrowhill ★

Blairhill

Coatbridge
Sunnyside

Airdrie

QUEEN
STREET

Argyle St.

Bellgrove

Shettleston

Easterhouse

★ Coatdyke

Drumgelloch

St. Enoch

Bridgeton

Coatbridge
Central

Bridge Street

Dalmarnock

Rutherglen

Carmyle

Baillieston

Kirkwood

Mount Vernon

Bargeddie

Whifflet

Cambuslang

RIVER CLYDE

Newton

nields East

Kirkhill

Uddingston

Bellshill

Holytown

Cleland

Shotts

Park

Burnside

Carfin

Hartwood

EDINBURGH

Croftfoot

Blantyre

Limited Service

Florida   King's Park

Hamilton West

Motherwell

Shieldmuir ★

Hamilton Central

Thorntonhall

East Kilbride

Airbles

Wishaw

Busby   Hairmyres

Carluke

Lanark

Carstairs

EDINBURGH

	Interchange with other operators		Glasgow International Airport		Bus route ★ close to station, unless marked*
	Glasgow Underground		Prestwick International Airport		Bus link
	Travelator link		Interchange with ferries		Park-and-Ride car parks
	other rail services		Catamaran Troon to Belfast		Cycle lockers for hire

CARLISLE

Current at November 1999

Glasgow International Airport

Glasgow International Airport is located eight miles (13km) west of Glasgow alongside the M8 motorway at Junction 28. It is linked by a bus service to Buchanan Bus Station, which runs every 10 minutes from 8.00 a.m.-5.00p.m. Monday to Saturday and less frequently at off peak times. There is a frequent coach service linking the Airport with all major bus and rail terminals in the City. Gilmour Street railway station in Paisley is 2 miles away and is linked by a frequent local bus service or by taxi.

Car parking is available with a graduated scale of charges. The Airport telephone number is 0141 887 1111

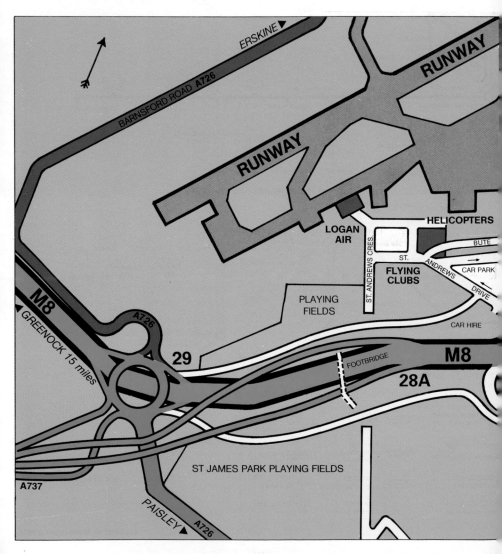

Airlines

Aer Lingus Flights to: Dublin
Reservations 0645 737 747
Air Canada Flights to: Toronto
Reservations 0990 247 226
KLM U.K. Flights to: Amsterdam and
London Stansted.
Reservations 0870 507 4074
British Airways Flights to:
London Gatwick, London Heathrow,
Manchester, Birmingham, Bristol,
Cardiff, Belfast, Londonderry and Inter
Scottish Routes.
Reservations 0345 222111

British Midland Flights to: London
Heathrow, East Midlands, Manchester,
Leeds Bradford, Jersey and
Copenhagen
Reservations 0870 607 0555
Easy Jet Flights to: London Luton.
Reservatons 01582 445566
Icelandair Flights to: Reykjavik.
Reservations 020 7874 1000
Manx Airlines Flights to: Isle of Man
Reservations 0845 725 6256
Sabena Flights to: Brussels
Reservations 0845 601 0933

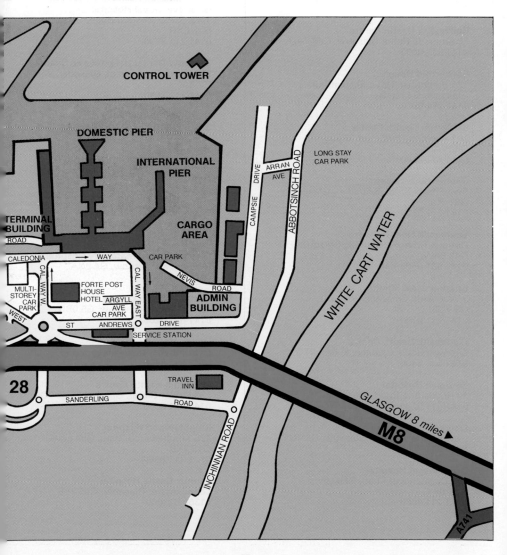

Hospitals and Health Centres

Greater Glasgow Health Board
(Administration)
Dalian House, P.O. Box 15329, 350 St.
Vincent Street, Glasgow, G3 8YZ
0141 201 4444

Acorn Street Psychiatric Day Hospital
23 Acorn Street, Bridgeton, Glasgow, G40
4AA
0141 556 4789

Baillieston Health Centre
20 Muirside Road, Glasgow, G69 7AD
0141 531 8000

Blawarthill Hospital
129 Holehouse Drive, Blawarthill,
Glasgow, G13 3TG
0141 954 9000

Bridgeton Health Centre
201 Abercromby Street, Glasgow,
G40 2AD
0141 531 6500

Canniesburn Hospital
Switchback Road, Bearsden, Glasgow,
G61 1QL
0141 211 5600

Castlemilk Health Centre
Dougrie Drive, Castlemilk, Glasgow,
G45 9AW
0141 531 8500

Charing Cross Clinic
8 Woodside Crescent, Glasgow,
G3 7UL
0141 211 8100

Clydebank Health Centre
Kilbowie Road, Clydebank, G81 2TQ
0141 531 6400

Cowglen Hospital
10 Boydstone Road, Glasgow, G53 6XJ
0141 211 9200

Douglas Inch Centre
2 Woodside Terrace, Glasgow, G3 7UY
0141 211 8000

Drumchapel Hospital
129 Drumchapel Road, Glasgow,
G15 6PX
0141 211 6000

Easterhouse Health Centre
9 Auchinlea Road, Glasgow, G34 9QU
0141 531 8100

Gartnavel General Hospital
1053 Great Western Road, Glasgow,
G12 0YN
0141 211 3000

Gartnavel Royal Hospital
1055 Great Western Road, Glasgow,
G12 0XH
0141 211 3600

Glasgow Dental Hospital and School
378 Sauchiehall Street, Glasgow,
G2 3JZ
0141 211 9600

Glasgow Eye Infirmary
3 Sandyford Place, Glasgow, 63 7NB
0141 211 3000

Glasgow Homeopathic Hospital
1053 Great Western Road, Glasgow,
G12 0XQ
0141 211 1600

Glasgow Royal Infirmary
84 Castle Street, Glasgow, G4 0SF
0141 211 4000

Glasgow Royal Maternity Hospital
Rottenrow, Glasgow, G4 0NA
0141 211 5400

Gorbals Health Centre
45 Pine Place, Glasgow, G5 0BQ
0141 531 8200

Govan Health Centre
5 Drumoyne Road, Glasgow G51 4BJ
0141 531 8400

Govanhill Health Centre
233 Calder Street, Glasgow, G42 7DR
0141 531 8300

Knightswood Hospital
125 Knightswood Road, Glasgow,
G13 2XB
0141 211 6900

Lennox Castle Hospital
Lennoxtown, Glasgow, G65 7LB
01360 313000

Lenzie Hospital
Auchinloch Road, Kirkintilloch, Glasgow,
G66 5UF
0141 211 8200

Leverndale Hospital
510 Crookston Road, Glasgow,
G53 7TU
0141 211 6400

Lightburn Hospital
966 Carntyne Road, Glasgow, G32 6ND
0141 221 1500

Maryhill Health Centre
41 Shawpark Street, Glasgow, G20 9DR
0141 531 8700

Mansionhouse Geriatric Unit
100 Mansionhouse Road, Glasgow,
G44 3DX
0141 201 6111

Parkhead Health Centre
101 Salamanca Street, Glasgow,
G31 5NA
0141 531 9000

Parkhead Hospital
81 Salamanca Street, Glasgow,
G31 5ES
0141 211 8300

Pollock Health Centre
21 Cowglen Road, Glasgow, G53 6EQ
0141 531 6800

Possilpark Health Centre
85 Denmark Street, Glasgow, G22 5EG
0141 531 6120

Queen Mother's Hospital
Yorkhill, Glasgow, G3 8SJ
0141 201 0550

Royal Hospital for Sick Children
Yorkhill, Glasgow, G3 8SJ
0141 201 0000

Rutherglen Health Centre
130 Stonelaw Road, Rutherglen,
Glasgow, G73 2PQ
0141 531 6000

Rutherglen Maternity Hospital
120 Stonelaw Road, Rutherglen,
Glasgow, G73 2PG   0141 201 6060

Shettleston Health Centre
420 Old Shettleston Road, Glasgow,
G32 7JZ
0141 531 6200

Southern General Hospital
1345 Govan Road, Glasgow, G51 4TF
0141 201 1100

Springburn Health Centre
200 Springburn Way, Glasgow, G21 1RT
0141 531 6700

Stobhill Hospital
133 Balornock Road, Glasgow, G21 3UW
0141 201 3000

Thornliebank Health Centre
20 Kennishead Road, Glasgow, G46 8NY
0141 531 6900

Townhead Health Centre
16 Alexandra Parade, Glasgow, G31 2ES
0141 531 8900

Victoria Infirmary
Langside Road, Glasgow, G42 9TY
0141 201 6000

Western Infirmary
Dumbarton Road, Partick, Glasgow,
G11 6NT
0141 211 2000

Woodilee Hospital
Lenzie, Glasgow, G66 3UG
0141 531 3100

Woodside Health Centre
Barr Street, Glasgow, G20 7LR
0141 531 9200

Renfrew District

A selection of leisure, recreational and cultural attractions in Renfrew District:

Barrhead Sports' Centre
The Centre contains swimming pools, sports halls, activity rooms and saunasuite. Bar and restaurant facilities add to the wide range of sporting and leisure activities available.
0141 580 1175

Barshaw Park, Glasgow Road, Paisley
The park is extensive with formal and informal areas. It adjoins the public golf course and incorporates a boating pond, playgrounds, model "ride-on" railway and a nature corner. 0141 840 2908

Braehead Shopping & Leisure Centre, King's Inch Road
Retail and leisure centre opened in 1999 including over 100 shops, 4000 seat ice arena, skating and curling rinks.
0141 885 4600

Castle Semple Visitor Centre, Lochwinnoch
Castle Semple Loch is a popular feature for sailing and fishing. Canoes, rowing boats and sailing boards for hire. Fishing permits available. 01505 842882

Coats Observatory
The Observatory has traditionally recorded astronomical and meteorological information since 1882. Now installed with a satellite picture receiver, it is one of the best equipped Observatories in the country. Open Tuesday - Saturday 10 a.m. - 5 p.m.
Sunday 2p.m. - 5p.m.
0141 889 2013

Erskine Bridge (Toll)
The bridge is an impressive high level structure opened by HRH Princess Anne in 1971 and provides a direct link from Renfrew District to Loch Lomond and the Trossachs. The bridge replaced the Erskine Ferry and affords extensive views up and down river to pedestrian users.

Finlaystone Country Estate
Off the A8 at Langbank. Gardens and woodland walks. The house has connections with John Knox and Robert Burns and is open by appointment only. Estate open all year round 10.30a.m. -5p.m. 0147 540505

Gleniffer Braes Country Park, Glenfield Road, Paisley
1,000 breathtaking acres including Glen Park

nature trail, picnic and children's play areas. Open dawn till dusk, the park affords extensive walks and spectacular views from this elevated moorland area, and contains an area reserved for model aero flying.
0141 884 3794

Houston Village
Houston was developed in the 18th century as an estate village. The traditional smiddy building, village pubs and terraced houses combine to create a quiet, sleepy atmosphere which has successfully survived the development of extensive modern housing on its periphery.

Inchinnan Bridges
Early 19th century stone bridges over the White Cart and Black Cart rivers close to St. Conval's stone, and the site of the Inchinnan Church which houses the graves of the Knights Templar, whose order was introduced to Scotland in 1153 by King David I.

Johnstone Castle
The remnants of a 1700 building formerly a much larger structure but demolished in the 1950's. The castle has significant historical links with the Cochrane and Houston families, major landowners who were instrumental in the development of the Burgh of Johnstone.

Kilbarchan Village
A good example of an 18th Century weaving village with many original buildings still fronting the narrow streets. A focal point is the steeple building in the square, originally a school and meal market and now used as public meeting rooms. A cycle route/footpath system links it to Glasgow and the Clyde Coast.

Lagoon Leisure Centre, Paisley
Ultra-modern complex housing superb ice rink and extensive "fun" pool featuring artificial wave machine and water slides. Also has cafe/bar facilities. Unique within the area, the complex is easily reached by public transport and has ample parking.
Monday - Friday 10 a.m. - 10 p.m.,
Saturday and Sunday 9.30 a.m. - 5.00 p.m.
0141 889 4000

Linwood Sports Centre
A wide range of indoor and outdoor sporting activities include football and rugby pitches, running track, games hall, squash courts, BMX track, fitness trail, tennis courts and conditioning suite.
01505 329 461

Lochwinnoch Village
An attractive rural village close to the Castle Semple Water Park, Muirshiel Country Park and the R.S.P.B. nature reserve, Lochwinnoch contains a small local museum with displays reflecting agricultural, social and industrial aspects of village life. Museum open Monday, 10 a.m. - 1 p.m., 2 - 5 p.m. and 6 - 8 p.m. Saturday 10 a.m. - 1 p.m. and 2- 5 p.m.
01505 842615

Muirshiel Country Park
Four miles north of Lochwinnoch, the park features trails of varying length radiating from the Information Centre. Open daily 9a.m.-4.30 p.m. (Winter), 9a.m. - 7.30 p.m. (Summer). 01505 842803

Paisley Abbey
Birthplace of the Stewart Dynasty, the Abbey dates, in part, to the 12th century and features regimental flags, relics, the Barochan Cross and beautiful stained glass windows.
Monday - Saturday 10 a.m. - 3.30 p.m., Sunday1.30- 3.30 p.m.
0141 889 3630

Paisley Arts Centre
Converted 18th century church the Laigh Kirk. Performing arts, works by local artists and participatory events, includes bar and bistro. Open Monday - Saturday 10a.m. - 8p.m. Further information
0141 887 1010

Paisley Museum and Art Gallery, High Street, Paisley
In addition to the world famous collection of Paisley shawls, the Museum traces the history of the Paisley pattern, the development of weaving techniques and houses collections of local and natural history, ceramics and paintings.
Tuesday- Saturday 10 a.m - 5 p.m.
Sunday 2p.m. - 5p.m.
0141 889 3151

Paisley Town Hall
A Renaissance style building by the River Cart in the heart of Paisley, it features a slim clock tower and houses a Tourist Information Centre. It accommodates many exhibitions during the year and it is also available for conferences and functions.
Monday - Friday 9 a.m. - 5 p.m.
0141 887 1007

Paisley Town Trail
An easy to follow route taking in the town's historic and architecturally significant buildings. Visitors can spend an hour or two walking round the trail and referring to a printed guide and wall plaques on the main buildings.

Renfrew Town Hall
The Town Hall has a "fairy-tale" style to its 105 feet high spire and was the administrative centre of the Royal Burgh of Renfrew. Originally the principal town in the area, Renfrew was strategically placed on the River Clyde, and a passenger ferry continues to operate daily.

Robert Tannahill, Weaver Poet
The works of Tannahill rank with those of Burns. Born in 1774 he took his own life in 1810 and is buried in a nearby graveyard. Visitors can visit his early home, site of his death, and his grave, and read his works in Paisley Library.

Royal Society for Protection of Birds,Lochwinnoch
An interesting visitor centre with observation tower, hides, displays and gift shop. Open every day 10a.m. - 5 p.m.
01505 842663

Sma' Shot Cottages, Paisley
Fully restored and furnished artisan's house of the Victorian era; exhibition room displaying photographs plus artefacts of local interest. 18th Century weaver's loomshop with combined living quarters.
Open Wednesday & Saturday April- September 1-5 p.m. Group visits arranged by appointment.
0141 889 1708

The Clyde Estuary
Visitors travelling along the rural route to the Old Greenock Road above Langbank village at the western end of the District are able to take advantage of extensive views of the upper and lower Clyde Estuary, the Gareloch and the mountains beyond.

Thomas Coats Memorial Church
Another gift from the Coats family to Paisley, the church was built in 1894 and constructed of red sandstone, is one of the finest Baptist Churches in the country.
Open May - September
Monday, Wednesday and Friday 2-4p.m.
Sunday 11a.m.-12 midday
0141 889 9980

Wallace Monument, Elderslie
The monument was erected in 1912 and marks the birthplace of the Scottish Patriot, Sir William Wallace. It stands adjacent to the reconstructed foundation plan of the Wallace Buildings which dated from the 17th Century.

Weaver's Cottage, Kilbarchan
This cottage, built in 1723, houses the last of the village's 800 looms and demonstrations are still given. It contains displays of weaving and domestic utensils, with Cottage garden and refreshments.
Open daily May - September and weekends in October 1.30p.m. - 5.30p.m.
01505 705588

INDEX TO STREETS

General Abbreviations

Arc.	Arcade	Dr.	Drive	Lo.	Lodge	St.	Street,Saint
Av.	Avenue	E.	East	Mans.	Mansions	Sta.	Station
Bk.	Bank	Est.	Estate	Ms.	Mews	Ter.	Terrace
Bldgs.	Buildings	Ex.	Exchange	N.	North	Trd.	Trading
Boul.	Boulevard	Fm.	Farm	Par.	Parade	Twr.	Tower
Bri.	Bridge	Gdns.	Gardens	Pas.	Passage	Vill.	Villa
Cen.	Centre,Central	Gra.	Grange	Pk.	Park	Vills.	Villas
Cft.	Croft	Grn.	Green	Pl.	Place	Vw.	View
Circ.	Circus	Gro.	Grove	Quad.	Quadrant	W.	West
Clo.	Close	Ho.	House	Rd.	Road	Wd.	Wood
Cor.	Corner	Hts.	Heights	Ri.	Rise	Wds.	Woods
Cotts.	Cottages	Ind.	Industrial	S.	South	Wf.	Wharf
Cres.	Crescent	La.	Lane	Sch.	School	Wk.	Walk
Ct.	Court	Ln.	Loan	Sq.	Square		

Postal Town Abbreviations

Clyde.	Clydebank	Ersk.	Erskine	Pais.	Paisley
Coat.	Coatbridge	John.	Johnstone	Renf.	Renfrew

Locality Abbreviations

Abbots.	Abbotsinch	Clark.	Clarkston	Kirk.	Kirkintilloch
Bail.	Baillieston	Cumb.	Cumbernauld	Linw.	Linwood
Barr.	Barrhead	Cumb.V.	Cumbernauld Village	Mill.Pk.	Milliken Park
Bears.	Bearsden	Dunt.	Duntocher	Mood.	Moodiesburn
Bishop.	Bishopbriggs	Elder.	Elderslie	Muir.	Muirhead
Blan.	Blantyre	Gart.	Gartcosh	Old Kil.	Old Kilpatrick
Both.	Bothwell	Giff.	Giffnock	Ruther.	Rutherglen
Camb.	Cambuslang	Inch.	Inchinnan	Thorn.	Thornliebank
Chry.	Chryston	Kilb.	Kilbarchan	Udd.	Uddingston

NOTES

Postal district information is included for all streets and so Abbey Dr. is to be found in postal district G14. In some cases the additional locality information is included in brackets following the street name. Where this has been abbreviated please consult the locality abbreviations listed above. For streets outwith the Glasgow post town area, the appropriate post town abbreviation is also used with the postal district. Thus Abbey Close is located within the Paisley post town, district PA1 and it will be found on page 46 in square K14.

This index contains some street names in standard text which are followed by another street named in italics. In these cases the street in standard text does not actually appear on the map due to insufficient space but can be located close to the street named in italics. Thus Abbot St. G41 is to be found off Frankfort St. page 51 grid square U15.

Entry	Map	Grid
Ardgour Dr. (Linw.), Pais. PA3	28	E13
Ardgowan Av., Pais. PA2	46	K14
Ardgowan Dr. (Udd.) G71	57	GG16
Ardgowan St., Pais. PA2	46	K15
Ardgowan Ter. La. G3	34	T11
Gray St.		
Ardholm St. G32	38	BB13
Ardhu Pl. G15	6	N6
Ardlamont Sq. (Linw.), Pais. PA3	28	F13
Ardlaw St. G51	33	R13
Ardle Rd. G43	63	U17
Ardlui St. G32	54	AA14
Ardmaleish Cres. G45	64	X19
Ardmaleish Rd. G45	64	X19
Ardmaleish St. G45	64	X19
Ardmaleish Ter. G45	64	X19
Ardmay Cres. G44	52	W16
Ardmillan St. G33	38	AA12
Ardmory Av. G42	52	W16
Ardmory La. G42	52	X16
Ardmory Pl. G42	52	X16
Ardnahoe Av. G42	52	W16
Ardnahoe Pl. G42	52	W16
Ardneil Rd. G51	33	R13
Ardnish St. G51	33	R12
Ardo Gdns. G51	34	S13
Ardoch Gro. (Camb.) G72	66	AA17
Ardoch Rd. (Bears.) G61	8	S5
Ardoch St. G22	22	W10
Ardoch Way (Chry.) G69	15	GG7
Braeside Av.		
Ardshiel Rd. G51	33	R12
Ardsloy La. G14	18	P10
Ardsloy Pl.		
Ardsloy Pl. G14	18	P10
Ardtoe Cres. G33	25	DD9
Ardtoe Pl. G33	25	DD9
Arduthie Rd. G51	33	R12
Ardwell Rd. G52	49	R14
Argosy Way, Renf. PA4	31	M11
Britannia Way		
Argyle St. G2	35	V12
Argyle St. G3	34	T11
Argyle St., Pais. PA1	46	J14
Argyll Arc. G2	35	V12
Argyll Av. (Abbots.), Pais. PA3	30	K11
Argyll Av., Renf. PA4	17	L10
Argyll Rd., Clyde. G81	5	M7
Arisaig Dr. G52	49	R14
Arisaig Dr. (Bears.) G61	8	S6
Arisaig Pl. G52	49	R14
Ark La. G31	36	X12
Arkle Ter. (Camb.) G72	66	AA18
Arkleston Cres., Pais. PA3	31	L12
Arkleston Rd., Pais. PA1	31	L13
Arkleston Rd., Pais. PA3	31	M12
Arkleston Rd., Renf. PA4	31	L12
Arklet Rd. G51	33	R13
Arkwrights Way, Pais. PA1	45	H14
Turners Av.		
Arlington St. G3	35	U11
Armadale Ct. G31	37	Y12
Townmill Rd.		
Armadale Path G31	37	Y12
Armadale Pl. G31	37	Y12
Armadale St. G31	37	Y12
Armaleish Dr. G45	64	X19
Armour Pl., John. PA5	44	E14
Armour Sq., John. PA5	44	E14
Armour St. G31	36	X13
Armour St., John. PA5	44	E14
Armstrong Cres. (Udd.) G71	57	HH16
Arngask Rd. G51	33	R12
Arnhall Pl. G52	49	R14
Arnhem St. (Camb.) G72	67	CC17
Arnholm Pl. G52	49	R14
Arnisdale Pl. G34	40	EE12
Arnisdale Rd. G34	40	EE12
Arnisdale Way (Ruther.) G73	65	Y18
Shieldaig Dr.		
Arniston St. G32	38	AA12
Arniston Way, Pais. PA3	31	L12
Arnol Pl. G33	39	DD12
Arnold Av. (Bishop.) G64	11	Y7
Arnold St. G20	21	V9
Arnott Way (Camb.) G72	66	BB17
Arnprior Cres. G45	64	W18
Arnprior Gdns. (Chry.) G69	15	GG7
Braeside Av.		
Arnprior Quad. G45	64	W18
Arnprior Rd. G45	64	W18
Arnprior St. G45	64	W18
Arnside Av. (Giff.) G46	62	T18
Arnwood Dr. G12	20	S9
Aron Ter. (Camb.) G72	66	AA18
Aros Dr. G52	49	R15
Aros La. G52	49	Q15
Aros Dr.		
Arran Av. (Abbots.), Pais. PA3	30	K11
Arran Dr. (Giff.) G46	62	S19
Arran Dr. G52	49	R14
Arran Dr. (Cumb.) G67	70	MM4
Arran Dr., John. PA5	43	C15
Arran Dr., Pais. PA2	46	K16
Arran La. (Chry.) G69	15	HH7
Burnbrae Av.		
Arran Pl., Clyde. G81	5	M7
Arran Pl. (Linw.), Pais. PA3	28	E13
Arran Rd., Renf. PA4	31	M11
Arran Ter. (Ruther.) G73	64	X17
Arran Way (Both.) G71	69	GG19
Arriochmill Rd. G20	20	T10
Kelvin Dr.		
Arrochar Ct. G23	21	U8
Sunningdale Rd.		
Arrochar Dr. G23	8	T7
Arrochar St. G23	20	T8
Arrol Pl. G40	53	Y14
Arrol Rd. G40	53	Y14
Arrol St. G52	32	N12
Arrowsmith Av. G13	19	Q8
Arthur Av. (Barr.) G78	59	L19
Arthur Rd., Pais. PA2	46	K16
Arthur St. G3	34	T11
Arthur St., Pais. PA1	30	J13
Arthurlie Av. (Barr.) G78	59	M19
Arthurlie Dr. (Giff.) G46	62	T19
Arthurlie St. G51	33	R12
Arthurlie St. (Barr.) G78	59	M19
Arundel Dr. G42	51	V16
Arundel Dr. (Bishop.) G64	11	Y6
Asbury Ct. (Linw.), Pais. PA3	28	F13
Ascaig Cres. G52	49	R15
Ascog Rd. (Bears.) G61	7	R7
Ascog St. G42	51	V15
Ascot Av. G12	19	R9
Ascot Ct. G12	20	S9
Ash Gro. (Bishop.) G64	11	Y7
Ash Gro. (Kirk.) G66	12	BB5
Ash Gro. (Bail.) G69	41	GG13
Ash Gro. (Udd.) G71	57	HH16
Ash Pl., John. PA5	44	E15
Ash Rd. (Cumb.) G67	71	QQ1
Ash Rd. (Bail.) G69	56	EE14
Ash Rd., Clyde. G81	4	K5
Ash Wk. (Ruther.) G73	65	Z18
Ash Wynd (Camb.) G72	67	DD18
Ashburton La. G12	20	S9
Ashburton Rd.		
Ashburton Rd. G12	20	S9
Ashby Cres. G13	7	R7
Ashcroft Dr. G44	64	X17
Ashdale Dr. G52	49	R14
Ashdene Rd. G22	21	V8
Ashfield (Bishop.) G64	11	Y6
Ashfield St. G22	22	W10
Ashgill Pl. G22	22	W9
Ashgill Rd. G22	21	V9
Ashgrove (Mood.) G69	41	GG13
Ashgrove St. G40	53	Y15
Ashkirk Dr. G52	49	R14
Ashlea Dr. (Giff.) G46	62	T18
Ashley Dr. (Both.) G71	69	HH19
Ashley La. G3	35	U11
Woodlands Rd.		
Ashley St. G3	35	U11
Ashmore Rd. G43	63	U17
Ashmore Rd. G44	63	U17
Ashton Gdns. G12	34	T11
University Av.		
Ashton Gdns. (Gart.) G69	27	GG9
Ashton La. G12	34	T11
University Av.		
Ashton La. N. G12	34	T11
University Av.		
Ashton Pl. G12	20	T10
Byres Rd.		
Ashton Rd. G12	34	T11
University Av.		
Ashton Rd. (Ruther.) G73	53	Y15
Ashton Ter. G12	34	T11
University Av.		
Ashton Way, Pais. PA2	45	G16
Ashtree Rd. G43	50	T16
Ashvale Cres. G21	22	X10
Ashwood Gdns. G13	19	R9
Aspen Dr. G21	23	Y10
Foresthall Dr.		
Aspen Pl. (Camb.) G72	67	DD18
Aspen Pl., John. PA5	44	E15
Aster Dr. G45	65	Y18
Aster Gdns. G53	61	Q18
Waukglen Cres.		
Athelstane Dr. (Cumb.) G67	70	MM4
Athelstane Rd. G13	19	Q8
Athena Way (Udd.) G71	57	HH16
Athol Av. G52	32	N12
Athole Gdns. G12	20	T10
Athole La. G12	20	T10
Saltoun St.		
Atholl Cres., Pais. PA1	32	N13
Atholl Gdns. (Bishop.) G64	11	Y6
Atholl Gdns. (Ruther.) G73	66	AA18
Atholl La. (Chry.) G69	15	HH7
Atholl Pl. (Linw.), Pais. PA3	28	E13
Atholl Ter. (Udd.) G71	57	GG15
Atlas Pl. G21	22	X10
Atlas Rd. G21	22	X10
Atlas Sq. G21	22	X10
Ayr St.		
Atlas St., Clyde. G81	17	L8
Cart St.		
Attlee Av., Clyde. G81	5	M7
Attlee Pl., Clyde. G81	5	M7
Attlee Av.		
Attow Rd. G43	62	S17
Auburn Dr. (Barr.) G78	59	M19
Auchans Rd. (Houston), John. PA6	28	E12
Auchenbothie Cres. G21	24	AA9
Auchenbothie Pl. G21	24	AA9
Auchencrow St. G34	40	FF12
Auchengeich Rd. (Mood.) G69	14	FF6
Auchenglen Dr. (Chry.) G69	15	GG7
Auchengreoch Av., John. PA5	43	C16
Auchengreoch Rd., John. PA5	43	C16
Auchenlodmont Rd., John. PA5	44	E15
Auchentorlie Quad., Pais. PA1	47	L14
Auchentorlie St. G11	33	R11
Dumbarton Rd.		
Auchentoshan Av., Clyde. G81	4	K5
Auchentoshan Ter. G21	36	X11
Auchentoshen Cotts. (Old Kil.) G60	4	J5
Auchinairn Rd. (Bishop.) G64	22	X8
Auchinbee Way (Cumb.) G68	70	LL2
Auchingill Path G34	40	FF11
Auchingill Rd.		
Auchingill Pl. G34	40	FF11
Auchingill Rd. G34	40	FF11
Auchinlea Rd. G34	39	DD11
Auchinleck Av. G33	24	AA9
Auchinleck Cres. G33	24	AA9
Auchinleck Dr. G33	24	AA9
Auchinleck Gdns. G33	24	AA9
Auchinleck Rd. G33	24	AA8
Auchinloch Rd. (Lenzie) G66	13	CC6
Auchinloch St. G21	22	X10
Auchmannoch Av., Pais. PA1	32	N13
Auckland Pl., Clyde. G81	4	J6
Auckland St. G22	21	V10
Auld Rd., The (Cumb.) G67	71	PP2
Auld St., Clyde. G81	4	K6
Auldbar Rd. G52	49	R14
Auldbar Ter., Pais. PA2	47	L15
Auldburn Rd. G43	62	S17
Auldburn Rd.		
Auldburn Rd. G43	62	S17
Auldearn Rd. G21	23	Z8
Auldgirth Rd. G52	49	R14
Auldhouse Av. G43	62	S17
Thornliebank Rd.		
Auldhouse Gdns. G43	62	S17
Auldhouse Rd. G43	62	S17
Auldhouse Ter. G43	62	T17
Auldhouse Rd.		
Auldkirk Rd. (Camb.) G72	67	CC18
Aultbea St. G22	21	V8
Aultmore Rd. G33	39	DD12
Aurs Cres. (Barr.) G78	59	M19
Aurs Dr. (Barr.) G78	59	M19

Aurs Glen (Barr.) G78   59   M19

Aurs Glen (Barr.) G78	59	M19
Aurs Pl. (Barr.) G78	59	M19
Aurs Rd. (Barr.) G78	59	M18
Aursbridge Cres. (Barr.) G78	59	M19
Aursbridge Dr. (Barr.) G78	59	M19
Austen La. G13	19	R9
Skaterig La.		
Austen Rd. G13	19	R9
Avenel Rd. G13	7	R7
Avenue, The (Kilb.), John.	42	B15
PA10		
Low Barholm		
Avenue End Rd. G33	24	BB10
Avenue St. G40	37	Y13
Avenue St. (Ruther.) G73	53	Y15
Avenuehead Rd. (Chry.) G69	15	GG7
Avenuepark St. G20	21	U10
Aviemore Gdns. (Bears.) G61	8	S5
Aviemore Rd. G52	49	R15
Avoch Dr. (Thorn.) G46	61	R18
Avoch St. G34	40	EE11
Avon Av. (Bears.) G61	8	S6
Avon Dr. (Bishop.) G64	23	Y8
Avon Dr. (Linw.), Pais. PA3	28	E13
Avon Rd. (Giff.) G46	62	S19
Avon Rd. (Bishop.) G64	23	Y8
Avon St. G5	35	U13
Avonbank Rd. (Ruther.) G73	52	X16
Avondale Dr., Pais. PA1	31	L13
Avondale St. G33	38	BB11
Avonhead Av. (Cumb.) G67	70	MM4
Avonhead Gdns. (Cumb.)	70	MM4
G67		
Avonhead Pl. (Cumb.) G67	70	MM4
Avonhead Rd. (Cumb.) G67	70	MM4
Avonspark St. G21	23	Y10
Aylmer Rd. G43	63	U17
Ayr Rd. (Giff.) G46	62	S19
Ayr St. G21	22	X10
Aytoun Rd. G41	50	T14
Azalia Gdns. (Camb.) G72	67	DD17

B

Back Causeway G31	37	Z13
Back Sneddon St., Pais. PA3	30	K13
Backmuir Rd. G15	6	P6
Bagnell St. G21	22	X9
Baillie Dr. (Both.) G71	69	HH18
Baillie Wynd (Udd.) G71	57	HH16
Baillieston Rd. G32	55	CC14
Baillieston Rd. (Udd.) G71	56	EE14
Bain Sq. G40	36	X13
Bain St.		
Bain St. G40	36	X13
Bainsford St. G32	38	AA13
Baird Av. G52	32	N12
Baird Ct., Clyde. G81	5	L7
North Av.		
Baird Dr. (Bears.) G61	7	Q5
Baird St. G4	36	W11
Bairdsbrae G4	21	V10
Possil Rd.		
Baker Pl. G41	51	U15
Baker St.		
Baker St. G41	51	U15
Bakewell Rd. (Bail.) G69	40	EE13
Balaclava St. G2	35	V13
McAlpine St.		
Balado Rd. G33	39	DD12
Balbeg St. G51	33	R13
Balbeggie Pl. G32	55	CC14
Balbeggie St. G32	55	CC14
Balblair Rd. G52	49	R15
Balcarres Av. G12	20	T9
Balcomie St. G33	38	BB11
Balcurvie Rd. G34	40	EE11
Baldinnie Rd. G34	40	EE12
Baldorran Cres. (Cumb.) G68	70	LL2
Baldovan Cres. G33	39	DD12
Baldovie Rd. G52	49	Q14
Baldragon Rd. G34	40	EE11
Baldric Rd. G13	19	Q9
Baldwin Av. G13	7	Q7
Balerno Dr. G52	49	R14
Balfluig St. G34	39	DD11
Balfour St. G20	20	T9
Balfron Rd. G51	33	R12
Balfron Rd., Pais. PA1	31	M13
Balgair Dr., Pais. PA1	31	L13
Balgair St. G22	21	V9
Balgair Ter. G32	38	BB13

Balglass St. G22	21	V10
Balgonie Av., Pais. PA2	45	H15
Balgonie Dr., Pais. PA2	46	J15
Balgonie Rd. G52	49	R14
Balgonie Wds., Pais. PA2	46	J15
Balgownie Cres. (Thorn.) G46	62	S19
Balgray Cres. (Barr.) G78	60	N19
Balgraybank St. G21	23	Y10
Balgrayhill Rd. G21	22	X9
Balintore St. G32	38	BB13
Baliol La. G3	35	U11
Woodlands Rd.		
Baliol St. G3	35	U11
Ballaig Av. (Bears.) G61	7	Q5
Ballaig Cres. (Stepps) G33	25	CC9
Ballantay Quad. G45	65	Y18
Ballantay Rd. G45	65	Y18
Ballantay Ter. G45	65	Y18
Ballantyne Rd. G52	32	P12
Ballater Dr. (Bears.) G61	7	R7
Ballater Dr., Pais. PA2	47	L15
Ballater Dr. (Inch.), Renf. PA4	16	J9
Ballater Pl. G5	52	W14
Ballater St. G5	36	W13
Ballayne Dr. (Chry.) G69	15	HH7
Ballindalloch Dr. G31	37	Y12
Ballindarroch La. G31	37	Y12
Meadowpark St.		
Balloch Gdns. G52	49	R14
Balloch Loop Rd. (Cumb.)	70	MM2
G68		
Balloch Vw. (Cumb.) G67	70	NN3
Ballochmill Rd. (Ruther.) G73	53	Z16
Ballochmyle Cres. G53	48	P16
Ballochmyle Dr. G53	48	P15
Ballochmyle Gdns. G53	48	P15
Ballogie Rd. G44	51	V16
Balmartin Rd. G23	8	T7
Balmerino Pl. (Bishop.) G64	23	Z8
Balmoral Cres. G42	51	V15
Queens Dr.		
Balmoral Cres. (Inch.), Renf.	16	K9
PA4		
Balmoral Dr. G32	54	BB16
Balmoral Dr. (Bears.) G61	8	S7
Balmoral Dr. (Camb.) G72	66	AA17
Balmoral Gdns. (Udd.) G71	57	GG15
Balmoral Gdns. (Blan.) G72	68	FF19
Balmoral Rd. (Elder.), John.	44	E15
PA5		
Balmoral St. G14	18	P10
Balmore Pl. G22	21	V9
Balmore Rd.		
Balmore Rd. G22	21	V8
Balmore Rd. G23	9	U7
Balmore Rd. (Milngavie) G62	9	U5
Balmore Sq. G22	21	V9
Balmuildy Rd. G23	9	V6
Balmuildy Rd. (Bishop.) G64	9	V6
Balornock Rd. G21	23	Y9
Balruddery Pl. (Bishop.) G64	23	Z8
Balshagray Av. G11	19	R10
Balshagray Cres. G14	33	R11
Dumbarton Rd.		
Balshagray Dr. G11	19	R10
Balshagray La. G11	19	R10
Balshagray Pl. G11	19	R10
Balshagray Dr.		
Baltic Ct. G40	53	Y14
Baltic St.		
Baltic La. G40	53	Y14
Baltic Pl. G40	52	X14
Baltic St. G40	53	Y14
Balure St. G31	37	Z12
Balvaird Cres. (Ruther.) G73	53	Y16
Balvaird Dr. (Ruther.) G73	53	Y16
Balveny St. G33	39	CC11
Balvicar Dr. G42	51	U15
Balvicar St. G42	51	U15
Balvie Av. G15	6	P7
Balvie Av. (Giff.) G46	62	T19
Banavie Rd. G11	20	S10
Banchory Av. G43	62	S17
Banchory Av. (Inch.), Renf.	16	J8
PA4		
Banchory Cres. (Bears.) G61	8	S7
Banff St. G33	38	BB11
Bangorshill St. (Thorn.) G46	61	R18
Bank Rd. G32	55	CC16
Bank St. G12	35	U11
Bank St. (Camb.) G72	66	BB17
Bank St. (Barr.) G78	59	M19

Bank St., Pais. PA1	46	K14
Bankbrae Av. G53	60	P17
Bankend St. G33	38	BB11
Bankfoot Dr. G52	48	P14
Bankfoot Rd. G52	48	P14
Bankfoot Rd., Pais. PA3	29	H13
Bankglen Rd. G15	6	P6
Bankhall St. G42	51	V15
Bankhead Av. G13	18	P9
Bankhead Dr. (Ruther.) G73	53	Y16
Bankhead Rd. (Ruther.) G73	64	X17
Bankier St. G40	36	X13
Banknock St. G32	38	AA13
Bankside Av., John. PA5	43	D14
Banktop Pl., John. PA5	43	D14
Banling Grn. Rd. G44	63	V17
Clarkston Rd.		
Bannatyne Av. G31	37	Y12
Banner Dr. G13	7	Q7
Banner Rd. G13	7	Q7
Bannercross Av. (Bail.) G69	40	EE13
Bannercross Dr. (Bail.) G69	40	EE13
Bannercross Gdns. (Bail.) G69	40	EE13
Bannercross Dr.		
Bannerman Pl., Clyde. G81	5	M7
Bannerman St., Clyde. G81	5	L7
Bantaskin St. G20	20	T8
Banton Pl. G33	40	EE12
Barassie Ct. (Both.) G71	69	GG19
Barassie Cres. (Cumb.) G68	70	NN1
Barbae Pl. (Both.) G71	69	HH18
Hume Dr.		
Barberry Av. G53	60	P19
Barberry Gdns. G53	60	P19
Barberry Av.		
Barberry Pl. G53	60	P19
Barberry Av.		
Barbreck Rd. G42	51	U15
Pollokshaws Rd.		
Barcaldine Av. (Chry.) G69	14	EE7
Barclay Av. (Elder.), John.	44	E15
PA5		
Barclay Sq., Renf. PA4	31	L11
Barclay St. G21	22	X9
Lenzie St.		
Barcraigs Dr., Pais. PA2	46	K16
Bard Av. G13	18	P8
Bardowie St. G22	21	V10
Bardrain Av. (Elder.), John.	44	F15
PA5		
Bardrain Rd., Pais. PA2	46	J16
Bardrill Dr. (Bishop.) G64	10	X7
Bardykes Rd. (Blan.) G72	68	FF19
Barfillan Dr. G52	33	R13
Barfillan Rd. G52	33	R13
Bargany Rd. G53	48	P15
Bargaran Rd. G53	48	P14
Bargarron Dr., Pais. PA3	31	L12
Bargeddie St. G33	37	Z11
Barholm Sq. G33	39	CC11
Barke Rd. (Cumb.) G67	71	PP2
Barlanark Av. G32	39	CC12
Barlanark Cres. G33	39	CC12
Barlanark Dr. G33	39	CC12
Barlanark Pl. G32	39	CC13
Hallhill Rd.		
Barlanark Pl. G33	39	DD12
Barlanark Rd. G33	39	CC12
Barlia Dr. G45	64	X18
Barlia St. G45	64	X18
Barlia Ter. G45	64	X18
Barloch St. G22	22	W10
Barlogan Av. G52	33	R13
Barlogan Quad. G52	33	R13
Barmulloch Rd. G21	23	Y10
Barn Av. (Kilb.), John.	42	B14
PA10		
Barnard Gdns. (Bishop.) G64	11	Y6
Barnard Ter. G40	53	Y14
Barnbeth Rd. G53	48	P15
Barnes Rd. G20	21	V9
Barnes St. (Barr.) G78	59	L19
Barness Pl. G33	38	BB12
Barnflat St. (Ruther.) G73	53	Y15
Barnhill Dr. G21	23	Y10
Foresthall Dr.		
Barnkirk Av. G15	6	P6
Barns St., Clyde. G81	5	M7
Barnsford Av. (Inch.), Renf.	16	J9
PA4		
Barnsford Rd. (Abbots.),	29	H12
Pais. PA3		

Bentinck St. G3 35 U11
Bents Rd. (Bail.) G69 40 EE13
Benvie Gdns. (Bishop.) G64 11 Y7
Benview St. G20 21 U10
Benview Ter., Pais. PA2 47 L15
Berelands Cres. (Ruther.) G73 52 X16
Berelands Pl. (Ruther.) G73 52 X16
Beresford Av. G14 19 R10
Berkeley St. G3 35 U12
Berkeley Ter. La. G3 35 U11
  Elderslie St.
Berkley Dr. (Blan.) G72 68 FF19
Bernard Path G40 53 Y14
Bernard St. G40 53 Y14
Bernard Ter. G40 53 Y14
Berneray St. G22 22 W8
Berridale Av. G44 63 V17
Berriedale Av. (Bail.) G69 56 EE14
Berryburn Rd. G21 23 Z10
Berryhill Dr. (Giff.) G46 62 S19
Berryhill Rd. (Giff.) G46 62 S19
Berryhill Rd. (Cumb.) G67 70 NN3
Berryknowes Av. G52 33 Q13
Berryknowes Av. (Chry.) G69 26 FF8
Berryknowes La. G52 33 Q13
Berryknowes Rd. G52 49 Q14
Bertram St. G41 51 U15
Bertrohill Ter. G33 39 CC12
  Stepps Rd.
Bervie St. G51 33 R13
Berwick Cres. (Linw.), Pais. 28 E12
  PA3
Berwick Dr. G52 48 P14
Berwick Dr. (Ruther.) G73 53 Z16
Betula Dr., Clyde. G81 5 L5
Bevan Gro., John. PA5 43 C15
Beverley Rd. G43 62 T17
Bevin Av., Clyde. G81 5 M7
Bideford Cres. G32 55 CC14
Biggar St. G31 37 Y13
Bigton St. G33 38 BB11
Bilsland Ct. G20 21 V9
  Bilsland Dr.
Bilsland Dr. G20 21 U9
Binend Rd. G53 49 Q16
Binnie Pl. G40 36 X13
Binniehill Rd. (Cumb.) G68 70 MM2
Binns Rd. G33 39 CC11
Birch Cres., John. PA5 44 E15
Birch Dr. (Lenzie) G66 13 CC5
Birch Dr. (Camb.) G72 67 CC17
Birch Gro. (Udd.) G71 57 HH16
  Burnhead St.
Birch Knowe (Bishop.) G64 11 Y7
Birch Pl. (Camb.) G72 67 DD18
Birch Rd., Clyde. G81 5 L5
Birch St. G5 52 W14
  Silverfir St.
Birch Vw. (Bears.) G61 8 S5
Birchend Dr. G21 37 Y11
Birchend Pl. G21 37 Y11
Birchfield Dr. G14 18 P10
Birchlea Dr. (Giff.) G46 62 T18
Birchwood Av. G32 55 DD14
Birchwood Dr., Pais. PA2 45 H15
Birchwood Pl. G32 55 DD14
Birdston Rd. G21 23 Z9
Birgidale Av. G45 64 W19
Birgidale Rd. G45 64 W19
Birgidale Ter. G45 64 W19
Birkdale Ct. (Both.) G71 69 GG19
Birken Rd. (Lenzie) G66 13 DD6
Birkenshaw St. G31 37 Y12
Birkenshaw Way, Pais. PA3 30 K12
  Abbotsburn Way
Birkhall Av. G52 48 N14
Birkhall Av. (Inch.), Renf. PA4 16 J8
Birkhall Dr. (Bears.) G61 7 R7
Birkhill Av. (Bishop.) G64 11 Y6
Birkhill Gdns. (Bishop.) G64 11 Z6
Birkmyre Rd. G51 33 R13
Birks Rd., Renf. PA4 31 L11
  Tower Dr.
Birkwood St. G40 53 Y15
Birmingham Rd., Renf. PA4 31 L11
Birnam Av. (Bishop.) G64 11 Y6
Birnam Cres. (Bears.) G61 8 S5
Birnam Gdns. (Bishop.) G64 11 Y7
Birnam Rd. G31 53 Z14
Birness Dr. G43 50 T16
Birness St. G43 50 T16
Birnie Ct. G21 23 Z10

Birnie Rd. G21 23 Z10
Birnock Av., Renf. PA4 32 N11
Birsay Rd. G22 21 V8
Bishop Gdns. (Bishop.) G64 10 X7
Bishop St. G3 35 V12
Bishopmill Pl. G21 23 Z10
Bishopmill Rd. G21 23 Z10
Bishopsgate Dr. G21 22 X8
Bishopsgate Gdns. G21 22 X8
Bishopsgate Pl. G21 22 X8
Bishopsgate Rd. G21 22 X8
Bissett Cres., Clyde. G81 4 K5
Black St. G4 36 W11
Blackburn Sq. (Barr.) G78 59 M19
Blackburn St. G51 34 T13
Blackbyres Ct. (Barr.) G78 59 M18
Blackbyres Rd. (Barr.) G78 59 M17
Blackcraig Av. G15 6 P6
Blackcroft Gdns. G32 55 CC14
Blackcroft Rd. G32 55 CC14
Blackfaulds Rd. (Ruther.) G73 52 X16
Blackford Rd., Pais. PA2 47 L15
Blackfriars St. G1 36 W12
Blackhall La., Pais. PA1 46 K14
Blackhall St., Pais. PA1 46 K14
Blackhill Cotts. G23 9 V7
Blackhill Pl. G33 37 Z11
Blackhill Rd. G23 8 T7
Blackie St. G3 34 T11
Blackland Gro., Pais. PA2 46 J16
Blacklands Pl. (Lenzie) G66 13 DD6
Blacklaw La., Pais. PA3 30 K13
Blackstone Av. G53 49 Q16
Blackstone Cres. G53 49 Q15
Blackstone Rd., Pais. PA3 29 H12
Blackstoun Av. (Linw.), Pais. 28 E13
  PA3
Blackstoun Oval, Pais. PA3 29 H13
Blackstoun Rd., Pais. PA3 29 H13
Blackthorn Av. (Kirk.) G66 12 BB5
Blackthorn Gro. (Kirk.) G66 12 BB5
Blackthorn Rd. (Cumb.) G67 71 QQ2
Blackthorn St. G22 22 X9
Blackwood Av. (Linw.), Pais. 28 E13
  PA3
Blackwood St. G13 19 R8
Blackwood St. (Barr.) G78 59 L19
Blackwood Ter., John. PA5 43 C16
Blackwoods Cres. (Mood.) 15 GG7
  G69
Blacurvie Rd. G34 40 EE11
Bladda La., Pais. PA1 46 K14
Blades Ct. (Gart.) G69 27 HH9
Bladnoch Dr. G15 7 Q7
  Moraine Av.
Blaeloch Av. G45 64 W19
Blaeloch Dr. G45 64 W19
Blaeloch Ter. G45 64 W19
Blair Cres. (Bail.) G69 56 EE14
Blair Rd., Pais. PA1 32 N13
Blair St. G32 38 AA13
Blairatholl Av. G11 20 S10
Blairatholl Gdns. G11 20 S10
Blairbeth Dr. G44 51 V16
Blairbeth Rd. (Ruther.) G73 65 Y17
Blairbeth Ter. (Ruther.) G73 65 Y18
Blairdardie Rd. G13 7 Q7
Blairdardie Rd. G15 6 P7
Blairdenan Av. (Chry.) G69 15 HH6
Blairdenon Dr. (Cumb.) G68 70 MM2
Blairgowrie Rd. G52 49 Q14
Blairhall Av. G41 51 U16
Blairhill Av. (Kirk.) G66 14 EE5
Blairlogie St. G33 38 BB11
Blairmore Av., Pais. PA1 31 M13
Blairston Av. (Both.) G71 69 HH19
Blairston Gdns. (Both.) G71 69 HH19
  Blairston Av.
Blairtum Dr. (Ruther.) G73 65 Y17
Blairtummock Rd. G33 39 CC12
Blake Rd. (Cumb.) G67 71 PP3
Blane St. G4 36 W11
Blantyre Mill Rd. (Both.) G71 69 GG19
Blantyre Rd. (Both.) G71 69 HH19
Blantyre St. G3 34 T11
Blaven Ct. (Bail.) G69 56 FF14
  Bracadale Rd.
Blawarthill St. G14 18 N9
Blenheim Av. (Stepps) G33 25 CC9
Blenheim Ct. (Stepps) G33 25 DD9
  Blenheim Av.
Blenheim Ct., Pais. PA1 30 J13

Blenheim La. (Stepps) G33 25 DD9
Blesdale Ct., Clyde. G81 5 L7
Blochairn Rd. G21 37 Y11
Bluebell Gdns. G45 65 Y19
Bluevale St. G31 37 Y13
Blyth Pl. G33 39 CC13
Blyth Rd. G33 39 DD13
Blythswood Av., Renf. PA4 17 M10
Blythswood Ct. G2 35 V12
  Cadogan St.
Blythswood Dr., Pais. PA3 30 J13
Blythswood Rd., Renf. PA4 17 M9
Blythswood Sq. G2 35 V12
Blythswood St. G2 35 V12
Bobbins Gate, Pais. PA1 45 H14
Boclair Av. (Bears.) G61 7 R6
Boclair Cres. (Bears.) G61 8 S6
Boclair Cres. (Bishop.) G64 11 Y7
Boclair Rd. (Bears.) G61 8 S6
Boclair Rd. (Bishop.) G64 11 Y7
Boclair St. G13 19 R8
Boden St. G40 53 Y14
Bodmin Gdns. (Chry.) G69 15 GG6
  Gartferry Rd.
Bogany Ter. G45 64 X19
Bogbain Rd. G34 40 EE12
Boggknowe (Udd.) G71 56 FF16
  Old Edinburgh Rd.
Boghall Rd. (Udd.) G71 56 EE15
Boghall St. G33 38 BB11
Boghead Rd. G21 23 Y10
Boghead Rd. (Kirk.) G66 12 BB6
Bogleshole Rd. (Camb.) G72 54 AA16
Bogmoor Rd. G51 33 Q12
Bogside Pl. (Bail.) G69 40 FF12
  Whamflet Av.
Bogside Rd. G33 24 BB9
Bogside St. G40 53 Y14
Bogton Av. G44 63 U18
Bogton Av. La. G44 63 U18
  Bogton Av.
Boleyn Rd. G41 51 U15
Bolivar Ter. G42 52 W16
Bolton Dr. G42 51 V16
Bon Accord Sq., Clyde. G81 17 L8
Bonawe St. G20 21 U10
Boness St. G40 53 Y14
Bonhill St. G22 21 V10
Bonnar St. G40 53 Y14
Bonnaughton Rd. (Bears.) G61 6 P5
Bonnyholm Av. G53 48 P14
Bonnyrigg Dr. G43 62 S17
Bonyton Av. G13 18 N9
Boon Dr. G15 6 P7
Boquhanran Pl., Clyde. G81 5 L6
  Albert Rd.
Boquhanran Rd., Clyde. G81 4 K7
Borden La. G13 19 R9
Borden Rd. G13 19 R9
Boreland Dr. G13 18 P8
Boreland Pl. G13 18 P9
Borgie Cres. (Camb.) G72 66 BB17
Borland Rd. (Bears.) G61 8 S6
Borron St. G4 22 W10
Borthwick St. G33 38 BB11
Boswell Ct. G42 51 U16
Boswell Sq. G52 32 N12
Botanic Cres. G20 20 T10
Bothlin Dr. (Stepps) G33 25 CC9
Bothlyn Cres. (Gart.) G69 27 GG8
Bothlyn Rd. (Chry.) G69 26 FF8
Bothwell La. G2 35 V12
  West Campbell St.
Bothwell Pk. Rd. (Both.) G71 69 HH19
Bothwell Rd. (Udd.) G71 69 GG17
Bothwell St. G2 35 V12
Bothwell St. (Camb.) G72 66 AA17
Bothwell Ter. G12 35 U11
  Bank St.
Bothwellpark Ind. Est. (Udd.) 69 HH18
  G71
Bothwick Way, Pais. PA2 45 G16
Boundary Rd. (Ruther.) G73 52 X15
  Rutherglen Rd.
Bourne Ct. (Inch.), Renf. PA4 16 J8
Bourne Cres. (Inch.), Renf. 16 J8
  PA4
Bourock Sq. (Barr.) G78 60 N19
Bourtree Dr. (Ruther.) G73 65 Z18
Bouverie St. G14 18 N9
Bouverie St. (Ruther.) G73 52 X16
Bowden Dr. G52 32 P13

Street	Ref		Street	Ref		Street	Ref	
Bower St. G12	21	U10	Braidfauld St. G32	54	AA15	Broadloan, Renf. PA4	31	M11
Bowes Cres. (Bail.) G69	55	DD14	Braidfield Gro., Clyde. G81	5	L5	Broadwood Dr. G44	63	V17
Bowfield Av. G52	32	N13	Braidfield Rd., Clyde. G81	5	L5	Brock Oval G53	61	Q17
Bowfield Cres. G52	32	N13	Braidholm Cres. (Giff.) G46	62	T18	Brock Pl. G53	49	Q16
Bowfield Dr. G52	32	N13	Braidholm Rd. (Giff.) G46	62	T18	Brock Rd. G53	49	Q16
Bowfield Pl. G52	32	N13	Braidpark Cres. (Giff.) G46	62	T18	Brock Ter. G53	61	Q17
Bowfield Ter. G52	32	N13	Braidpark Dr. (Giff.) G46	62	T18	Brock Way (Cumb.) G67	71	PP3
Bowfield Cres.			Braids Dr. G53	48	N15	*North Carbrain Rd.*		
Bowhouse Way (Ruther.) G73	65	Y18	Braids Gait, Pais. PA2	46	J15	Brockburn Rd. G53	48	P15
Bowling Grn. La. G14	19	Q10	Braids Rd., Pais. PA2	46	K15	Brockburn Ter. G53	49	Q16
Westland Dr.			Bramley Pl. (Lenzie) G66	13	DD6	Brockville St. G32	38	AA13
Bowling Grn. Rd. G14	19	Q10	Branchock Av. (Camb.) G72	67	CC18	Brodick Sq. (Bishop.) G64	23	Y8
Bowling Grn. Rd. G32	55	CC14	Brand Pl. G51	34	T13	Brodick St. G21	37	Y11
Bowling Grn. Rd. G44	63	V17	Brand St. G51	34	T13	Brodie Pk. Av., Pais. PA2	46	K15
Bowling Grn. Rd. (Chry.) G69	26	FF8	Brandon Gdns. (Camb.) G72	66	AA17	Brodie Pk. Cres., Pais. PA2	46	J15
Bowman St. G42	51	V15	Brandon St. G31	36	X13	Brodie Pk. Gdns., Pais. PA2	46	K15
Bowmont Gdns. G12	20	T10	Branscroft (Kilb.), John. PA10	42	B14	Brodie Pl., Renf. PA4	31	L11
Bowmont Hill (Bishop.) G64	11	Y6	Brassey St. G20	21	U9	Brodie Rd. G21	23	Z8
Bowmont Ter. G12	20	T10	Breadalbane Gdns. (Ruther.) G73	65	Z18	Brogknowe (Udd.) G71	56	FF16
Bowmore Cres. (Udd.) G71	57	GG16	Breadalbane St. G3	35	U12	*Glasgow Rd.*		
Bowmore Gdns. (Ruther.) G73	66	AA18	*St. Vincent St.*			Bron Way (Cumb.) G67	71	PP3
Bowmore Rd. G52	33	R13	Brechin Rd. (Bishop.) G64	11	Z7	Brook St. G40	36	X13
Boyd St. G42	51	V15	Brechin St. G3	35	U12	Brookfield Av. G33	23	Z8
Boydstone Pl. (Thorn.) G46	61	R17	Breck Av., Pais. PA2	44	F16	Brookfield Cor. G33	23	Z8
Boydstone Rd. G43	61	R17	Brediland Rd., Pais. PA2	45	G15	Brookfield Dr. G33	23	Z8
Boydstone Rd. (Thorn.) G46	61	R17	Brediland Rd. (Linw.), Pais. PA3	28	E13	Brookfield Gdns. G33	23	Z8
Boydstone Rd. G53	61	R17	Bredisholm Dr. (Bail.) G69	56	FF14	Brookfield Gate G33	23	Z8
Boyle St., Clyde. G81	17	M8	Bredisholm Rd. (Bail.) G69	56	FF14	Brookfield Pl. G33	23	Z8
Boylestone Rd. (Barr.) G78	59	L18	Bredisholm Ter. (Bail.) G69	56	FF14	Brooklands Av. (Udd.) G71	57	GG16
Boyndie Path G34	40	EE12	Brenfield Av. G44	63	U18	Brooklea Dr. (Giff.) G46	62	T17
Boyndie St. G34	40	EE12	Brenfield Dr. G44	63	U18	Brookside St. G40	37	Y13
Brabl004 Cres., Pais. PA3	30	K13	Brenfield Rd. G44	63	U18	Broom Cres. (Barr.) G78	59	L17
Bracadale Dr. (Bail.) G69	56	FF14	Brent Av. (Thorn.) G46	61	R17	Broom Dr., Clyde. G81	5	L6
Bracadale Gdns. (Bail.) G69	56	FF14	Brent Dr. (Thorn.) G46	61	R17	Broom Gdns. (Kirk.) G66	12	BB5
Bracadale Gro. (Bail.) G69	56	FF14	Brent Gdns. (Thorn.) G46	62	S17	Broom Path (Bail.) G69	55	DD14
Bracadale Rd. (Bail.) G69	56	FF14	Brent Rd. (Thorn.) G46	61	R17	*Tudor St.*		
Bracken St. G22	21	V9	Brent Way (Thorn.) G46	61	R17	Broom Rd. G43	62	T17
Bracken Ter. (Both.) G71	69	HH18	Brentwood Av. G53	60	P18	Broom Rd. (Cumb.) G67	71	QQ1
Brackenbrae Av. (Bishop.) G64	10	X7	Brentwood Dr. G53	60	P18	Broom Ter., John. PA5	43	D15
Brackenbrae Rd. (Bishop.) G64	10	X7	Brentwood Sq. G53	60	P18	Broomdyke Way, Pais. PA3	30	J12
Brackenrig Rd. (Thorn.) G46	61	R19	*Brentwood Dr.*			Broomfield Av. G21	23	Y10
Brackla Av. G13	18	N8	Brereton St. G42	52	W15	*Broomfield Rd.*		
Brackla Av., Clyde. G81	18	N8	Bressey Rd. G33	39	DD13	Broomfield Av. (Camb.) G72	53	Z16
Bracora Pl. G20	20	T9	Brewery St., John. PA5	43	D14	Broomfield La. G21	22	X9
Glenfinnan Dr.			Brewster Av., Pais. PA3	31	L12	*Broomfield Rd.*		
Bradan Av. G13	18	N8	Briar Dr., Clyde. G81	5	L6	Broomfield Pl. G21	22	X9
Bradan Av., Clyde. G81	18	N8	Briar Gdns. G43	62	T17	*Broomfield Rd.*		
Bradda Av. (Ruther.) G73	65	Z18	Briar Gro. G43	62	T17	Broomfield Rd. G21	22	X9
Bradfield Av. G12	20	T9	Briar Neuk (Bishop.) G64	23	Y8	Broomfield Ter. (Udd.) G71	57	GG15
Brady Cres. (Mood.) G69	15	HH6	Briar Rd. G43	62	T17	Broomhill Av. G11	33	R11
Braeface Rd. (Cumb.) G67	70	NN3	Briarcroft Dr. G33	23	Z8	Broomhill Av. G32	54	BB16
Braefield Dr. (Thorn.) G46	62	S18	Briarcroft Pl. G33	24	AA9	Broomhill Dr. G11	19	R10
Braefoot Cres., Pais. PA2	46	K16	Briarcroft Rd. G33	23	Z9	Broomhill Dr. (Ruther.) G73	65	Y17
Braehead Rd. (Cumb.) G67	71	PP2	Briarlea Dr. (Giff.) G46	62	T18	Broomhill Gdns. G11	19	R10
Braehead Rd., Pais. PA2	58	J17	Briarwood Ct. G32	55	DD15	Broomhill La. G11	19	R10
Braehead St. G5	52	W14	Briarwood Gdns. G32	55	DD15	Broomhill Path G11	33	R11
Braemar Av., Clyde. G81	4	K6	*Woodend Rd.*			*Broomhill Ter.*		
Braemar Ct. G44	63	U18	Brick La., Pais. PA3	30	K13	Broomhill Pl. G11	19	R10
Braemar Cres. (Bears.) G61	7	R7	Bridge of Weir Rd. (Linw.), Pais. PA3	28	E13	Broomhill Ter. G11	33	R11
Braemar Cres., Pais. PA2	46	K16	Bridge St. G5	35	V13	Broomieknowe Dr. (Ruther.) G73	65	Y17
Braemar Dr. (Elder.), John. PA5	44	E15	Bridge St. (Camb.) G72	66	BB17	Broomieknowe Rd. (Ruther.) G73	65	Y17
Braemar Rd. (Ruther.) G73	66	AA18	Bridge St., Clyde. G81	4	K6	Broomielaw G1	35	V13
Braemar Rd. (Inch.), Renf. PA4	16	J8	Bridge St., Pais. PA1	46	K14	Broomknowe (Cumb.) G68	70	MM2
Braemar St. G42	51	U16	Bridge St. (Linw.), Pais. PA3	28	F13	Broomknowe Pl. (Lenzie) G66	13	DD6
Braemar Vw., Clyde. G81	4	K5	Bridgeburn Dr. (Chry.) G69	15	GG7	Broomknowes Rd. G21	23	Y10
Braemount Av., Pais. PA2	58	J17	Bridgegate G1	36	W13	Broomlands Av., Ersk. PA8	16	J8
Braes Av., Clyde. G81	17	M8	Bridgend Cres. (Mood.) G69	15	GG7	Broomlands Cres., Ersk. PA8	16	J8
Braeside Av. (Chry.) G69	15	GG7	Bridgend Pl. (Mood.) G69	15	GG7	Broomlands Gdns., Ersk. PA8	16	J8
Braeside Av. (Ruther.) G73	53	Z16	Bridgeton Cross G40	36	X13	Broomlands Rd. (Cumb.) G67	71	PP4
Braeside Cres. (Bail.) G69	41	GG13	Brigham Pl. G23	21	U8	Broomlands St., Pais. PA1	46	J14
Braeside Cres. (Barr.) G78	60	N19	*Broughton Rd.*			Broomlands Way, Ersk. PA8	16	K8
Braeside Dr. (Barr.) G78	59	M19	Bright St. G21	36	X11	Broomlea Cres. (Inch.), Renf. PA4	16	J8
Braeside Pl. (Camb.) G72	66	BB18	Brighton Pl. G51	34	S13	Broomley Dr. (Giff.) G46	62	T19
Braeside St. G20	21	U10	Brighton St. G51	34	S13	Broomley La. (Giff.) G46	62	T19
Braeview Av., Pais. PA2	45	H16	Brightside Av. (Udd.) G71	69	HH17	Broomloan Ct. G51	34	S13
Braeview Dr., Pais. PA2	45	H16	Brisbane Ct. (Giff.) G46	62	T18	Broomloan Pl. G51	34	S13
Braeview Gdns., Pais. PA2	45	H16	*Braidpark Dr.*			Broomloan Rd. G51	34	S13
Braeview Rd., Pais. PA2	45	H16	Brisbane St. G42	51	V16	Broompark Circ. G31	36	X12
Braid Sq. G4	35	V11	Brisbane St., Clyde. G81	4	J6	Broompark Dr. G31	36	X12
Braid St. G4	35	V11	Britannia Way, Renf. PA4	31	M11	Broompark Dr. (Inch.), Renf. PA4	16	J8
Braidbar Fm. Rd. (Giff.) G46	62	T18	Briton St. G51	34	S13	Broompark La. G31	36	X12
Braidbar Rd. (Giff.) G46	62	T18	Broad Pl. G40	36	X13	*Craigpark*		
Braidcraft Pl. G53	49	Q16	*Broad St.*			Broompark St. G31	36	X12
Braidcraft Rd. G53	49	Q15	Broad St. G40	36	X13	Broomton Rd. G21	23	Z8
Braidfauld Gdns. G32	54	AA14	Broadford St. G4	36	W11	Broomward Dr., John. PA5	44	E14
Braidfauld Pl. G32	54	AA15	*Harvey St.*			Brora Dr. (Giff.) G46	62	T19
			Broadholm St. G22	21	V9	Brora Dr. (Bears.) G61	8	S6
			Broadleys Av. (Bishop.) G64	10	X6	Brora Dr., Renf. PA4	18	N10
			Broadlie Dr. G13	18	P9			

Brora Gdns. (Bishop.) G64	11	Y7
Brora La. G33	37	Z11
Brora St.		
Brora Rd. (Bishop.) G64	11	Y7
Brora St. G33	37	Z11
Broughton Dr. G23	21	U8
Broughton Gdns. G23	9	U7
Broughton Rd. G23	21	U8
Brown Av., Clyde. G81	17	M8
Brown Pl. (Camb.) G72	66	BB17
Allison Dr.		
Brown Rd. (Cumb.) G67	70	NN3
Brown St. G2	35	V12
Brown St., Pais. PA1	30	J13
Brown St., Renf. PA4	31	L11
Brownhill Rd. G43	62	S18
Brownlie St. G42	51	V16
Browns La., Pais. PA1	46	K14
Brownsdale Rd. (Ruther.) G73	52	X16
Brownside Av. (Camb.) G72	66	AA17
Brownside Av. (Barr.) G78	59	L17
Brownside Av., Pais. PA2	46	J16
Brownside Cres. (Barr.) G78	59	L17
Brownside Dr. G13	18	N9
Brownside Dr. (Barr.) G78	59	L17
Brownside Gro. (Barr.) G78	59	L17
Brownside Ms. (Camb.) G72	66	AA17
Brownside Rd. (Camb.) G72	65	Z17
Brownside Rd. (Ruther.) G73	65	Z17
Bruce Av., John. PA5	43	D16
Bruce Av., Pais. PA3	31	L12
Bruce Rd. G41	51	U14
Bruce Rd., Pais. PA3	31	L13
Bruce Rd., Renf. PA4	31	L11
Bruce St., Clyde. G81	5	L7
Bruce Ter. (Blan.) G72	69	GG19
Brucefield Pl. G34	40	FF12
Brunstane Rd. G34	40	EE11
Brunswick Ho., Clyde. G81	4	J5
Perth Cres.		
Brunswick La. G1	36	W12
Brunswick St.		
Brunswick St. G1	36	W12
Brunton St. G44	63	V17
Brunton Ter. G44	63	U18
Bruntsfield Av. G53	60	P18
Bruntsfield Gdns. G53	60	P18
Bruntsfield Av.		
Brydson Pl. (Linw.), Pais. PA3	28	E13
Fulwood Av.		
Buccleuch Av. G52	32	N12
Buccleuch La. G3	35	V11
Scott St.		
Buccleuch St. G3	35	V11
Buchan St. G5	35	V13
Norfolk St.		
Buchan Ter. (Camb.) G72	66	AA18
Buchanan Cres. (Bishop.) G64	23	Z8
Buchanan Dr. (Bears.) G61	8	S6
Buchanan Dr. (Bishop.) G64	23	Z8
Buchanan Dr. (Lenzie) G66	13	CC6
Buchanan Dr. (Camb.) G72	66	AA17
Buchanan Dr. (Ruther.) G73	65	Y17
Buchanan Gdns. G32	55	DD15
Buchanan Gro. (Bail.) G69	40	EE13
Buchanan St. G1	35	V12
Buchanan St. (Bail.) G69	56	EE14
Buchanan St., John. PA5	43	D15
Buchley (Bishop.) G64	10	W5
Buchlyvie Gdns. (Bishop.) G64	22	X8
Buchlyvie Path G34	40	EE12
Buchlyvie Rd., Pais. PA1	32	N13
Buchlyvie St. G34	40	EE12
Buckingham Bldgs. G12	20	T10
Great Western Rd.		
Buckingham Dr. G32	54	BB16
Buckingham Dr. (Ruther.) G73	53	Z16
Buckingham St. G12	20	T10
Buckingham Ter. G12	20	T10
Bucklaw Gdns. G52	49	Q14
Bucklaw Pl. G52	49	Q14
Bucklaw Ter. G52	49	Q14
Buckley St. G22	22	W9
Bucksburn Rd. G21	23	Z10
Buckthorne Pl. G53	60	P18
Buddon St. G40	53	Z14
Budhill Av. G32	38	BB13
Bulldale Ct. G14	18	N9
Bulldale Rd. G14	18	N9
Bulldale St. G14	18	N9
Bullionslaw Dr. (Ruther.) G73	65	Z17
Bulloch Av. (Giff.) G46	62	T19
Bullwood Av. G53	48	N15
Bullwood Ct. G53	48	N15
Bullwood Dr. G53	48	N15
Bullwood Gdns. G53	48	N15
Bullwood Pl. G53	48	N15
Bunessan St. G52	33	R13
Bunhouse Rd. G3	34	T11
Burgh Hall La. G11	34	S11
Fortrose St.		
Burgh Hall St. G11	34	S11
Burgh La. G12	20	T10
Vinicombe St.		
Burghead Dr. G51	33	R12
Burghead Pl. G51	33	R12
Burgher St. G31	37	Z13
Burleigh Rd. (Both.) G71	69	HH18
Burleigh St. G51	34	S12
Burlington Av. G12	20	S9
Burmola St. G22	21	V10
Burn Pl. (Camb.) G72	54	AA16
Burn Ter.		
Burn Ter. (Camb.) G72	54	AA16
Burn Vw. (Cumb.) G67	71	QQ2
Burnacre Gdns. (Udd.) G71	57	GG16
Burnawn Gdns. G33	23	Z8
Brookfield Dr.		
Burnawn Pl. G33	23	Z8
Brookfield Av.		
Burnbank Dr. (Barr.) G78	59	M19
Burnbank Gdns. G20	35	U11
Burnbank Pl. G4	36	X12
Drygate		
Burnbank Ter. G20	35	U11
Burnbrae, Clyde. G81	5	L5
Burnbrae Av. (Mood.) G69	15	HH7
Burnbrae Av. (Linw.), Pais. PA3	28	F13
Bridge St.		
Burnbrae Ct. (Lenzie) G66	13	CC6
Auchinloch Rd.		
Burnbrae Dr. (Ruther.) G73	65	Z17
East Kilbride Rd.		
Burnbrae Rd. (Kirk.) G66	13	DD7
Burnbrae Rd. (Chry.) G69	14	EE7
Burnbrae Rd. (Linw.), Pais. PA3	44	F14
Burnbrae St. G21	23	Y10
Burncleuch Av. (Camb.) G72	66	BB18
Burncrooks Ct., Clyde. G81	4	K5
Burndyke Ct. G51	34	T12
Burndyke Sq. G51	34	T12
Burndyke St. G51	34	S12
Burnett Rd. G33	39	DD12
Burnfield Av. (Thorn.) G46	62	S18
Burnfield Cotts. (Thorn.) G46	62	S18
Burnfield Dr. G43	62	S18
Burnfield Gdns. (Giff.) G46	62	T18
Burnfield Rd.		
Burnfield Rd. G43	62	S17
Burnfield Rd. (Thorn.) G46	62	S18
Burnfoot Cres. (Ruther.) G73	65	Z17
Burnfoot Cres., Pais. PA2	46	J16
Burnfoot Dr. G52	32	P13
Burngreen Ter. (Cumb.) G67	71	PP1
Burnham Rd. G14	18	P10
Burnham Ter. G14	18	P10
Burnham Rd.		
Burnhead Rd. G43	63	U17
Burnhead Rd. (Cumb.) G68	70	MM3
Burnhead Rd. (Udd.) G71	57	HH16
Burnhill Quad. (Ruther.) G73	52	X16
Burnhill St. (Ruther.) G73	52	X16
Burnhouse St. G20	20	T9
Kelvindale Rd.		
Burnmouth Ct. G33	39	DD13
Pendeen Rd.		
Burnmouth Pl. (Bears.) G61	8	S5
Burnmouth Rd. G33	39	DD13
Burnpark Av. (Udd.) G71	56	FF16
Burns Dr., John. PA5	43	D16
Burns Gdns. (Blan.) G72	68	FF19
Burns Gro. (Thorn.) G46	62	S19
Burns Rd. (Cumb.) G67	71	PP3
Burns St. G4	35	V11
Burns St., Clyde. G81	4	K6
Burnside Av. (Barr.) G78	59	L18
Burnside Ct., Clyde. G81	4	K6
Scott St.		
Burnside Gdns. (Mill.Pk.), John. PA10	42	B15
Burnside Gate (Ruther.) G73	65	Z17
Burnside Gro., John. PA5	43	D15
Quarrelton Rd.		
Burnside Pl., Pais. PA3	29	H12
Burnside Rd. (Ruther.) G73	65	Z17
Burnside Rd. (Elder.), John. PA5	44	F15
Burntbroom Dr. (Bail.) G69	55	DD14
Burntbroom Gdns. (Bail.) G69	55	DD14
Burntbroom St. G33	39	CC12
Burntshields Rd. (Kilb.), John. PA10	42	A15
Burra Gdns. (Bishop.) G64	11	Z6
Solway Rd.		
Burrells La. G4	36	X12
High St.		
Burrelton Rd. G43	63	U17
Burton La. G42	51	V15
Langside Rd.		
Bushes Av., Pais. PA2	46	J15
Busheyhill St. (Camb.) G72	66	BB17
Bute Av., Renf. PA4	31	M11
Bute Cres. (Old Kil.) G60	4	J5
Bute Cres. (Bears.) G61	7	R7
Bute Cres., Pais. PA2	46	J16
Bute Dr. (Old Kil.) G60	4	J5
Bute Dr., John. PA5	43	C15
Bute Gdns. G12	34	T11
Bute Gdns. G44	63	U18
Bute Gdns. (Old Kil.) G60	4	J5
Bute La. G12	34	T11
Great George St.		
Bute Rd. (Abbots.), Pais. PA3	30	J11
Bute Ter. (Udd.) G71	57	HH16
Bute Ter. (Ruther.) G73	65	Y17
Butterbiggins Rd. G42	51	V14
Butterfield Pl. G41	51	U15
Pollokshaws Rd.		
Byrebush Rd. G53	49	Q15
Byres Av., Pais. PA3	31	L13
Byres Cres., Pais. PA3	31	L13
Byres Rd. G11	34	T11
Byres Rd. G12	34	T11
Byres Rd. (Elder.), John. PA5	44	F15
Byron Ct. (Both.) G71	69	HH19
Shelley Dr.		
Byron St. G11	33	R11
Byron St., Clyde. G81	4	K6
Byshot St. G22	22	W10

C

Cable Depot Rd., Clyde. G81	4	K7
Cadder Ct. (Bishop.) G64	11	Y5
Cadder Gro. G20	21	U8
Cadder Rd.		
Cadder Pl. G20	21	U8
Cadder Rd. G20	21	U8
Cadder Rd. G23	21	U8
Cadder Rd. (Bishop.) G64	11	Y5
Cadder Way (Bishop.) G64	11	Y5
Cadoc St. (Camb.) G72	66	BB17
Cadogan St. G2	35	V12
Cadzow Dr. (Camb.) G72	66	AA17
Cadzow St. G2	35	V12
Cadogan St.		
Caird Dr. G11	34	S11
Cairn Av., Renf. PA4	32	N11
Cairn Dr. (Linw.), Pais. PA3	28	E13
Cairn La., Pais. PA3	30	J12
Mosslands Rd.		
Cairn St. G21	22	X9
Cairnban St. G51	33	Q13
Cairnbrook Rd. G34	40	FF12
Cairncraig St. G31	53	Z14
Cairndow Av. G44	63	U18
Cairndow Ct. G44	63	U18
Cairngorm Cres. (Bears.) G61	6	P5
Cairngorm Cres. (Barr.) G78	59	M19
Cairngorm Cres., Pais. PA2	46	K15
Cairngorm Rd. G43	62	T17
Cairnhill Circ. G52	48	N14
Cairnhill Dr. G52	48	N14
Cairnhill Pl. G52	48	N14
Cairnhill Circ.		
Cairnhill Rd. (Bears.) G61	7	R7
Cairnlea Dr. G51	34	S13
Cairnoch Hill (Cumb.) G68	70	MM3
Cairns Av. (Camb.) G72	66	BB17
Cairns Rd. (Camb.) G72	66	BB18

102

Carrick Gro. G32	55	DD14
Carrick Rd. (Bishop.) G64	11	Z7
Carrick Rd. (Cumb.) G67	71	PP2
Carrick Rd. (Ruther.) G73	64	X17
Carrick St. G2	35	V12
Carrickarden Rd. (Bears.) G61	7	R6
Carrickstone Rd. (Cumb.) G68	70	NN1
Carrickstone Vw. (Cumb.) G68	70	NN1
Carriden Pl. G33	39	DD12
Carrington St. G4	35	U11
Carroglen Gdns. G32	39	CC13
Carroglen Gro. G32	39	CC13
Carron Ct. (Camb.) G72	67	CC17
Carron Cres. G22	22	W9
Carron Cres. (Bears.) G61	7	Q6
Carron Cres. (Bishop.) G64	11	Y7
Carron Cres. (Lenzie) G66	13	DD6
Carron La., Pais. PA3	31	L12
Kilearn Rd.		
Carron Pl. G22	22	X9
Carron St. G22	22	X9
Carrour Gdns. (Bishop.) G64	10	X7
Carsaig Dr. G52	33	R13
Carse Vw. Dr. (Bears.) G61	8	S5
Carsebrook Av. (Kirk.) G66	14	EE5
Chryston Rd.		
Carsegreen Av., Pais. PA2	45	H16
Carstairs St. G40	53	Y15
Carswell Gdns. G41	51	U15
Cart St., Clyde. G81	17	L8
Cartbank Gdns. G44	63	V18
Cartbank Rd.		
Cartbank Gro. G44	63	V18
Cartbank Rd. G44	63	V18
Cartcraigs Rd. G43	62	S17
Cartha Cres., Pais. PA2	47	L14
Cartha St. G41	51	U16
Cartside Av., John. PA5	43	C15
Cartside Quad. G42	51	V16
Cartside St. G42	51	U16
Cartside Ter. (Mill.Pk.), John.	43	C15
PA10		
Kilbarchan Rd.		
Cartvale La., Pais. PA3	30	K13
Cartvale Rd. G42	51	U16
Caskie Dr. (Blan.) G72	69	GG19
Cassley Av., Renf. PA4	32	N11
Castle Av. (Udd.) G71	69	GG17
Castle Av. (Elder.), John. PA5	44	E15
Castle Chimmins Av.	67	CC18
(Camb.) G72		
Castle Chimmins Rd.	67	CC18
(Camb.) G72		
Castle Cres. N. Ct. G1	36	W12
Royal Ex. Sq.		
Castle Gait, Pais. PA1	46	J14
Castle Gdns. (Chry.) G69	15	GG7
Castle Gdns., Pais. PA2	45	H14
Castle Gate (Udd.) G71	69	GG17
Castle Pl. (Udd.) G71	69	GG17
Ferry Rd.		
Castle Rd. (Elder.), John. PA5	44	F14
Castle Sq., Clyde. G81	4	K6
Castle St. G4	36	X12
Castle St. G11	34	T11
Benalder St.		
Castle St. (Bail.) G69	56	EE14
Castle St. (Ruther.) G73	53	Y16
Castle St., Clyde. G81	4	K6
Castle St., Pais. PA1	46	J14
Castle Vw., Clyde. G81	5	L6
Granville St.		
Castle Way (Cumb.) G67	71	QQ2
Castle Way (Bail.) G69	41	GG13
Dukes Rd.		
Castlebank Ct. G13	19	R9
Castlebank Cres. G11	34	S11
Meadowside St.		
Castlebank Gdns. G13	19	R9
Castlebank St. G11	33	R11
Castlebank Vills. G13	19	R9
Castlebay Dr. G22	10	W7
Castlebay Pl. G22	22	W8
Castlebay St. G22	22	W8
Castlecroft Gdns. (Udd.) G71	69	GG17
Castlefern Rd. (Ruther.) G73	65	Y18
Castlehill Cres., Renf. PA4	17	M10
Ferry Rd.		
Castlehill Rd. (Bears.) G61	6	P5
Castlelaw Gdns. G32	38	BB13
Castlelaw Pl. G32	38	BB13
Castlelaw St. G32	38	BB13
Castlemilk Cres. G44	64	X17
Castlemilk Dr. G45	64	X18
Castlemilk Ms. G44	64	X17
Castlemilk Rd.		
Castlemilk Rd. G44	52	X16
Castleton Av. (Bishop.) G64	22	X8
Colston Rd.		
Castleton Ct. G45	64	X19
Castleview Av., Pais. PA2	45	H16
Castleview Dr., Pais. PA2	45	H16
Castleview Pl., Pais. PA2	45	H16
Cathay St. G22	22	W8
Cathcart Cres., Pais. PA2	47	L14
Cathcart Pl. (Ruther.) G73	52	X16
Cathcart Rd. G42	51	V16
Cathcart Rd. (Ruther.) G73	52	X16
Cathedral Ct. G4	36	W12
Rottenrow E.		
Cathedral La. G4	36	W12
Cathedral St.		
Cathedral Sq. G4	36	X12
Cathedral St. G1	36	W12
Cathedral St. G4	36	W12
Catherine Pl. G3	35	U12
Hydepark St.		
Cathkin Av. (Camb.) G72	66	AA17
Cathkin Av. (Ruther.) G73	53	Z16
Cathkin Bypass (Ruther.) G73	65	Z18
Cathkin Ct. G45	64	X19
Cathkin Cres. (Cumb.) G68	70	NN2
Cathkin Gdns. (Udd.) G71	57	GG15
Cathkin Pl. (Camb.) G72	66	AA17
Cathkin Rd. G42	51	U16
Cathkin Rd. (Udd.) G71	57	GG15
Cathkin Rd. (Ruther.) G73	65	Y19
Cathkin Rd. (Clark.) G76	65	Y19
Cathkin Vw. G32	54	BB16
Cathkinview Pl. G42	51	V16
Cathkinview Rd. G42	51	V16
Catrine Ct. G53	48	P16
Catrine Gdns. G53	48	P16
Catrine Pl. G53	48	P16
Catrine Rd. G53	48	P16
Causewayside Cres. G32	54	BB15
Causewayside St. G32	54	BB15
Causeyside St., Pais. PA1	46	K14
Cavendish Pl. G5	51	V14
Cavendish St. G5	51	V14
Cavin Dr. G45	64	X18
Cavin Rd. G45	64	X18
Cawder Ct. (Cumb.) G68	70	MM1
Cawder Pl. (Cumb.) G68	70	MM1
Cawder Rd. (Cumb.) G68	70	MM2
Cawder Vw. (Cumb.) G68	70	MM1
Cawder Way (Cumb.) G68	70	MM1
Cayton Gdns. (Bail.) G69	55	DD14
Cecil Pl. G51	35	U13
Paisley Rd. W.		
Cecil St. G12	20	T10
Cedar Av., Clyde. G81	4	J6
Cedar Av., John. PA5	44	E16
Cedar Ct. G20	35	V11
Cedar Ct. (Kilb.), John. PA10	42	B14
Cedar Dr. (Lenzie) G66	13	CC5
Cedar Gdns. (Ruther.) G73	65	Z18
Cedar Pl. (Blan.) G72	68	FF19
Cedar Pl. (Barr.) G78	59	M19
Cedar Rd. (Bishop.) G64	23	Y8
Cedar Rd. (Cumb.) G67	71	QQ2
Cedar St. G20	35	V11
Cedar Wk. (Bishop.) G64	23	Y8
Cedric Pl. G13	19	Q8
Cedric Rd. G13	19	Q8
Celtic St. G20	20	T8
Cemetery Rd. G52	49	Q14
Paisley Rd. W.		
Centenary Ct., Clyde. G81	5	L7
Bruce St.		
Central Av. G11	33	R11
Broomhill Ter.		
Central Av. G32	55	CC14
Central Av. (Camb.) G72	66	AA17
Central Av., Clyde. G81	5	L7
Central Chambers G2	35	V12
Hope St.		
Central Gro. G32	55	CC14
Central Gro. (Camb.) G72	66	AA17
Central Path G32	55	DD14
Central Rd., Pais. PA1	30	K13
Central Sta. G1	35	V12
Central Way (Cumb.) G67	70	NN4
Central Way, Pais. PA1	30	K13
Centre, The (Barr.) G78	59	L19
Centre St. G5	35	V13
Centre Way (Barr.) G78	59	L18
Ceres Gdns. (Bishop.) G64	11	Z7
Cessnock Pl. (Camb.) G72	67	CC17
Cessnock Rd. G33	24	BB9
Cessnock St. G51	34	T13
Chachan Dr. G51	33	R12
Skipness Dr.		
Chalmers Ct. G40	36	X13
Chalmers Gate G40	36	X13
Claythorn St.		
Chalmers Pl. G40	36	X13
Claythorn St.		
Chalmers St. G40	36	X13
Chalmers St., Clyde. G81	5	L7
Chamberlain La. G13	19	R9
Chamberlain Rd. G13	19	R9
Chancellor St. G11	34	S11
Chapel Rd., Clyde. G81	5	L5
Chapel St. G20	21	U9
Chapel St. (Ruther.) G73	52	X16
Chapelhill Rd., Pais. PA2	47	L15
Chapelton Av. (Bears.) G61	7	R6
Chapelton Gdns. (Bears.) G61	7	R6
Chapelton St. G22	21	V9
Chaplet Av. G13	19	Q8
Chapman St. G42	51	V15
Allison St.		
Chappell St. (Barr.) G78	59	L18
Charing Cross G2	35	U11
Charing Cross La. G3	35	U12
Granville St.		
Charles Av., Renf. PA4	17	M10
Charles Cres. (Lenzie) G66	13	CC6
Charles St. G21	36	X11
Charlotte La. G1	36	W13
London Rd.		
Charlotte La. S. G1	36	W13
Charlotte St.		
Charlotte La. W. G1	36	W13
London Rd.		
Charlotte Pl., Pais. PA2	46	K15
Charlotte St. G1	36	W13
Charnwood Av., John. PA5	43	C16
Chatelherault Av. (Camb.)	66	AA17
G72		
Chatton St. G23	8	T7
Cheapside St. G3	35	U12
Chelmsford Dr. G12	20	S9
Cherry Bk. (Kirk.) G66	12	BB5
Cherry Cres., Clyde. G81	5	L6
Cherry Pl. (Bishop.) G64	23	Y8
Cherry Pl., John. PA5	44	E15
Cherrybank Rd. G43	63	U17
Cherrytree Dr. (Camb.) G72	67	DD18
Cherrywood Rd. (Elder.),	44	F15
John. PA5		
Chester St. G32	38	BB13
Chesterfield Av. G12	20	S9
Chesters Pl. (Ruther.) G73	53	Y16
Chesters Rd. (Bears.) G61	7	Q6
Chestnut Dr. (Kirk.) G66	12	BB5
Chestnut Dr., Clyde. G81	5	L5
Chestnut Pl., John. PA5	44	E16
Chestnut St. G22	22	W9
Chestnut Way (Camb.) G72	67	DD18
Cheviot Av. (Barr.) G78	59	M19
Cheviot Rd. G43	62	T17
Cheviot Rd., Pais. PA2	46	K16
Chirmorie Pl. G53	48	P15
Dalmellington Rd.		
Chirnside Pl. G52	32	P13
Chirnside Rd. G52	32	P13
Chisholm St. G1	36	W13
Chrighton Grn. (Udd.) G71	57	HH16
Christian St. G43	50	T16
Christie La., Pais. PA3	30	K13
New Sneddon St.		
Christie Pl. (Camb.) G72	66	BB17
Christie St., Pais. PA1	30	K13
Christopher St. G21	37	Y11
Chryston Rd. (Kirk.) G66	14	FF5
Chryston Rd. (Chry.) G69	26	FF8
Church Av. (Stepps) G33	25	CC9
Church Av. (Ruther.) G73	65	Z17
Church Dr. (Kirk.) G66	13	CC5
Church Hill, Pais. PA1	30	K13
Church La. G42	51	V15
Victoria Rd.		
Church Rd. (Giff.) G46	62	T19
Church Rd. (Muir.) G69	26	FF8

Church St. G11	34	T11
Church St. (Bail.) G69	56	FF14
Church St. (Udd.) G71	69	GG17
Church St., Clyde. G81	5	L6
Church St., John. PA5	43	D14
Church St. (Kilb.), John. PA10	42	B14
Church Vw. (Camb.) G72	54	BB16
Churchill Av., John. PA5	43	C16
Churchill Cres. (Both.) G71	69	HH18
Churchill Dr. G11	19	R10
Churchill Pl. (Kilb.), John. PA10	42	B14
Churchill Way (Bishop.) G64	10	X7
Kirkintilloch Rd.		
Circus Dr. G31	36	X12
Circus Pl. G31	36	X12
Circus Pl. La. G31	36	X12
Circus Pl.		
Cityford Cres. (Ruther.) G73	52	X16
Cityford Dr. (Ruther.) G73	52	X16
Clachan Dr. G51	33	R12
Skipness Dr.		
Claddens Pl. (Lenzie) G66	13	DD6
Claddens Quad. G22	22	W9
Claddens St. G22	21	V9
Claddens Wynd (Kirk.) G66	13	DD6
Claddon Vw., Clyde. G81	5	M6
Kirkoswald Dr.		
Clair Rd. (Bishop.) G64	11	Z7
Clairinsh Gdns., Renf. PA4	31	M11
Sandy Rd.		
Clairmont Gdns. G3	35	U11
Clare St. G21	37	Y11
Claremont Pas. G3	35	U11
Claremont Ter.		
Claremont Pl. G3	35	U11
Claremont Ter.		
Claremont St. G3	35	U12
Claremont Ter. G3	35	U11
Claremont Ter. La. G3	35	U11
Clifton St.		
Claremount Av. (Giff.) G46	62	T19
Clarence Dr. G11	20	S10
Clarence Dr. G12	20	S10
Clarence Dr., Pais. PA1	47	L14
Clarence Gdns. G11	20	S10
Clarence La. G12	20	S10
Hyndland Rd.		
Clarence St., Clyde. G81	5	M6
Clarence St., Pais. PA1	31	L13
Clarendon La. G20	35	V11
Clarendon St.		
Clarendon Pl. G20	35	V11
Clarendon Pl. (Stepps) G33	25	CC9
Clarendon St. G20	35	V11
Clarion Cres. G13	18	P8
Clarion Rd. G13	18	P8
Clark St. G41	35	U13
Tower St.		
Clark St., Clyde. G81	4	K6
Clark St., John. PA5	43	D14
Clark St., Pais. PA3	30	J13
Clark St., Renf. PA4	17	L10
Clarkston Av. G44	63	U18
Clarkston Rd. G44	63	U18
Clarkston Rd. (Clark.) G76	63	U19
Clathic Av. (Bears.) G61	8	S6
Claud Rd., Pais. PA3	31	L13
Claude Av. (Camb.) G72	67	DD18
Clavens Rd. G52	32	N13
Claverhouse Pl., Pais. PA2	47	L14
Claverhouse Rd. G52	32	N12
Clavering St. E., Pais. PA1	30	J13
Well St.		
Clavering St. W., Pais. PA1	30	J13
King St.		
Clayhouse Rd. G33	25	DD9
Claypotts Pl. G33	38	BB11
Claypotts Rd. G33	38	BB11
Clayslaps Rd. G3	34	T11
Argyle St.		
Claythorn Av. G40	36	X13
Claythorn Circ. G40	36	X13
Claythorn Av.		
Claythorn Ct. G40	36	X13
Claythorn Pk.		
Claythorn Pk. G40	36	X13
Claythorn St. G40	36	X13
Claythorn Ter. G40	36	X13
Claythorn Pk.		
Clayton Ter. G31	36	X12
Cleddans Cres., Clyde. G81	5	M5
Cleddans Rd., Clyde. G81	5	M5
Cleddens Ct. (Bishop.) G64	11	Y7
Cleeves Pl. G53	60	P17
Cleeves Quad. G53	60	P17
Cleeves Rd. G53	60	P17
Cleghorn St. G22	21	V10
Cleland La. G5	36	W13
Cleland St.		
Cleland St. G5	36	W13
Clelland Av. (Bishop.) G64	23	Y8
Clerwood St. G32	37	Z13
Cleveden Cres. G12	20	S9
Cleveden Cres. La. G12	20	S9
Cleveden Dr.		
Cleveden Dr. G12	20	S9
Cleveden Dr. (Ruther.) G73	65	Z17
Cleveden Gdns. G12	20	T9
Cleveden La. G12	20	S9
Burlington Av.		
Cleveden Pl. G12	20	S9
Cleveden Rd. G12	20	S9
Cleveland St. G3	35	U11
Cliff Rd. G3	35	U11
Clifford Gdns. G51	34	S13
Clifford La. G51	34	T13
North Gower St.		
Clifford Pl. G51	34	T13
Clifford St.		
Clifford St. G51	34	S13
Clifton Pl. G3	35	U11
Clifton St.		
Clifton Rd. (Giff.) G46	62	S18
Clifton St. G3	35	U11
Clifton Ter. (Camb.) G72	66	AA18
Clifton Ter., John. PA5	44	E15
Clincart Rd. G42	51	V16
Clincarthill Rd. (Ruther.) G73	53	Y16
Clippens Rd. (Linw.), Pais. PA3	28	E13
Cloan Av. G15	6	P7
Cloan Cres. (Bishop.) G64	11	Y6
Cloberhill Rd. G13	7	Q7
Cloch St. G33	38	BB12
Clochoderick Av. (Mill.Pk.), John. PA10	42	B15
Mackenzie Dr.		
Clonbeith St. G33	39	DD11
Closeburn St. G22	22	W9
Cloth St. (Barr.) G78	59	M19
Clouden Rd. (Cumb.) G67	71	PP3
Cloudhowe Ter. (Blan.) G72	68	FF19
Clouston Ct. G20	21	U10
Clouston La. G20	20	T10
Clouston St.		
Clouston St. G20	20	T10
Clova Pl. (Udd.) G71	69	GG17
Clova St. (Thorn.) G46	61	R18
Clover Av. (Bishop.) G64	10	X7
Cloverbank St. G21	37	Y11
Clovergate (Bishop.) G64	10	X7
Clunie Rd. G52	49	R14
Cluny Av. (Bears.) G61	8	S7
Cluny Dr. (Bears.) G61	8	S7
Cluny Dr., Pais. PA3	31	L13
Cluny Gdns. G14	19	R10
Cluny Gdns. (Bail.) G69	56	EE14
Cluny Vills. G14	19	Q10
Westland Dr.		
Clutha St. G51	35	U13
Paisley Rd. W.		
Clyde Av. (Both.) G71	69	GG19
Clyde Av. (Barr.) G78	59	M19
Clyde Ct., Clyde. G81	4	K6
Littleholm		
Clyde Pl. G5	35	V13
Clyde Pl. (Camb.) G72	67	CC18
Clyde Pl., John. PA5	43	C16
Clyde Rd., Pais. PA3	31	L12
Clyde St. G1	35	V13
Clyde St., Clyde. G81	17	L8
Clyde St., Renf. PA4	17	M9
Clyde Ter. (Both.) G71	69	HH19
Clyde Tunnel G14	33	R11
Clyde Tunnel G51	33	R11
Clyde Tunnel Expressway G51	33	Q12
Clyde Vale (Both.) G71	69	HH19
Clyde Vw., Pais. PA2	47	L15
Clydebrae Dr. (Both.) G71	69	HH19
Clydebrae St. G51	34	S12
Clydeford Dr. G32	54	AA14
Clydeford Dr. (Udd.) G71	56	FF16
Clydeford Rd. (Camb.) G72	54	BB16
Clydeholm Rd. G14	33	Q11
Clydeholm Ter., Clyde. G81	17	M8
Clydeneuk Dr. (Udd.) G71	56	FF16
Clydesdale Av., Pais. PA3	31	L11
Clydeside Expressway G3	34	T11
Clydeside Expressway G14	19	Q10
Clydeside Rd. (Ruther.) G73	52	X15
Clydesmill Dr. G32	54	BB16
Clydesmill Gro. G32	54	BB16
Clydesmill Pl. G32	54	BB16
Clydesmill Rd. G32	54	BB16
Clydeview G11	34	S11
Dumbarton Rd.		
Clydeview La. G11	33	R11
Broomhill Ter.		
Clydeview Ter. G32	55	CC16
Clydeview Ter. G40	52	X14
Newhall St.		
Clynder St. G51	34	S13
Clyth Dr. (Giff.) G46	62	T19
Coalhill St. G31	37	Y13
Coatbridge Rd. (Bail.) G69	41	GG13
Coatbridge Rd. (Gart.) G69	27	GG10
Coats Cres. (Bail.) G69	40	EE13
Coats Dr., Pais. PA2	45	H14
Coatshill Av. (Blan.) G72	68	FF19
Cobblerigg Way (Udd.) G71	69	GG17
Cobden Rd. G21	36	X11
Cobington Pl. G33	38	BB11
Cobinshaw St. G32	38	BB13
Coburg St. G5	35	V13
Cochno St., Clyde. G81	17	M8
Cochran St., Pais. PA1	46	K14
Cochrane Sq. (Linw.), Pais. PA3	28	E13
Cochrane St. G1	36	W12
Cochrane St. (Barr.) G78	59	L19
Cochranemill Rd., John. PA5	43	C15
Cockels Ln., Renf. PA4	31	L11
Cockenzie St. G32	38	BB13
Cockmuir St. G21	23	Y10
Cogan Pl. (Barr.) G78	59	L19
Cogan Rd. G43	62	T17
Cogan St. G43	50	T16
Cogan St. (Barr.) G78	59	L19
Colbert St. G40	52	X14
Colbreggan Ct., Clyde. G81	5	M5
St. Helena Cres.		
Colbreggan Gdns., Clyde. G81	5	M5
Colchester Dr. G12	20	S9
Coldingham Av. G14	18	N9
Coldstream Dr. (Ruther.) G73	65	Z17
Coldstream Dr., Pais. PA2	45	H15
Coldstream Pl. G21	22	W10
Keppochhill Rd.		
Coldstream Rd., Clyde. G81	5	L7
Colebrook St. (Camb.) G72	66	BB17
Colebrooke La. G12	21	U10
Colebrooke St.		
Colebrooke Pl. G12	21	U10
Belmont St.		
Colebrooke St. G12	21	U10
Colebrooke Ter. G12	21	U10
Colebrooke St.		
Coleridge (Both.) G71	69	HH18
Colfin St. G34	40	FF11
Colgrain St. G20	21	V9
Colgrave Cres. G32	54	AA14
Colinbar Circle (Barr.) G78	59	L19
Colinslee Av., Pais. PA2	46	K15
Colinslee Cres., Pais. PA2	46	K15
Colinslee Dr., Pais. PA2	46	K15
Colinslie Rd. G53	49	Q16
Colinton Pl. G32	38	BB12
Colintraive Av. G33	24	AA10
Colintraive Cres. G33	24	AA10
Coll Av., Renf. PA4	31	M11
Coll Pl. G21	37	Y11
Coll St. G21	37	Y11
Colla Gdns. (Bishop.) G64	11	Z7
College La. G1	36	W13
High St.		
College La., Pais. PA1	46	J14
College St. G1	36	W12
Collessie Dr. G33	39	CC11
Collier St., John. PA5	43	D14
Collina St. G20	20	T9
Collins St. G4	36	X12
Collylin Rd. (Bears.) G61	7	R6
Colmonell Av. G13	18	N8

104

Street	Page	Grid
Colonsay Av., Renf. PA4	31	M11
Colonsay Rd. G52	33	R13
Colonsay Rd., Pais. PA2	46	J16
Colquhoun Av. G52	32	P12
Colquhoun Dr. (Bears.) G61	7	Q5
Colston Av. (Bishop.) G64	22	X8
Colston Dr. (Bishop.) G64	22	X8
Colston Gdns. (Bishop.) G64	22	X8
Colston Path (Bishop.) G64	22	X8
Colston Gdns.		
Colston Pl. (Bishop.) G64	22	X8
Colston Rd.		
Colston Rd. (Bishop.) G64	22	X8
Coltmuir Av. (Bishop.) G64	22	X8
Coltmuir Dr.		
Coltmuir Cres. (Bishop.) G64	22	X8
Coltmuir Dr. (Bishop.) G64	22	X8
Coltmuir Gdns. (Bishop.) G64	22	X8
Coltmuir Dr.		
Coltmuir St. G22	21	V9
Coltness La. G33	39	CC12
Coltness St. G33	39	CC12
Coltpark Av. (Bishop.) G64	22	X8
Coltpark La. (Bishop.) G64	22	X8
Coltsfoot Dr. G53	60	P18
Columba Path, Clyde. G81	5	M7
Onslow Rd.		
Columba St. G51	34	S12
Colvend Dr. (Ruther.) G73	65	Y18
Colvend St. G40	52	X14
Colville Dr. (Ruther.) G73	65	Z17
Colwood Av. G53	60	P18
Colwood Gdns. G53	60	P18
Colwood Av.		
Colwood Path G53	60	P18
Parkhouse Rd.		
Colwood Pl. G53	60	P18
Colwood Sq. G53	60	P18
Colwood Av.		
Comedie Rd. G33	25	DD10
Comelypark St. G31	37	Y13
Comley Pl. G31	37	Y13
Gallowgate		
Commerce St. G5	35	V13
Commercial Ct. G5	36	W13
Commercial Rd. G5	52	W14
Commercial Rd. (Barr.) G78	59	M18
Commonhead Rd. G34	40	FF12
Commore Av. (Barr.) G78	59	M19
Commore Dr. G13	18	P8
Comrie Rd. G33	25	CC9
Comrie St. G32	54	BB14
Cona St. (Thorn.) G46	61	R18
Conan Ct. (Camb.) G72	67	CC17
Condorrat Ring Rd. (Cumb.) G67	70	MM4
Congleton St. G53	60	N17
Nitshill Rd.		
Congress Rd. G3	35	U12
Congress Way G3	35	U12
Conifer Pl. (Kirk.) G66	12	BB5
Conisborough Path G34	39	DD11
Balfluig St.		
Conisborough Rd. G34	39	DD11
Conistone Cres. (Bail.) G69	55	DD14
Connal St. G40	53	Y14
Conniston St. G32	38	AA12
Connor Rd. (Barr.) G78	59	L18
Conon Av. (Bears.) G61	7	Q6
Consett La. G33	39	CC12
Consett St. G33	39	CC12
Consett La.		
Contin Pl. G12	20	T9
Convair Way, Renf. PA4	31	M11
Lismore Av.		
Conval Way, Pais. PA3	30	J12
Abbotsburn Way		
Cook St. G5	35	V13
Cooperage Ct. G14	17	M9
Coopers Well La. G11	34	T11
Dumbarton Rd.		
Coopers Well St. G11	34	T11
Dumbarton Rd.		
Copland Pl. G51	34	S13
Copland Quad. G51	34	S13
Copland Rd. G51	34	S13
Coplaw St. G42	51	V14
Copperfield La. (Udd.) G71	57	HH16
Hamilton Vw.		
Corbett St. G32	54	BB14
Corbiston Way (Cumb.) G67	71	PP3
Cordiner St. G44	51	V16
Corkerhill Gdns. G52	49	R14
Corkerhill Pl. G52	49	Q15
Corkerhill Rd. G52	49	Q15
Corlaich Av. G42	52	X16
Corlaich Dr. G42	52	X16
Corn St. G4	35	V11
Cornaig Rd. G53	48	P16
Cornalee Gdns. G53	48	P16
Cornalee Pl. G53	48	P16
Cornalee Rd. G53	48	P16
Cornhill St. G21	23	Y9
Cornoch St. G23	8	T7
Torrin Rd.		
Cornock Cres., Clyde. G81	5	L6
Cornock St., Clyde. G81	5	L6
Cornwall Av. (Ruther.) G73	65	Z17
Cornwall St. G41	34	T13
Cornwall St. S. G41	34	T13
Coronation Pl. (Gart.) G69	27	GG8
Coronation Way (Bears.) G61	8	S7
Corpach Pl. G34	40	FF11
Corran St. G33	38	AA12
Corrie Dr., Pais. PA1	48	N14
Corrie Gro. G44	63	U18
Corrie Pl. (Lenzie) G66	13	DD6
Corrour Rd. G43	50	T16
Corse Rd. G52	32	N13
Corsebar Av., Pais. PA2	46	J15
Corsebar Cres., Pais. PA2	46	J15
Corsebar Dr., Pais. PA2	46	J15
Corsebar La., Pais. PA2	45	H15
Balgonie Av.		
Corsebar Rd., Pais. PA2	45	H15
Corsebar Way, Pais. PA2	46	J14
Corseford Av., John. PA5	43	C16
Corsehill Pl. G34	40	FF12
Corsehill St. G34	40	FF12
Corselet Rd. G53	60	P18
Corsewall Av. G32	55	DD14
Corsford Dr. G53	61	Q17
Corsock St. G31	37	Z12
Corston St. G33	37	Z12
Cortachy Pl. (Bishop.) G64	11	Z7
Coruisk Way, Pais. PA2	45	G16
Spencer Dr.		
Corunna St. G3	35	U12
Coshneuk Rd. G33	24	BB9
Cottar St. G20	21	U8
Cotton Av. (Linw.), Pais. PA3	28	E13
Cotton St. G40	53	Y15
Cotton St., Pais. PA1	46	K14
Coulin Gdns. G22	22	W10
Coulters La. G40	36	X13
Countess Way (Bail.) G69	41	HH13
Park Rd.		
Counting Ho., The, Pais. PA1	45	H14
County Av. (Camb.) G72	53	Z16
County Pl., Pais. PA1	30	K13
Moss St.		
County Sq., Pais. PA1	30	K13
Couper St. G4	36	W11
Courthill (Bears.) G61	7	Q5
Courthill Av. G44	63	V17
Coustonhill St. G43	50	T16
Pleasance St.		
Coustonholm Rd. G43	50	T16
Coventry Dr. G31	37	Y12
Cowal Dr. (Linw.), Pais. PA3	28	E13
Cowal Rd. G20	20	T8
Cowal St. G20	20	T8
Cowan Clo. (Barr.) G78	59	M18
Cowan Cres. (Barr.) G78	59	M19
Cowan La. G12	35	U11
Cowan St.		
Cowan Rd. (Cumb.) G68	70	MM3
Cowan St. G12	35	U11
Cowan Wilson Av. (Blan.) G72	68	FF19
Cowan Wynd (Udd.) G71	57	HH16
Cowcaddens Rd. G4	35	V11
Cowcaddens St. G2	35	V12
Renfield St.		
Cowden Dr. (Bishop.) G64	11	Y6
Cowden St. G51	33	Q12
Cowdenhill Circ. G13	19	Q8
Cowdenhill Pl. G13	19	Q8
Cowdenhill Rd. G13	19	Q8
Cowdray Cres., Renf. PA4	17	M10
Cowell Vw., Clyde. G81	5	L6
Granville St.		
Cowglen Pl. G53	49	Q16
Cowglen Rd.		
Cowglen Rd. G53	49	Q16
Cowglen Ter. G53	49	Q16
Cowlairs Rd. G21	22	X10
Coxhill St. G21	22	W10
Coxton Pl. G33	39	CC11
Coylton Rd. G43	63	U17
Craggan Dr. G14	18	N9
Crags Av., Pais. PA2	46	K15
Crags Cres., Pais. PA2	46	K15
Crags Rd., Pais. PA2	46	K15
Craig Rd. G44	63	V17
Craigallian Av. (Camb.) G72	67	CC18
Craiganour La. G43	62	T17
Craiganour Pl. G43	62	T17
Craigard Pl. (Ruther.) G73	66	AA18
Inverclyde Gdns.		
Craigbank Dr. G53	60	P17
Craigbank St. G22	22	W10
Craigbarnet Cres. G33	24	BB10
Craigbo Av. G23	8	T7
Craigbo Ct. G23	20	T8
Craigbo Dr. G23	20	T8
Craigbo Pl. G23	20	T8
Craigbo Rd. G23	20	T8
Craigbo St. G23	8	T7
Craigbog Av., John. PA5	43	C15
Craigdonald Pl., John. PA5	43	D14
Craigellan Rd. G43	62	T17
Craigenbay Cres. (Lenzie) G66	13	CC5
Craigenbay Rd. (Lenzie) G66	13	CC6
Craigenbay St. G21	23	Y10
Craigencart Ct., Clyde. G81	4	K5
Gentle Row		
Craigend Pl. G13	19	R9
Craigend St. G13	19	R9
Craigendmuir Rd. G33	25	DD10
Craigendmuir St. G33	37	Z11
Craigendon Oval, Pais. PA2	58	J17
Craigendon Rd., Pais. PA2	58	J17
Craigends Dr. (Kilb.), John. PA10	42	B14
High Barholm		
Craigenfeoch Av., John. PA5	43	C15
Craigfaulds Av., Pais. PA2	45	H15
Craigflower Gdns. G53	60	P18
Craigflower Rd. G53	60	P18
Craighalbert Rd. (Cumb.) G68	70	MM2
Craighalbert Way (Cumb.) G68	70	MM2
Craighall Rd. G4	35	V11
Craighead Av. G33	23	Z10
Craighead St. (Barr.) G78	59	L19
Craighead Way (Barr.) G78	59	L19
Craighouse St. G33	38	BB11
Craigie Pk. (Lenzie) G66	13	DD5
Craigie St. G42	51	V15
Craigiebar Dr., Pais. PA2	46	J16
Craigieburn Gdns. G20	20	S8
Craigieburn Rd. (Cumb.) G67	70	NN3
Craigiehall Pl. G51	34	T13
Craigiehall St. G51	35	U13
Craigiehall Pl.		
Craigielea Dr., Pais. PA3	29	H13
Craigielea Pk., Renf. PA4	17	L10
Craigielea Rd., Renf. PA4	17	M10
Craigielea St. G31	37	Y12
Craigiolinn Av., Pais. PA2	58	J17
Craigievar St. G33	39	DD11
Craigleith St. G32	38	AA13
Craiglockhart St. G33	39	CC11
Craigmaddie Ter. La. G3	35	U12
Derby St.		
Craigmillar Rd. G42	51	V16
Craigmont Dr. G20	21	U9
Craigmont St. G20	21	U9
Craigmore St. G31	37	Z13
Craigmount Av., Pais. PA2	58	J17
Craigmuir Cres. G52	32	N13
Craigmuir Pl. G52	32	N13
Craigmuir Rd.		
Craigmuir Rd. G52	32	N13
Craigneil St. G33	39	DD11
Craignestock Pl. G40	36	X13
London Rd.		
Craignestock St. G40	36	X13
Craignethan Gdns. G11	34	S11
Lawrie St.		
Craignure Rd. (Ruther.) G73	65	Y18
Craigpark G31	37	Y12
Craigpark Dr. G31	37	Y12
Craigpark Ter. G31	37	Y12
Craigpark		

Cumlodden Dr. G20 20 T8
Cumming Dr. G42 51 V16
Cumnock Dr. (Barr.) G78 59 M19
Cumnock Rd. G33 24 AA9
Cunard St., Clyde. G81 17 L8
Cunningham Dr. (Giff.) G46 63 U18
Cunningham Dr., Clyde. G81 4 K5
Cunningham Rd. G52 32 N12
Cunningham Rd. (Ruther.) 53 Z16
G73
Cunninghame Rd. (Kilb.), 42 B14
John. PA10
Curfew Rd. G13 7 Q7
Curle St. G14 33 Q11
Curlew Pl., John. PA5 43 C16
Curling Cres. G44 52 W16
Currie St. G20 21 U9
Curtis Av. G44 52 W16
Curtis Av. (Ruther.) G73 52 W16
Curzon St. G20 21 U9
Custom Ho. Quay G1 36 W12
Cut, The (Udd.) G71 69 GG17
Cuthbert St. (Udd.) G71 57 HH16
Cuthbertson St. G42 51 V15
Cuthelton Dr. G31 54 AA14
Cuthelton St.
Cuthelton St. G31 53 Z14
Cuthelton Ter. G31 53 Z14
Cypress Av. (Udd.) G71 57 HH16
Cypress Av. (Blan.) G72 68 FF19
Cypress Ct. (Kirk.) G66 12 BB5
Cypress St. G22 22 W9
Cypress Way (Camb.) G72 67 DD18
Cyprus Av. (Elder.), John. 44 E15
PA5
Cyril St., Pais. PA1 47 L14

D

Daer Av., Renf. PA4 32 N11
Dairsie Ct. G44 63 U18
Dairsie Gdns. (Bishop.) G64 23 Z8
Dairsie St. G44 63 U18
Daisy St. G42 51 V15
Dakota Way, Renf. PA4 31 M11
Friendship Way
Dalbeth Rd. G32 54 AA15
Dalcharn Path G34 40 EE12
Dalcharn Pl.
Dalcharn Pl. G34 40 EE12
Dalcraig Cres. (Blan.) G72 68 FF19
Dalcross La. G11 34 T11
Byres Rd.
Dalcross St. G11 34 T11
Dalcruin Gdns. (Mood.) G69 15 HH6
Daldowie Av. G32 55 CC14
Daldowie Rd. (Udd.) G71 56 EE15
Dale St. G40 52 X14
Dale Way (Ruther.) G73 65 Y18
Daleview Av. G12 20 S9
Dalfoil Ct., Pais. PA1 48 N14
Dalgarroch Av., Clyde. G81 18 N8
Dalgleish Av., Clyde. G81 4 K5
Dalhouse Rd. (Udd.) G71 56 EE15
Dalhousie Gdns. (Bishop.) 10 X7
G64
Dalhousie La. G3 35 V11
Scott St.
Dalhousie La. W. G3 35 V11
Buccleuch St.
Dalhousie Rd. (Mill.Pk.), 42 B15
John. PA10
Dalhousie St. G3 35 V11
Dalilea Dr. G34 40 FF11
Dalilea Path G34 40 FF11
Dalilea Dr.
Dalilea Pl. G34 40 FF11
Dalintober St. G5 35 V13
Dalkeith Av. G41 50 S14
Dalkeith Av. (Bishop.) G64 11 Y6
Dalkeith Rd. (Bishop.) G64 11 Y6
Dalmahoy St. G32 38 AA12
Dalmally St. G20 21 U10
Dalmarnock Bri. G40 53 Y15
Dalmarnock Bri. (Ruther.) 53 Y15
G73
Dalmarnock Ct. G40 53 Y14
Baltic St.
Dalmarnock Rd. G40 52 X14
Dalmarnock Rd. (Ruther.) 53 Y15
G73
Dalmary Dr., Pais. PA1 31 L13

Dalmellington Dr. G53 48 P16
Dalmellington Rd. G53 48 P16
Dalmeny Av. (Giff.) G46 62 T18
Dalmeny Dr. (Barr.) G78 59 L19
Dalmeny St. G5 52 X15
Dalmuir Ct., Clyde. G81 4 K6
Stewart St.
Dalnair St. G3 34 T11
Dalness Pas. G32 54 BB14
Ochil St.
Dalness St. G32 54 BB14
Dalreoch Av. (Bail.) G69 40 FF13
Dalriada St. G40 53 Z14
Dalry Rd. (Udd.) G71 57 HH16
Myrtle Rd.
Dalry St. G32 54 BB14
Dalserf Cres. (Giff.) G46 62 S19
Dalserf St. G31 37 Y13
Dalsetter Av. G15 6 N7
Dalsetter Pl. G15 6 P7
Dalsholm Av. G20 20 S8
Dalsholm Rd. G20 20 S8
Dalskeith Av., Pais. PA3 29 H13
Dalskeith Cres., Pais. PA3 29 H13
Dalskeith Rd., Pais. PA3 45 H14
Dalswinton Pl. G34 40 FF12
Dalswinton St.
Dalswinton St. G34 40 FF12
Dalton Av., Clyde. G81 5 M7
Dalton St. G31 38 AA13
Dalveen Ct. (Barr.) G78 59 M19
Dalveen Dr. (Udd.) G71 57 GG16
Dalveen St. G32 38 AA13
Dalveen Way (Ruther.) G73 65 Z18
Dalwhinnie Av. (Blan.) G72 68 FF19
Daly Gdns. (Blan.) G72 69 GG19
Dalziel Dr. G41 50 T14
Dalziel Quad. G41 50 T14
Dalziel Dr.
Dalziel Rd. G52 32 N12
Damshot Cres. G53 49 Q15
Damshot Rd. G53 49 Q16
Danby Rd. (Bail.) G69 55 DD14
Danes Av. G14 19 Q10
Danes Cres. G14 18 P9
Danes Dr. G14 18 P9
Danes La. N. G14 19 Q10
Upland Rd.
Danes La. S. G14 19 Q10
Dunglass Av.
Dargarvel Av. G41 50 S14
Darkwood Ct., Pais. PA3 29 H13
Darkwood Cres., Pais. PA3 29 H13
Darkwood Dr., Pais. PA3 29 H13
Darkwood Cres.
Darleith St. G32 38 AA13
Darley Mains Rd. G53 61 Q18
Darley Rd. (Cumb.) G68 70 NN1
Darnaway Av. G33 39 CC11
Darnaway Dr. G33 39 CC11
Darnaway St. G33 39 CC11
Darnick St. G21 23 Y10
Hobden St.
Darnley Cres. (Bishop.) G64 10 X6
Darnley Gdns. G41 51 U15
Darnley Path (Thorn.) G46 61 R17
Kennisholm Av.
Darnley Pl. G41 51 U15
Darnley Rd.
Darnley Rd. G41 51 U15
Darnley Rd. (Barr.) G78 60 N18
Darnley St. G41 51 U15
Darroch Way (Cumb.) G67 71 PP2
Dartford St. G22 21 V10
Darvel Cres., Pais. PA1 47 M14
Darvel St. G53 60 N17
Darwin Pl., Clyde. G81 4 J6
Dava St. G51 34 S12
Davaar Dr., Pais. PA2 46 K16
Davaar Rd., Renf. PA4 31 M11
Davaar St. G40 53 Y14
Daventry Dr. G12 20 S9
David Pl. (Bail.) G69 55 DD14
David Pl., Pais. PA3 31 L12
Killarn Way
David St. G40 37 Y13
David Way, Pais. PA3 31 L12
Killarn Way
Davidson Gdns. G14 19 Q10
Westland Dr.
Davidson Pl. G32 39 CC13
Davidson St. G40 53 Y15

Davidson St., Clyde. G81 18 N8
Davidston Pl. (Kirk.) G66 13 DD6
Davieland Rd. (Giff.) G46 62 S19
Daviot St. G51 33 Q13
Dawes La. N. G14 19 Q10
Upland Rd.
Dawson Pl. G4 21 V10
Dawson Rd.
Dawson Rd. G4 21 V10
Deaconsbank Av. (Thorn.) 61 Q19
G46
Deaconsbank Cres. (Thorn.) 61 Q19
G46
Deaconsbank Gdns. (Thorn.) 61 R19
G46
Deaconsbank Gro. (Thorn.) 61 Q19
G46
Deaconsbank Av.
Deaconsbank Pl. (Thorn.) 61 Q19
G46
Dealston Rd. (Barr.) G78 59 L18
Dean Cres. (Muir.) G69 14 FF7
Dean Pk. Dr. (Camb.) G72 67 CC18
Dean Pk. Rd., Renf. PA4 32 N11
Dean St., Clyde. G81 5 M7
Deanbrae St. (Udd.) G71 69 GG17
Deanfield Quad. G52 32 N13
Deans Av. (Camb.) G72 67 CC18
Deanside La. G4 36 W12
Rottenrow
Deanside Rd. G52 32 P12
Deanston Av. (Barr.) G78 59 L19
Deanston Dr. G41 51 U16
Deanston Gdns. (Barr.) G78 59 L19
Deanston Pk. (Barr.) G78 59 L19
Deanwood Av. G44 63 U18
Deanwood Rd. G44 63 U18
Debdale Cotts. G13 19 R9
Whittingehame Dr.
Dechmont Av. (Camb.) G72 67 CC18
Dechmont Gdns. (Udd.) G71 57 GG15
Dechmont Gdns. (Blan.) G72 68 FF19
Dechmont Pl. (Camb.) G72 67 CC18
Dechmont Rd. (Udd.) G71 57 GG15
Dechmont St. G31 53 Z14
Dechmont Vw. (Udd.) G71 57 HH16
Hamilton Vw.
Dee Av., Pais. PA2 45 G15
Dee Av., Renf. PA4 18 N10
Dee Dr., Pais. PA2 45 G15
Dee Pl., John. PA5 43 C16
Dee St. G33 37 Z11
Deepdene Rd. (Bears.) G61 7 Q7
Deepdene Rd. (Chry.) G69 15 HH7
Delburn St. G31 53 Z14
Delhi Av., Clyde. G81 4 J6
Delny Pl. G33 39 DD12
Delvin Rd. G44 63 V17
Denbeck St. G32 38 AA13
Denbrae St. G32 38 AA13
Dene Wk. (Bishop.) G64 23 Z8
Denewood Av., Pais. PA2 46 J16
Denham St. G22 21 V10
Denholm Dr. (Giff.) G46 62 T19
Denkenny Sq. G15 6 N6
Denmark St. G22 22 W10
Denmilne Path G34 40 FF12
Denmilne Pl. G34 40 FF12
Denmilne Rd. (Bail.) G69 40 FF12
Denmilne St. G34 40 FF12
Derby St. G3 35 U12
Derby Ter. La. G3 35 U12
Derby St.
Derwent St. G22 21 V10
Despard Av. G32 55 DD14
Despard Gdns. G32 55 DD14
Deveron Av. (Giff.) G46 62 T19
Deveron Rd. (Bears.) G61 7 Q7
Deveron St. G33 37 Z11
Devol Cres. G53 48 P16
Devon Gdns. G12 20 S10
Hyndland Rd.
Devon Gdns. (Bishop.) G64 10 X6
Devon Pl. G41 51 V14
Devon St. G5 51 V14
Devondale Av. (Blan.) G72 68 FF19
Devonshire Gdns. G12 20 S10
Devonshire Gdns. La. G12 20 S10
Hyndland Rd.
Devonshire Ter. G12 20 S10
Devonshire Ter. La. G12 20 S10
Hughenden Rd.

Street	Page	Grid
Dewar Clo. (Udd.) G71	57	HH15
Diana Av. G13	18	P8
Dick St. G20	21	U10
Henderson St.		
Dickens Av., Clyde. G81	4	K6
Dilwara Av. G14	33	R11
Dimity St., John. PA5	43	D15
Dinard Dr. (Giff.) G46	62	T18
Dinart St. G33	37	Z11
Dinduff St. G34	40	FF11
Dingwall St. G3	34	T12
Kelvinhaugh St.		
Dinmont Pl. G41	51	U15
Norham St.		
Dinmont Rd. G41	50	T15
Dinwiddie St. G21	37	Z11
Dipple Pl. G15	6	P7
Dirleton Dr. G41	51	U16
Dirleton Dr., Pais. PA2	45	H15
Dirleton Gate (Bears.) G61	7	Q7
Dixon Av. G42	51	V15
Dixon Rd. G42	52	W15
Dixon St. G1	35	V13
Dixon St., Pais. PA1	46	K14
Dobbies Ln. G4	35	V11
Dobbies Ln. Pl. G4	36	W12
Dochart Av., Renf. PA4	32	N11
Dochart St. G33	38	AA11
Dock St., Clyde. G81	17	M8
Dodhill Pl. G13	18	P9
Dodside Gdns. G32	55	CC14
Dodside Pl. G32	55	CC14
Dodside St. G32	55	CC14
Dolan St. (Bail.) G69	40	EE13
Dollar Ter. G20	20	T8
Crosbie St.		
Dolphin Rd. G41	50	T15
Don Av., Renf. PA4	32	N11
Don Dr., Pais. PA2	45	G15
Don Pl., John. PA5	43	C16
Don St. G33	37	Z12
Donald Way (Udd.) G71	57	HH16
Donaldson Dr., Renf. PA4	17	M10
Ferguson St.		
Donaldson Grn. (Udd.) G71	57	HH16
Donaldswood Pk., Pais. PA2	46	J16
Donaldswood Rd., Pais. PA2	46	J16
Doncaster St. G20	21	V10
Doon Cres. (Bears.) G61	7	Q6
Doon Side (Cumb.) G67	71	PP3
Doon St., Clyde. G81	5	M6
Doonfoot Rd. G43	62	T17
Dora St. G40	53	Y14
Dorchester Av. G12	20	S9
Dorchester Ct. G12	20	S9
Dorchester Av.		
Dorchester Pl. G12	20	S9
Dorlin Rd. G33	25	DD9
Dormanside Ct. G53	48	P14
Dormanside Gate G53	48	P14
Dormanside Gro. G53	48	P14
Dormanside Rd. G53	48	P14
Dornal Av. G13	18	N8
Dornford Av. G32	55	CC15
Dornford Rd. G32	55	CC15
Dornie Dr. G32	55	CC16
Dornie Dr. (Thorn.) G46	61	R18
Dornoch Av. (Giff.) G46	62	T19
Dornoch Pl. (Bishop.) G64	11	Z7
Dornoch Pl. (Chry.) G69	14	FF7
Dornoch Rd. (Bears.) G61	7	Q7
Dornoch St. G40	36	X13
Dornoch Way (Cumb.) G68	71	PP1
Dorset Sq. G3	35	U12
Dorset St.		
Dorset St. G3	35	U12
Dosk Av. G13	18	N8
Dosk Pl. G13	18	N8
Dougalston Rd. G23	9	U7
Douglas Av. G32	54	BB15
Douglas Av. (Giff.) G46	62	T19
Douglas Av. (Lenzie) G66	13	CC5
Douglas Av. (Ruther.) G73	65	Z17
Douglas Av. (Elder.), John. PA5	44	E15
Douglas Ct. (Lenzie) G66	13	CC5
Douglas Cres. (Udd.) G71	57	HH16
Douglas Dr. G15	6	N7
Douglas Dr. (Bail.) G69	39	DD13
Douglas Dr. (Both.) G71	69	HH19
Douglas Dr. (Camb.) G72	66	AA17
Douglas Gdns. (Giff.) G46	62	T19
Douglas Gdns. (Bears.) G61	7	R6
Douglas Gdns. (Lenzie) G66	13	CC5
Douglas Gdns. (Udd.) G71	69	GG17
Douglas Gate (Camb.) G72	66	BB17
Douglas La. G2	35	V12
West George St.		
Douglas Pk. Cres. (Bears.) G61	8	S5
Douglas Pl. (Bears.) G61	7	R5
Douglas Pl. (Kirk.) G66	13	CC5
Douglas Av.		
Douglas Rd., Renf. PA4	31	L12
Douglas St. G2	35	V12
Douglas St. (Udd.) G71	57	HH16
Douglas St., Pais. PA1	30	J13
Douglas Ter. G41	51	U15
Glencairn Dr.		
Douglas Ter., Pais. PA3	30	K11
Dougray Pl. (Barr.) G78	59	M19
Dougrie Dr. G45	64	W18
Dougrie Gdns. G45	64	W19
Dougrie Pl. G45	64	X18
Dougrie Rd. G45	64	W19
Dougrie St. G45	64	X18
Dougrie Ter. G45	64	W19
Doune Cres. (Bishop.) G64	11	Y6
Doune Gdns. G20	21	U10
Doune Quad. G20	21	U10
Dove St. G53	60	P17
Dovecot G43	50	T16
Shawhill Rd.		
Dovecothall St. (Barr.) G78	59	M18
Dover St. G3	35	U12
Dowanfield Rd. (Cumb.) G67	70	NN3
Dowanhill St. G11	34	T11
Dowanhill St. G12	34	T11
Dowanside La. G12	20	T10
Byres Rd.		
Dowanside Rd. G12	20	T10
Dowanvale Ter. G11	34	S11
White St.		
Downcraig Dr. G45	64	W19
Downcraig Gro. G45	64	W19
Downcraig Rd. G45	64	W19
Downcraig Ter. G45	64	W19
Downfield Gdns. (Both.) G71	69	GG19
Downfield St. G32	54	AA14
Downie Clo. (Udd.) G71	57	HH16
Downiebrae Rd. (Ruther.) G73	53	Y15
Downs St. G21	22	X10
Dowrie Cres. G53	48	P15
Dows Pl. G4	21	V10
Possil Rd.		
Drainie St. G34	40	EE12
Westerhouse Rd.		
Drake St. G40	36	X13
Drakemire Av. G45	64	W18
Drakemire Dr. G44	64	W18
Drakemire Dr. G45	64	W18
Dreghorn St. G31	37	Z12
Drem Pl. G11	34	S11
Merkland St.		
Drimnin Rd. G33	25	DD9
Drive Rd. G51	33	R12
Drochil St. G34	40	EE11
Drumbeg Dr. G53	60	P17
Drumbeg Pl. G53	60	P17
Drumbottie Rd. G21	23	Y9
Drumby Cres. (Clark.) G76	62	T19
Drumcavel Rd. (Muir.) G69	26	FF8
Drumchapel Gdns. G15	6	P7
Drumchapel Pl. G15	6	P7
Drumchapel Rd. G15	6	P7
Drumclog Gdns. G33	24	AA9
Drumcross Rd. G53	49	Q15
Drumhead La. G32	54	AA15
Drumhead Pl. G32	54	AA15
Drumhead Rd. G32	54	AA15
Drumilaw Rd. (Ruther.) G73	65	Y17
Drumilaw Way (Ruther.) G73	65	Y17
Drumlaken Av. G23	8	T7
Drumlaken Ct. G23	8	T7
Drumlaken St. G23	8	T7
Drumlanrig Av. G34	40	FF11
Drumlanrig Pl. G34	40	FF11
Drumlochy Rd. G33	38	BB11
Drummond Av. (Ruther.) G73	52	X16
Drummond Dr., Pais. PA1	47	M14
Drummond Gdns. G13	19	R9
Crow Rd.		
Drummore Rd. G15	6	P5
Drumover Dr. G31	54	AA14
Drumoyne Av. G51	33	R12
Drumoyne Circ. G51	33	R13
Drumoyne Dr. G51	33	R12
Drumoyne Pl. G51	33	R13
Drumoyne Circ.		
Drumoyne Quad. G51	33	R13
Drumoyne Rd. G51	33	R13
Drumoyne Sq. G51	33	R12
Drumpark St. (Thorn.) G46	61	R18
Drumpark St., Coat. ML5	57	HH14
Dunnachie Dr.		
Drumpellier Av. (Bail.) G69	56	EE14
Drumpellier Pl. (Bail.) G69	56	EE14
Drumpellier Rd. (Bail.) G69	56	EE14
Drumpellier St. G33	37	Z11
Drumreoch Dr. G42	52	X16
Drumreoch Pl. G42	52	X16
Drumry Pl. G15	6	N7
Drumry Rd., Clyde. G81	5	L6
Drumry Rd. E. G15	5	M7
Drums Av., Pais. PA3	29	H13
Drums Cres., Pais. PA3	30	J13
Drums Rd. G53	48	P14
Drumsack Av. (Chry.) G69	26	FF8
Drumsargard Rd. (Ruther.) G73	65	Z17
Drumshaw Dr. G32	55	CC16
Drumvale Dr. (Chry.) G69	15	GG7
Drury St. G2	35	V12
Dryad St. (Thorn.) G46	61	R17
Dryburgh Av. (Ruther.) G73	53	Y16
Dryburgh Av., Pais. PA2	45	H15
Dryburgh Gdns. G20	21	U10
Dryburgh Rd. (Bears.) G61	7	Q5
Dryburgh Wk. (Mood.) G69	15	HH6
Dryburn Av. G52	32	P13
Drygate G4	36	X12
Drygrange Rd. G33	39	CC11
Drymen Pl. (Lenzie) G66	13	CC6
Drymen Rd. (Bears.) G61	7	Q5
Drymen St. G52	33	R13
Morven St.		
Drymen Wynd (Bears.) G61	7	R6
Drynoch Pl. G22	21	V8
Drysdale St. G14	18	N9
Duart Dr. (Elder.), John. PA5	44	E15
Duart St. G20	20	T8
Dubs Rd. (Barr.) G78	60	N18
Dubton Path G34	40	EE11
Dubton St. G34	40	EE11
Duchall Pl. G14	18	P10
Duchess Pl. (Ruther.) G73	53	Z16
Duchess Rd. (Ruther.) G73	53	Z16
Duchess Way (Bail.) G69	41	GG13
Park Rd.		
Duchray Dr., Pais. PA1	48	N14
Duchray La. G33	37	Z11
Duchray St.		
Duchray St. G33	37	Z11
Dudhope St. G33	39	CC11
Dudley Dr. G12	20	S10
Dudley La. G12	20	S10
Clarence Dr.		
Duffus Pl. G32	55	CC16
Duffus St. G34	40	EE11
Duffus Ter. G32	55	CC16
Duich Gdns. G23	9	U7
Duisdale Rd. G32	55	CC16
Duke St. G4	36	X12
Duke St. G31	36	X12
Duke St., Pais. PA2	46	K15
Duke St. (Linw.), Pais. PA3	28	F13
Dukes Gate (Both.) G71	69	GG18
Dukes Rd. (Bail.) G69	41	GG13
Dukes Rd. (Camb.) G72	65	Z17
Dukes Rd. (Ruther.) G73	65	Z17
Dulnain St. (Camb.) G72	67	DD17
Dulsie Rd. G21	23	Z9
Dumbarton Rd. G11	34	S11
Dumbarton Rd. G14	18	P10
Dumbarton Rd. (Old Kil.) G60	4	J6
Dumbarton Rd., Clyde. G81	4	J6
Dumbarton Rd. (Dunt.), Clyde. G81	4	K5
Dumbreck Av. G41	50	S14
Dumbreck Ct. G41	50	S14
Dumbreck Pl. (Kirk.) G66	13	DD6
Dumbreck Rd. G41	50	S14
Dumbreck Sq. G41	50	S14
Dumbreck Av.		

Dunagoil Gdns. G45 64 X19
Dunagoil St.
Dunagoil Pl. G45 64 X19
Dunagoil Rd. G45 64 W19
Dunagoil St. G45 64 X19
Dunagoil Ter. G45 64 X19
Dunalistair Dr. G33 24 BB9
Dunan Pl. G33 39 DD12
Dunard Rd. (Ruther.) G73 53 Y16
Dunard St. G20 21 U10
Dunard Way, Pais. PA3 30 J12
Mosslands Rd.
Dunaskin St. G11 34 T11
Dunbar Av. (Ruther.) G73 53 Z16
Dunbar Av., John. PA5 43 D16
Dunbar Rd., Pais. PA2 45 H15
Dunbeith Pl. G20 20 T9
Dunblane St. G4 35 V11
Dunbrach Rd. (Cumb.) G68 70 MM2
Duncan Av. G14 19 Q10
Duncan La. G14 19 Q10
Duncan Av.
Duncan La. N. G14 19 Q10
Ormiston Av.
Duncan La. S. G14 19 Q10
Duncan Av.
Duncan St., Clyde. G81 5 L6
Duncansby Rd. G33 39 CC13
Dunchattan Pl. G31 36 X12
Duke St.
Dunchattan St. G31 36 X12
Dunchurch Rd., Pais. PA1 31 M13
Dunclutha Dr. (Both.) G71 69 HH19
Dunclutha St. G40 53 Y15
Duncombe St. G20 20 T8
Duncombe Vw., Clyde. G81 5 M6
Kirkoswald Dr.
Duncraig Cres., John. PA5 43 C16
Duncrub Dr. (Bishop.) G64 10 X7
Duncruin St. G20 20 T8
Duncryne Av. G32 55 CC14
Duncryne Gdns. G32 55 DD14
Duncryne Pl. (Bishop.) G64 22 X8
Dundaff Hill (Cumb.) G68 70 MM3
Dundas La. G1 36 W12
Dundas St. G1 36 W12
Dundashill G4 35 V11
Dundasvale Ct. G4 35 V11
Maitland St.
Dundasvale Rd. G4 35 V11
Maitland St.
Dundee Dr. G52 48 P14
Dundee Path G52 49 Q14
Dundee Dr.
Dundonald Av., John. PA5 43 C15
Dundonald Rd. G12 20 T10
Dundonald Rd., Pais. PA3 31 L12
Dundrennan Rd. G42 51 U16
Dunearn Pl., Pais. PA2 47 L14
Dunearn St. G4 35 U11
Dunellan St. G52 33 R13
Dungeonhill Rd. G34 40 FF12
Dunglass Av. G14 19 Q10
Dunglass La. G14 19 Q10
Dunglass Av.
Dunglass La. N. G14 19 Q10
Verona Av.
Dunglass La. S. G14 19 Q10
Dunglass Av.
Dungoil Av. (Cumb.) G68 70 LL2
Dungoil Rd. (Lenzie) G66 13 DD6
Dungoyne St. G20 20 T8
Dunira St. G32 54 AA14
Dunivaig St. G33 39 DD12
Dunkeld Av. (Ruther.) G73 53 Y16
Dunkeld Dr. (Bears.) G61 8 S6
Dunkeld Gdns. (Bishop.) G64 11 Y7
Dunkeld La. (Chry.) G69 15 HH7
Burnbrae Av.
Dunkeld St. G31 53 Z14
Dunkenny Pl. G15 6 N6
Dunkenny Rd. G15 6 N6
Dunkenny Sq. G15 6 N6
Dunlin G12 20 S9
Dunlop Cres. (Both.) G71 69 HH19
Dunlop Cres., Renf. PA4 17 M10
Fulbar St.
Dunlop Gro. (Udd.) G71 57 HH15
Dunlop St. G1 36 W13
Dunlop St. (Camb.) G72 67 DD17
Dunlop St. (Linw.), Pais. 28 F13
PA3

Dunlop St., Renf. PA4 17 M10
Fulbar St.
Dunmore La. G5 35 V13
Norfolk St.
Dunmore St. G5 35 V13
Dunmore St., Clyde. G81 17 M8
Dunn St. G40 53 Y14
Dunn St., Clyde. G81 4 K6
Dunn St. (Dunt.), Clyde. G81 4 K5
Dunn St., Pais. PA1 47 L14
Dunnachie Dr., Coat. ML5 57 HH14
Dunnichen Gdns. (Bishop.) 11 Z7
G64
Dunnottar St. G33 38 BB11
Dunnottar St. (Bishop.) G64 11 Z7
Dunolly St. G21 37 Y11
Dunphail Dr. G34 40 FF12
Dunphail Rd. G34 40 FF12
Dunragit St. G31 37 Z12
Dunrobin Av. (Elder.), John. 44 F15
PA5
Dunrobin St. G31 37 Y13
Dunrod St. G32 54 BB14
Dunside Dr. G53 60 P17
Dunskaith Pl. G34 40 FF12
Dunskaith St. G34 40 FF12
Dunsmuir St. G51 34 S12
Dunster Gdns. (Bishop.) G64 11 Y6
Dunswin Av., Clyde. G81 4 K6
Dunswin Ct., Clyde. G81 4 K6
Dunswin Av.
Dunsyre Pl. G23 9 U7
Dunsyre St. G33 38 AA12
Duntarvie Av. G34 40 FF12
Duntarvie Clo. G34 40 FF12
Duntarvie Cres. G34 40 FF12
Duntarvie Dr. G34 40 EE12
Duntarvie Gdns. G34 40 FF12
Duntarvie Gro. G34 40 FF12
Duntarvie Pl. G34 40 EE12
Duntarvie Quad. G34 40 FF12
Duntarvie Rd. G34 40 EE12
Dunterlie Av. G13 18 P9
Dunterlie Ct. (Barr.) G78 59 M18
Duntiglennan Rd., Clyde. G81 5 L5
Duntocher Rd. (Bears.) G61 6 P5
Duntocher Rd., Clyde. G81 4 K6
Duntocher Rd. (Dunt.), Clyde. 5 L5
G81
Duntocher St. G21 22 X10
Northcroft Rd.
Duntreath Av. G13 18 N8
Duntreath Av. G15 18 N8
Duntreath Dr. G15 6 N7
Duntreath Gdns. G15 6 N7
Duntreath Gro. G15 6 N7
Duntroon St. G31 37 Y12
Dunure Dr. (Ruther.) G73 64 X17
Dunure St. G20 20 T8
Dunvegan Av. (Elder.), John. 44 F15
PA5
Dunvegan Ct. G13 18 P9
Kintillo Dr.
Dunvegan Dr. (Bishop.) G64 11 Y6
Dunvegan Quad., Renf. PA4 17 L10
Kirklandneuk Rd.
Dunwan Av. G13 18 N8
Dunwan Pl. G13 18 N8
Durban Av., Clyde. G81 4 J6
Durham St. G41 34 T13
Durness Av. (Bears.) G61 8 S5
Durno Path G33 39 DD12
Duror St. G32 38 BB13
Durris Gdns. G32 55 CC14
Durrockstock Cres., Pais. PA2 45 G16
Durrockstock Rd., Pais. PA2 45 G16
Durward Av. G41 50 T15
Durward Ct. G41 50 T15
Durward Cres., Pais. PA2 45 G15
Duthil St. G51 33 Q13
Dyce La. G11 34 S11
Dyers La. G1 36 W13
Turnbull St.
Dyers Wynd, Pais. PA1 30 K13
Gilmour St.
Dyke Pl. G13 18 P8
Dyke Rd. G13 18 N9
Dyke Rd. G14 18 N9
Dyke St. (Bail.) G69 40 FF13
Dykebar Av. G13 18 P9
Dykebar Cres., Pais. PA2 47 L15
Dykefoot Dr. G53 49 Q16

Dykehead La. G33 39 CC12
Dykehead Rd. (Bail.) G69 41 GG13
Dykehead St. G33 39 CC12
Dykemuir Pl. G21 23 Y10
Dykemuir Quad. G21 23 Y10
Dykemuir St.
Dykemuir St. G21 23 Y10

E
Eagle Cres. (Bears.) G61 6 P5
Eagle St. G4 36 W11
Eaglesham Ct. G51 35 U13
Blackburn St.
Eaglesham Pl. G51 35 U13
Earl Haig Rd. G52 32 N12
Earl La. G14 19 Q10
Harland St.
Earl Pl. G14 19 Q10
Earl St. G14 18 P10
Earlbank Av. G14 19 Q10
Earlbank La. N. G14 19 Q10
Earlbank La. S. G14 19 Q10
Verona Av.
Earls Gate (Both.) G71 69 GG18
Earls Hill (Cumb.) G68 70 LL2
Earlsburn Rd. (Lenzie) G66 13 DD6
Earlscourt (Mood.) G69 15 GG7
Langdale Av.
Earlspark Av. G43 51 U16
Earn Av. (Bears.) G61 8 S6
Earn Av., Renf. PA4 32 N11
Almond Av.
Earn St. G33 38 AA11
Earnock St. G32 23 Z10
Earnside St. G32 38 BB13
Easdale Dr. G32 54 BB14
East Av., Renf. PA4 17 M10
East Barns St., Clyde. G81 17 M8
East Bath La. G2 35 V12
Sauchiehall St.
East Buchanan St., Pais. PA1 30 K13
East Campbell St. G1 36 X13
East Greenlees Av. (Camb.) 67 CC18
G72
East Greenlees Cres. 66 BB18
(Camb.) G72
East Greenlees Dr. (Camb.) 66 BB18
G72
East Greenlees Gro. (Camb.) 66 BB18
G72
East Greenlees Rd. (Camb.) 66 BB18
G72
East Hallhill Rd. (Bail.) G69 40 EE13
East Kilbride Expressway 66 BB19
(Camb.) G72
East Kilbride Rd. (Ruther.) 65 Z17
G73
East La., Pais. PA1 47 L14
East Reid St. (Ruther.) G73 53 Z16
East Rd. (Kilb.), John. PA10 42 B14
East Springfield Ter. 23 Y8
(Bishop.) G64
East Thomson St., Clyde. G81 5 L6
East Wellington St. G31 37 Z13
East Whitby St. G31 53 Z14
Eastbank Dr. G12 20 T10
Eastbank Dr. G32 39 CC13
Eastbank Pl. G12 20 T10
Eastbank Pl. G32 39 CC13
Eastbank Ri. G12 20 T9
Eastbank Ri. G32 39 CC13
Eastburn Cres. G21 23 Y9
Eastburn Pl. G21 23 Y9
Eastburn Rd. G21 23 Y9
Eastcote Av. G14 19 R10
Eastcroft (Ruther.) G73 53 Y16
Eastcroft Ter. G21 23 Y10
Easter Av. (Udd.) G71 69 GG17
Easter Garngaber Rd. 13 DD5
(Lenzie) G66
Easter Ms. (Udd.) G71 69 GG17
Church St.
Easter Queenslie Rd. G33 39 DD12
Eastercraigs G31 37 Y12
Easterhill Pl. G32 54 AA14
Easterhill St. G32 54 AA14
Easterhouse Pl. G34 40 FF12
Easterhouse Rd.
Easterhouse Quad. G34 40 FF12
Easterhouse Rd.

Name	Page	Grid
Easterhouse Rd. G34	40	FF12
Easterhouse Rd. (Bail.) G69	40	FF12
Eastfield Av. (Camb.) G72	66	AA17
Eastfield Rd. G21	22	X10
Eastfield Rd. (Cumb.) G68	70	MM2
Eastgate (Gart.) G69	27	HH9
Easthall Pl. G33	39	DD12
Eastmuir St. G32	38	BB13
Eastvale Pl. G3	34	T12
Eastwood Av. G41	50	T16
Eastwood Av. (Giff.) G46	62	T19
Eastwood Ct. (Thorn.) G46	61	R18
Main St.		
Eastwood Cres. (Thorn.) G46	61	R18
Eastwood Rd. (Chry.) G69	15	GG7
Eastwood Vw. (Camb.) G72	67	DD17
Eastwoodmains Rd. (Giff.)	62	S19
G46		
Eastwoodmains Rd. (Clark.)	62	S19
G76		
Easwald Bk. (Mill.Pk.), John.	42	B15
PA10		
Eccles St. G22	22	X9
Eckford St. G32	54	BB14
Eday St. G22	22	W9
Edderton Pl. G34	40	EE12
Eddleston Pl. (Camb.) G72	67	DD17
Eddlewood Path G33	39	DD12
Eddlewood Pl. G33	39	DD12
Eddlewood Rd. G33	39	DD12
Edelweiss Ter. G11	34	S11
Gardner St.		
Eden La. G33	37	Z11
Eden Pk. (Both.) G71	69	GG19
Eden Pl. (Camb.) G72	67	CC17
Eden Pl., Renf. PA4	32	N11
Eden St. G33	37	Z11
Edenwood St. G31	38	AA13
Edgam Dr. G52	33	Q13
Edgefauld Av. G21	22	X10
Edgefauld Dr. G21	22	X10
Edgefauld Pl. G21	22	X9
Balgrayhill Rd.		
Edgefauld Rd. G21	22	X10
Edgehill La. G11	20	S10
Marlborough Av.		
Edgehill Rd. G11	20	S10
Edgehill Rd. (Bears.) G61	7	R5
Edgemont St. G41	51	U16
Edinbeg Av. G42	52	X16
Edinbeg Pl. G42	52	X16
Edinburgh Rd. G33	37	Z12
Edinburgh Rd. (Bail.) G69	39	DD12
Edington Gdns. (Chry.) G69	15	GG6
Edington St. G4	35	V11
Edison St. G52	32	N12
Edmiston Dr. G51	33	R13
Edmiston Dr. (Linw.), Pais.	28	E13
PA3		
Edmiston St. G31	53	Z14
Edmondstone Ct., Clyde. G81	17	M8
Yokerburn Ter.		
Edrom Path G32	38	AA13
Edrom St.		
Edrom St. G32	38	AA13
Edward Av., Renf. PA4	18	N10
Edward St. G3	34	T12
Lumsden St.		
Edward St. (Bail.) G69	41	GG13
Edward St., Clyde. G81	17	M8
Edwin St. G51	34	T13
Edzell Ct. G14	33	Q11
Edzell Dr. (Elder.), John. PA5	44	F15
Edzell Gdns. (Bishop.) G64	23	Z8
Edzell Pl. G14	33	Q11
Edzell St. G14	33	Q11
Egidia Av. (Giff.) G46	62	S19
Egilsay Cres. G22	22	W8
Egilsay Pl. G22	22	W8
Egilsay St. G22	22	W8
Egilsay Ter. G22	22	W8
Eglinton Av. (Udd.) G71	69	GG17
Eglinton Ct. G5	35	V13
Eglinton Dr. (Giff.) G46	62	T19
Eglinton La. G5	51	V14
Eglinton St.		
Eglinton St. G5	51	V14
Eider G12	20	S8
Eighth St. (Udd.) G71	57	GG15
Eildon Dr. (Barr.) G78	59	M19
Eileen Gdns. (Bishop.) G64	11	Y7
Elba La. G31	37	Z13
Elcho St. G40	36	X13
Elder Cres. (Camb.) G72	67	DD18
Elder Gro. (Udd.) G71	57	HH16
Elder St. G51	33	R12
Elderbank (Bears.) G61	7	R6
Elderpark Gdns. G51	33	R12
Elderpark Gro. G51	33	R12
Elderpark St. G51	33	R12
Elderslie St. G3	35	U11
Eldin Pl. (Elder.), John. PA5	44	E15
Eldon Gdns. (Bishop.) G64	10	X7
Eldon St. G3	35	U11
Eldon Ter. G11	34	S11
Caird Dr.		
Elgin St. G40	37	Y13
Elibank St. G33	38	BB11
Elie St. G11	34	T11
Elizabeth Cres. (Thorn.) G46	62	S18
Elizabeth St. G51	34	T13
Elizabethan Way, Renf. PA4	31	M11
Cockels Ln.		
Ellangowan Rd. G41	50	T16
Ellergreen Rd. (Bears.) G61	7	R6
Ellerslie St., John. PA5	44	E14
Ellesmere St. G22	21	V10
Ellinger Ct., Clyde. G81	4	K6
Scott St.		
Elliot Av. (Giff.) G46	62	T19
Elliot Av., Pais. PA2	45	G16
Elliot Dr. (Giff.) G46	62	T18
Elliot La. G3	35	U12
Elliot St.		
Elliot Pl. G3	35	U12
Elliot St. G3	35	U12
Ellisland Av., Clyde. G81	5	M6
Ellisland Cres. (Ruther.) G73	64	X17
Ellisland Rd. G43	62	T17
Ellisland Rd. (Cumb.) G67	71	PP3
Ellismuir Fm. Rd. (Bail.) G69	56	FF14
Ellismuir Pl. (Bail.) G69	56	FF14
Ellismuir Rd. (Bail.) G69	56	FF14
Ellismuir Way (Udd.) G71	57	HH15
Elliston Av. G53	61	Q17
Elliston Cres. G53	61	Q17
Elliston Dr. G53	61	Q17
Elliston Pl. G53	61	Q17
Ravenscraig Dr.		
Ellon Dr. (Linw.), Pais. PA3	28	E13
Ellon Way, Pais. PA3	31	L12
Elm Av. (Lenzie) G66	13	CC5
Elm Av., Renf. PA4	17	M10
Elm Bk. (Bishop.) G64	11	Y7
Elm Dr. (Camb.) G72	67	CC17
Elm Dr., John. PA5	43	D16
Elm Gdns. (Bears.) G61	7	R5
Elm La. E. G14	19	Q10
Elm St.		
Elm La. W. G14	19	Q10
Elm St.		
Elm Rd. (Ruther.) G73	65	Y18
Elm Rd., Clyde. G81	5	L5
Elm Rd., Pais. PA2	47	L15
Elm St. G14	19	Q10
Elm Wk. (Bears.) G61	7	R5
Elm Way (Camb.) G72	67	DD18
Elmbank Av. (Udd.) G71	57	HH16
Elmbank Cres. G2	35	V12
Elmbank St.		
Elmbank La. G3	35	U12
North St.		
Elmbank St. G2	35	V12
Elmbank St. La. G2	35	V12
Elmbank St.		
Elmfoot St. G5	52	W15
Elmira Rd. (Muir.) G69	26	FF8
Elmore Av. G44	63	V17
Elmore La. G44	63	V17
Elmslie Ct. (Bail.) G69	56	EE14
Elmvale Row G21	22	X10
Elmvale Row E. G21	22	X10
Elmvale Row		
Elmvale Row W. G21	22	X10
Elmvale Row		
Elmvale St. G21	22	X9
Elmwood Av. G11	19	R10
Elmwood Ct. (Both.) G71	69	HH19
Elmwood Gdns. G11	19	R10
Randolph Rd.		
Elmwood Gdns. (Kirk.)	12	BB5
G66		
Elmwood La. G11	19	R10
Elmwood Av.		
Elmwood Ter. G11	19	R10
Crow Rd.		
Elphin St. G23	8	T7
Invershiel Rd.		
Elphinstone Pl. G51	34	T12
Elrig Rd. G44	63	V17
Elspeth Gdns. (Bishop.) G64	11	Y7
Eltham St. G22	21	V10
Elvan Ct. G32	38	AA13
Edrom St.		
Elvan St. G32	38	AA13
Embo Dr. G13	18	P9
Emerson Rd. (Bishop.) G64	11	Y7
Emerson St. G20	21	V9
Emily Pl. G31	36	X13
Endfield Av. G12	20	S9
Endrick Bk. (Bishop.) G64	11	Y6
Endrick Dr. (Bears.) G61	7	R6
Endrick Dr., Pais. PA1	31	L13
Endrick St. G21	22	W10
Endsleigh Gdns. G11	20	S10
Partickhill Rd.		
Ensay St. G22	22	W8
Enterkin St. G32	54	AA14
Ericht Rd. G43	62	T17
Eriska Av. G14	18	P9
Eriskay Dr. (Old Kil.) G60	4	J5
Eriskay Pl. (Old Kil.) G60	4	J5
Erradale St. G22	21	V8
Erriboll Pl. G22	21	V8
Erriboll St. G22	21	V8
Errogie St. G34	40	EE12
Errol Gdns. G5	52	W14
Erskine Av. G41	50	S14
Erskine Sq. G52	32	N12
Erskine Vw., Clyde. G81	5	L6
Singer St.		
Erskinefauld Rd. (Linw.),	28	E13
Pais. PA3		
Ervie St. G34	40	FF12
Esk Av., Renf. PA4	32	N11
Esk Dr., Pais. PA2	45	G15
Esk St. G14	18	N9
Esk Way, Pais. PA2	45	G15
Eskbank St. G32	38	BB13
Eskdale Dr. (Ruther.) G73	53	Z16
Eskdale Rd. (Bears.) G61	7	Q7
Eskdale St. G42	51	V15
Esmond St. G3	34	T11
Espedair St., Pais. PA2	46	K14
Essenside Av. G15	7	Q7
Essex Dr. G14	19	R10
Essex La. G14	19	R10
Esslemont Av. G14	18	P9
Estate Quad. G32	55	CC16
Estate Rd. G32	55	CC16
Etive Av. (Bears.) G61	8	S6
Etive Ct., Clyde. G81	5	M5
Etive Cres. (Bishop.) G64	11	Y7
Etive Dr. (Giff.) G46	62	T19
Etive St. G32	38	BB13
Eton Gdns. G12	35	U11
Oakfield Av.		
Eton La. G12	35	U11
Great George St.		
Eton Pl. G12	35	U11
Oakfield Av.		
Eton Ter. G12	35	U11
Oakfield Av.		
Ettrick Av., Renf. PA4	32	N11
Ettrick Ct. (Camb.) G72	67	DD18
Gateside Av.		
Ettrick Cres. (Ruther.) G73	53	Z16
Ettrick Oval, Pais. PA2	45	G16
Ettrick Pl. G43	50	T16
Ettrick Ter., John. PA5	43	C16
Ettrick Way, Renf. PA4	32	N11
Eure Point Ct. G33	38	BB12
Sutherness Dr.		
Evan Cres. (Giff.) G46	62	T19
Evan Dr. (Giff.) G46	62	T19
Evanton Dr. (Thorn.) G46	61	R18
Evanton Pl. (Thorn.) G46	61	R18
Evanton Dr.		
Everard Ct. G21	22	X8
Everard Dr. G21	22	X8
Everard Pl. G21	22	X8
Everard Quad. G21	22	X8
Everglades, The (Chry.)	26	EE8
G69		
Eversley St. G32	54	BB14
Everton Rd. G53	49	Q15

110

Ewart Pl. G3	34	T12
Kelvinhaugh St.		
Ewing Pl. G31	37	Z13
Ewing St. (Ruther.) G73	53	Y16
Ewing St. (Kilb.), John. PA10	42	B14
Exchange Pl. G1	36	W12
Buchanan St.		
Exeter Dr. G11	34	S11
Exeter La. G11	34	S11
Exeter Dr.		
Eynort St. G22	21	V8

F

Fagan Ct. (Blan.) G72	69	GG19
Faifley Rd., Clyde. G81	5	L5
Fairbairn Cres. (Thorn.) G46	62	S19
Fairbairn Path G40	53	Y14
Ruby St.		
Fairbairn St. G40	53	Y14
Dalmarnock Rd.		
Fairburn St. G32	54	AA14
Fairfax Av. G44	64	W17
Fairfield Dr., Renf. PA4	31	M11
Fairfield Gdns. G51	33	R12
Fairfield Pl. G51	33	R12
Fairfield Pl. (Both.) G71	69	HH19
Fairfield St. G51	33	R12
Fairhaven Dr. G23	20	T8
Fairhill Av. G53	49	Q16
Fairholm St. G32	54	AA14
Fairley St. G51	34	S13
Fairlie Pk. Dr. G11	34	S11
Fairway Av., Pais. PA2	46	J16
Fairways (Bears.) G61	6	P5
Fairways Vw., Clyde. G81	5	M5
Fairyknowe Gdns. (Both.) G71	69	HH19
Falcon Cres., Pais. PA3	29	H13
Falcon Rd., John. PA5	43	C16
Falcon Ter. G20	20	T8
Falcon Ter. La. G20	20	T8
Falfield St. G5	51	V14
Falkland Cres. (Bishop.) G64	23	Z8
Falkland La. G12	20	S10
Clarence Dr.		
Falkland Mans. G12	20	S10
Clarence Dr.		
Falkland St. G12	20	S10
Falloch Rd. G42	51	V16
Falloch Rd. (Bears.) G61	7	Q7
Fallside Rd. (Both.) G71	69	HH19
Falside Av., Pais. PA2	46	K15
Falside Rd. G32	54	BB14
Falside Rd., Pais. PA2	46	J15
Fara St. G23	21	U8
Farie St. (Ruther.) G73	53	Y16
Farm Castle Ct. (Ruther.) G73	53	Z15
Farm Ct. (Both.) G71	69	HH18
Farm La. (Udd.) G71	69	HH17
Myers Cres.		
Farm Pk. (Lenzie) G66	13	CC6
Farm Rd. G41	50	S14
Farm Rd. (Blan.) G72	68	FF19
Farm Rd. (Dalmuir), Clyde. G81	4	J6
Farm Rd. (Dunt.), Clyde. G81	5	L5
Farme Cross (Ruther.) G73	53	Y15
Farmeloan Rd. (Ruther.) G73	53	Y16
Farmington Av. G32	39	CC13
Farmington Gdns. G32	39	CC13
Farmington Gate G32	39	CC13
Farmington Gro. G32	39	CC13
Farne Dr. G44	63	V18
Farnell St. G4	35	V11
Farrier Ct., John. PA5	43	D14
Faskally Av. (Bishop.) G64	10	X6
Faskin Cres. G53	48	N16
Faskin Pl. G53	48	N16
Faskin Rd. G53	48	N16
Fasque Pl. G15	6	N6
Fastnet St. G33	38	BB12
Fauldhouse St. G5	52	W14
Faulds (Bail.) G69	40	FF13
Faulds Gdns. (Bail.) G69	40	FF13
Fauldshead Rd., Renf. PA4	17	M10
Fauldspark Cres. (Bail.) G69	40	FF13
Fauldswood Cres., Pais. PA2	45	H15
Fauldswood Dr., Pais. PA2	45	H15
Fearnmore Rd. G20	20	T8

Felton Pl. G13	18	N8
Fendoch St. G32	54	BB14
Fenella St. G32	38	BB13
Fennsbank Av. (Ruther.) G73	65	Z18
Fenwick Dr. (Barr.) G78	59	M19
Fenwick Pl. (Giff.) G46	62	S19
Fenwick Rd. (Giff.) G46	62	T18
Fereneze Av. (Barr.) G78	59	L18
Fereneze Av., Renf. PA4	31	L12
Fereneze Cres. G13	18	P8
Fereneze Dr., Pais. PA2	46	J16
Fereneze Gro. (Barr.) G78	59	L18
Fereneze Rd. (Barr.) G78	58	J19
Fergus Av., Pais. PA3	29	H13
Westburn Av.		
Fergus Ct. G20	21	U10
Fergus Dr. G20	21	U10
Fergus Dr., Pais. PA3	29	H13
Woodvale Av.		
Ferguslie, Pais. PA1	45	H14
Ferguslie Pk. Av., Pais. PA3	29	H13
Ferguslie Pk. Cres., Pais. PA3	45	H14
Ferguslie Wk., Pais. PA1	45	H14
Ferguson Av., Renf. PA4	17	M10
Ferguson St., John. PA5	43	D14
Ferguson St., Renf. PA4	17	M10
Fergusson Rd. (Cumb.) G67	70	NN3
Ferguston Rd. (Bears.) G61	7	R6
Fern Av. (Bishop.) G64	23	Y8
Fern Av. (Lenzie) G66	13	CC5
Fern Dr. (Barr.) G78	59	L18
Fern Gro. (Gart.) G69	27	HH9
Inchnock Av.		
Fern La. G13	19	R9
Whittingehame Dr.		
Fernan St. G32	38	AA13
Fernbank Av. (Camb.) G72	67	CC18
Fernbank St. G21	22	X9
Fernbank St. G22	22	X9
Fernbrae Av. (Ruther.) G73	65	Z18
Fernbrae Way (Ruther.) G73	65	Y18
Ferncroft Dr. G44	64	W17
Ferndale Ct. G23	20	T8
Ferndale Dr. G23	20	T8
Ferndale Gdns. G23	20	T8
Ferndale Pl. G23	20	T8
Ferness Oval G21	23	Z8
Ferness Pl. G21	23	Z8
Ferness Rd. G21	23	Z9
Ferngrove Av. G12	20	S9
Fernhill Gra. (Both.) G71	69	HH19
Fernhill Rd. (Ruther.) G73	65	Y18
Fernie Gdns. G20	21	U8
Fernlea (Bears.) G61	7	R6
Fernleigh Pl. (Chry.) G69	15	GG7
Fernleigh Rd. G43	62	T17
Ferry Rd. G3	34	S12
Ferry Rd. (Both.) G71	69	HH19
Ferry Rd. (Udd.) G71	68	FF17
Ferry Rd., Renf. PA4	17	M10
Ferryden St. G14	33	R11
Fersit St. G43	62	T17
Fetlar Dr. G44	64	W17
Fettercairn Av. G15	6	N6
Fettercairn Gdns. (Bishop.) G64	11	Z7
Fettes St. G33	38	AA12
Fidra St. G33	38	AA12
Fielden Pl. G40	37	Y13
Fielden St. G40	37	Y13
Fieldhead Dr. G43	62	S17
Fieldhead Sq. G43	62	S17
Fife Av. G52	48	P14
Fife Cres. (Both.) G71	69	HH19
Fife Way (Bishop.) G64	23	Z8
Fifth Av. G12	19	R9
Fifth Av. (Stepps) G33	24	BB9
Fourth Av.		
Fifth Av. (Kirk.) G66	13	CC7
Fifth Av., Renf. PA4	31	M11
Fifty Pitches Pl. G51	33	Q12
Fifty Pitches Rd. G51	33	Q13
Finch Dr. G13	18	N8
Finch Pl., John. PA5	43	C16
Findhorn Av., Pais. PA2	45	G15
Findhorn Av., Renf. PA4	18	N10
Findhorn St. G33	37	Z12
Findochty St. G33	39	CC11
Fingal La. G20	20	T8
Fingal St.		

Fingal St. G20	20	T8
Fingask St. G32	55	CC14
Finglas Av., Pais. PA2	47	L15
Fingleton Av. (Barr.) G78	59	M19
Finhaven St. G32	54	AA14
Finlarig St. G34	40	FF12
Finlas St. G22	22	W10
Finlay Dr. G31	37	Y12
Finnart Dr., Pais. PA2	47	L15
Finnart Sq. G40	52	X14
Finnart St. G40	52	X14
Finnieston St.		
Finnieston Pl. G3	35	U12
Finnieston St.		
Finnieston Quay G3	35	U12
Finnieston Sq. G3	35	U12
Houldsworth St.		
Finnieston St. G3	35	U12
Finsbay St. G51	33	R13
Fintry Av., Pais. PA2	46	K16
Fintry Cres. (Bishop.) G64	11	Z7
Fintry Cres. (Barr.) G78	59	M19
Fintry Dr. G44	52	W16
Fir Ct. (Camb.) G72	67	DD18
Fir Pl. (Bail.) G69	56	EE14
Fir Pl. (Camb.) G72	67	CC17
Birch Dr.		
Fir Pl., John. PA5	44	E15
Firbank Ter. (Barr.) G78	60	N19
Firdon Cres. G15	6	P7
Firhill Rd. G20	21	V10
Firhill St. G20	21	V10
Firpark Pl. G31	36	X12
Firpark St.		
Firpark Rd. (Bishop.) G64	23	Y8
Firpark St. G31	36	X12
Firpark Ter. G31	36	X12
Ark La.		
First Av. (Millerston) G33	24	BB10
First Av. G44	63	U19
First Av. (Bears.) G61	8	S6
First Av. (Kirk.) G66	13	CC7
First Av. (Udd.) G71	57	GG16
First Av., Renf. PA4	31	M11
First Gdns. G41	50	S14
First St. (Udd.) G71	57	GG16
First Ter., Clyde. G81	5	L6
Firwood Dr. G44	64	W17
Fischer Gdns., Pais. PA1	29	G13
Fisher Av., Pais. PA1	45	G14
Fisher Ct. G31	36	X12
Fisher Cres., Clyde. G81	5	L5
Fisher Dr., Pais. PA1	45	G14
Fisher Way, Pais. PA1	45	G14
Fisher Dr.		
Fishers Rd., Renf. PA4	17	M9
Fishescoates Av. (Ruther.) G73	65	Z18
Fishescoates Gdns. (Ruther.) G73	65	Z17
Fishescoates Rd.		
Fishescoates Rd. (Ruther.) G73	65	Z17
Fitzalan Dr., Pais. PA3	31	L13
Fitzalan Rd., Renf. PA4	31	L11
Fitzroy La. G3	35	U12
North Claremont St.		
Fitzroy Pl. G3	35	U12
North Claremont St.		
Flax Rd. (Udd.) G71	69	HH17
Fleet Av., Renf. PA4	32	N11
Fleet St. G32	54	BB14
Fleming Av. (Chry.) G69	26	FF8
Fleming Av., Clyde. G81	17	M8
Fleming Rd. (Cumb.) G67	70	NN3
Fleming St. G31	37	Y13
Fleming St., Pais. PA3	30	K12
Flemington Rd. (Camb.) G72	67	DD19
Flemington St. G21	22	X10
Fleurs Av. G41	50	S14
Fleurs Rd. G41	50	S14
Floors St., John. PA5	43	D15
Floorsburn Cres., John. PA5	43	D15
Flora Gdns. (Bishop.) G64	11	Z7
Florence Dr. (Giff.) G46	62	T19
Florence Gdns. (Ruther.) G73	65	Z18
Florence St. G5	36	W13
Florentine Pl. G12	35	U11
Gibson St.		
Florentine Ter. G12	35	U11
Southpark Av.		
Florida Av. G42	51	V16
Florida Cres. G42	51	V16

Name	Page	Grid
Florida Dr. G42	51	V16
Florida Gdns. (Bail.) G69	40	EE13
Florida Sq. G42	51	V16
Florida St. G42	51	V16
Flowerdale Pl. G53	60	P19
Waukglen Dr.		
Flures Av., Ersk. PA8	16	K8
Flures Cres., Ersk. PA8	16	K8
Flures Dr., Ersk. PA8	16	K8
Flures Pl., Ersk. PA8	16	K8
Fochabers Dr. G52	33	Q13
Fogo Pl. G20	20	T9
Foinaven Dr. (Thorn.) G46	62	S17
Foinaven Gdns. (Thorn.) G46	62	S17
Foinaven Way (Thorn.) G46	62	S17
Forbes Dr. G40	36	X13
Forbes Pl., Pais. PA1	46	K14
Forbes St. G40	36	X13
Ford Rd. G12	20	T10
Fordneuk St. G40	37	Y13
Fordoun St. G34	40	FF12
Fordyce St. G11	34	S11
Fore St. G14	19	Q10
Forehouse Rd. (Kilb.), John. PA10	42	A14
Foremount Ter. La. G12	20	T10
Hyndland Rd.		
Forest Dr. (Both.) G71	69	HH18
Forest Gdns. (Kirk.) G66	12	BB6
Forest Pl. (Kirk.) G66	12	BB6
Forest Pl., Pais. PA2	46	K15
Brodie Pk. Av.		
Forest Rd. (Cumb.) G67	71	QQ3
Forest Vw. (Cumb.) G67	71	QQ2
Foresthall Cres. G21	23	Y10
Foresthall Dr. G21	23	Y10
Forfar Av. G52	48	P14
Forfar Cres. (Bishop.) G64	23	Z8
Forgan Gdns. (Bishop.) G64	23	Z8
Forge, The (Giff.) G46	62	T18
Braidpark Dr.		
Forge Pl. G21	37	Y11
Forge St. G21	37	Y11
Forglen St. G34	40	EE11
Formby Dr. G23	8	T7
Forres Av. (Giff.) G46	62	T18
Forres Gate (Giff.) G46	62	T19
Forres Av.		
Forres St. G23	9	U7
Tolsta St.		
Forrest Gate (Udd.) G71	57	HH15
Forrest St. G40	37	Y13
Forrester Ct. (Bishop.) G64	22	X8
Crowhill Rd.		
Forrestfield St. G21	37	Y11
Fortevoit Av. (Bail.) G69	40	FF13
Fortevoit Pl. (Bail.) G69	40	FF13
Forth Av., Pais. PA2	45	G15
Forth Pl., John. PA5	43	C16
Forth Rd. (Bears.) G61	7	Q7
Forth St. G41	51	U14
Forth St., Clyde. G81	17	M8
Forties Cres. (Thorn.) G46	61	R17
Forties Way (Thorn.) G46	62	S17
Fortingall Av. G12	20	T9
Grandtully Dr.		
Fortingall Pl. G12	20	T9
Fortrose St. G11	34	S11
Foswell Pl. G15	6	N5
Fotheringay La. G41	51	U15
Beaton Rd.		
Fotheringay Rd. G41	50	T15
Foulis La. G13	19	R9
Herschell St.		
Foulis St. G13	19	R9
Herschell St.		
Foundry La. (Barr.) G78	59	L19
Main St.		
Foundry St. G21	22	X10
Fountain Cres. (Inch.), Renf. PA4	16	J9
Fountain Dr. (Inch.), Renf. PA4	16	J9
Fountain St. G31	36	X13
Fountainwell Av. G21	36	W11
Fountainwell Dr. G21	36	W11
Fountainwell Pl. G21	36	W11
Fountainwell Rd. G21	36	W11
Fountainwell Sq. G21	36	X11
Fountainwell Ter. G21	36	X11
Fourth Av. G33	24	BB9
Fourth Av. (Kirk.) G66	13	CC7
Fourth Av., Renf. PA4	31	M11
Third Av.		
Fourth Gdns. G41	50	S14
Fourth St. (Udd.) G71	57	GG15
Fox La. G1	36	W13
Fox St. G1	35	V13
Foxbar Cres., Pais. PA2	45	G16
Foxbar Dr. G13	18	P9
Foxbar Dr., Pais. PA2	45	G16
Foxbar Rd. (Elder.), John. PA5	45	G16
Foxbar Rd., Pais. PA2	45	G16
Foxes Gro. (Lenzie) G66	13	DD5
Foxglove Pl. G53	60	P18
Foxhills Pl. G23	9	U7
Foxley St. G32	55	CC15
Foyers Ct. G13	18	P9
Kirkton Av.		
Foyers Ter. G21	23	Y10
Francis St. G5	51	V14
Frankfield Rd. G33	25	DD9
Frankfield St. G33	37	Z11
Frankfort St. G41	51	U15
Franklin St. G40	52	X14
Fraser Av. (Ruther.) G73	53	Z16
Fraser Av., John. PA5	44	E15
Fraser St. (Camb.) G72	66	AA17
Fraserbank St. G21	22	W10
Keppochhill Rd.		
Frazer St. G40	37	Y13
Freeland Ct. G53	60	P17
Freeland Dr. G53	60	P17
Freeland Dr. (Inch.), Renf. PA4	16	J9
Freelands Ct. (Old Kil.) G60	4	J5
Freelands Pl. (Old Kil.) G60	4	J6
Freelands Rd. (Old Kil.) G60	4	J5
French St. G40	52	X14
French St., Clyde. G81	4	K6
French St., Renf. PA4	31	L11
Freuchie St. G34	40	EE12
Friar Av. (Bishop.) G64	11	Y6
Friars Pl. G13	19	Q8
Friarscourt Av. G13	7	Q7
Friarscourt La. G13	19	Q8
Arrowsmith Av.		
Friarscourt Rd. (Chry.) G69	14	EE7
Friarton Rd. G43	63	U17
Friendship Way, Renf. PA4	31	M11
Fruin Pl. G22	22	W10
Fruin Rd. G15	6	N7
Fruin St. G22	22	W10
Fulbar Av., Renf. PA4	17	M10
Fulbar Ct., Renf. PA4	17	M10
Fulbar Av.		
Fulbar Cres., Pais. PA2	45	G15
Fulbar Gdns., Pais. PA2	45	G15
Peacock Dr.		
Fulbar La., Renf. PA4	17	M10
Fulbar Rd. G51	33	Q12
Fulbar Rd., Pais. PA2	45	G15
Fulbar Rd., Renf. PA4	17	M10
Fullarton Av. G32	54	BB15
Fullarton Dr. G32	54	BB15
Fullarton La. G32	54	BB15
Fullarton Rd. G32	54	AA16
Fullarton Rd. (Cumb.) G68	70	NN1
Fullerton St., Pais. PA3	30	J12
Fullerton Ter., Pais. PA3	30	K12
Fulmar Ct. (Bishop.) G64	22	X8
Fulmar Pl., John. PA5	43	C16
Fulton Cres. (Kilb.), John. PA10	42	B14
Fulton St. G13	19	Q8
Fulwood Av. G13	18	N8
Fulwood Av. (Linw.), Pais. PA3	28	E13
Fulwood Pl. G13	18	N8
Fyvie Av. G43	62	S17

G

Name	Page	Grid
Gadie Av., Renf. PA4	32	N11
Gadie St. G33	37	Z12
Gadloch Av. (Kirk.) G66	13	CC7
Gadloch Gdns. (Kirk.) G66	13	CC6
Gadloch St. G22	22	W9
Gadloch Vw. (Kirk.) G66	13	CC7
Gadsburn Ct. G21	23	Z9
Wallacewell Quad.		
Gadshill St. G21	36	X11
Gailes Pk. (Both.) G71	69	GG19
Gailes Rd. (Cumb.) G68	70	NN1
Gailes St. G40	53	Y14
Gairbraid Av. G20	20	T9
Gairbraid Ct. G20	20	T9
Gairbraid Pl. G20	20	T9
Gairbraid Ter. (Bail.) G69	41	HH13
Gairn St. G11	34	S11
Castlebank St.		
Gala Av., Renf. PA4	32	N11
Gala St. G33	38	AA11
Galbraith Av. G51	33	R12
Burghead Dr.		
Galbraith St. G51	33	Q12
Moss Rd.		
Galdenoch St. G33	38	BB11
Gallacher Av., Pais. PA2	45	H15
Gallan Av. G23	9	U7
Galloway Dr. (Ruther.) G73	65	Y18
Galloway St. G21	22	X9
Gallowflat St. (Ruther.) G73	53	Y16
Reid St.		
Gallowgate G1	36	W13
Gallowgate G4	36	W13
Gallowgate G31	37	Y13
Gallowgate G40	37	Y13
Gallowhill Av. (Lenzie) G66	13	CC5
Gallowhill Gro. (Kirk.) G66	13	CC5
Gallowhill Rd. (Kirk.) G66	13	CC5
Gallowhill Rd., Pais. PA3	30	K13
Galston St. G53	60	N17
Gamrie Dr. G53	48	P16
Gamrie Gdns. G53	48	P16
Gamrie Rd. G53	48	P16
Gannochy Dr. (Bishop.) G64	11	Z7
Gantock Cres. G33	38	BB12
Gardenside Av. G32	54	BB16
Gardenside Av. (Udd.) G71	69	GG17
Gardenside Cres. G32	54	BB16
Gardenside Gro. G32	54	BB16
Gardenside Pl. G32	54	BB16
Gardenside St. (Udd.) G71	69	GG17
Gardner Gro. (Udd.) G71	57	HH16
Gardner La. (Bail.) G69	56	FF14
Church St.		
Gardyne St. G34	40	EE11
Garfield St. G31	37	Y13
Garforth Rd. (Bail.) G69	55	DD14
Gargrave Av. (Bail.) G69	55	DD14
Garion Dr. G13	18	P9
Talbot Dr.		
Garlieston Rd. G33	39	DD13
Garmouth Ct. G51	33	R12
Garmouth St.		
Garmouth Gdns. G51	33	R12
Garmouth St. G51	33	R12
Garnet La. G3	35	V11
Garnet St.		
Garnet St. G3	35	V11
Garnethill St. G3	35	V11
Garngaber Av. (Lenzie) G66	13	CC5
Garngaber Ct. (Kirk.) G66	13	DD5
Woodilee Rd.		
Garnie Av., Ersk. PA8	4	J7
Garnie Cres., Ersk. PA8	4	J7
Garnie La., Ersk. PA8	4	J7
Garnie Oval, Ersk. PA8	4	J7
Garnie Pl., Ersk. PA8	4	J7
Garnieland Rd., Ersk. PA8	4	J7
Garnkirk La. G33	25	DD9
Garnkirk St. G21	36	X11
Garnock St. G21	36	X11
Garrell Way (Cumb.) G67	70	NN3
Garrioch Cres. G20	20	T9
Garrioch Dr. G20	20	T9
Garrioch Gate G20	20	T9
Garrioch Quad. G20	20	T9
Garrioch Rd. G20	20	T10
Garriochmill Rd. G20	21	U10
Raeberry St.		
Garriochmill Way G20	21	U10
Woodside Rd.		
Garrowhill Dr. (Bail.) G69	55	DD14
Garry Av. (Bears.) G61	8	S7
Garry Dr., Pais. PA2	45	H15
Garry St. G44	51	V16
Garscadden Rd. G15	6	P7
Garscadden Rd. S. G13	18	P8
Garscadden Vw., Clyde. G81	5	M6
Kirkoswald Rd.		
Garscube Cross G4	35	V11

Street	Page	Grid
Garscube Mill (Bears.) G61	8	S7
Maryhill Rd.		
Garscube Rd. G4	21	V10
Garscube Rd. G20	21	V10
Gartartan Rd., Pais. PA1	32	N13
Gartcarron Hill (Cumb.) G68	70	MM2
Dunbrach Rd.		
Gartconnell Dr. (Bears.) G61	7	R5
Gartconnell Gdns. (Bears.) G61	7	R5
Gartconnell Rd. (Bears.) G61	7	R5
Gartcosh Rd. (Gart.) G69	41	HH12
Gartcraig Path G33	38	AA11
Gartcraig Pl.		
Gartcraig Pl. G33	38	AA11
Gartcraig Rd. G33	38	AA12
Gartferry Av. (Chry.) G69	15	GG7
Gartferry Rd. (Mood.) G69	15	GG7
Gartferry St. G21	23	Y10
Garth St. G1	36	W12
Garthamlock Rd. G33	39	DD11
Garthland Dr. G31	37	Y12
Garthland La., Pais. PA1	30	K13
Gartliston Ter. (Bail.) G69	41	HH13
Gartloch Cotts. (Gart.) G69	27	GG10
Gartloch Cotts. (Muir.) G69	26	EE9
Gartloch Rd. G33	38	AA11
Gartloch Rd. G34	39	CC11
Gartloch Rd. (Gart.) G69	26	EE10
Gartly St. G44	63	U18
Clarkston Rd.		
Gartmore Gdns. (Udd.) G71	57	GG16
Gartmore La. (Chry.) G69	15	HH7
Gartmore Rd., Pais. PA1	47	L14
Gartmore Ter. (Camb.) G72	66	AA18
Gartness St. G31	37	Y12
Gartocher Dr. G32	39	CC13
Gartocher Rd. G32	39	CC13
Gartocher Ter. G32	39	CC13
Gartochmill Rd. G20	21	U10
Gartons Rd. G21	23	Z10
Gartshore Rd. (Kirk.) G66	15	GG5
Gartshore Rd. (Chry.) G69	15	GG5
Garturk St. G42	51	V15
Garvald Ct. G40	53	Y14
Baltic St.		
Garvald St. G40	53	Y14
Garve Av. G44	63	V18
Garvel Cres. G33	39	DD13
Garvel Rd. G33	39	DD13
Garvock Dr. G43	62	S17
Gas St., John. PA5	44	E14
Gask Pl. G13	18	N8
Gaskin Path G33	25	DD9
Clayhouse Rd.		
Gatehouse St. G32	38	BB13
Gateside Av. (Camb.) G72	67	CC17
Gateside Cres. (Barr.) G78	59	L19
Gateside Pl. (Kilb.), John. PA10	42	B14
Gateside Rd. (Barr.) G78	59	L19
Gateside St. G31	37	Y13
Gauldry Av. G52	49	Q14
Gauze St., Pais. PA1	30	K13
Gavins Rd., Clyde. G81	5	L5
Gavinton St. G44	63	U18
Gear Ter. G40	53	Y15
Geary St. G23	8	T7
Torrin Rd.		
Geddes Rd. G21	23	Z8
Gelston St. G32	54	BB14
General Terminus Quay G51	35	U13
Generals Gate (Udd.) G71	69	GG17
Cobblerigg Way		
Gentle Row, Clyde. G81	4	K5
George Av., Clyde. G81	5	M6
Robert Burns Av.		
George Cres., Clyde. G81	5	M6
George Gray St. (Ruther.) G73	53	Z16
George La., Pais. PA1	46	K14
George St.		
George Mann Ter. (Ruther.) G73	65	Y17
George Pl., Pais. PA1	46	K14
George Reith Av. G12	19	R9
George Sq. G2	36	W12
George St. G1	36	W12
George St. (Bail.) G69	56	EE14
George St. (Barr.) G78	59	L18
George St., John. PA5	43	D14
George St., Pais. PA1	46	J14
Gertrude Pl. (Barr.) G78	59	L19
Gibb St. G21	36	X11
Royston Rd.		
Gibson Cres., John. PA5	43	D15
Gibson Rd., Renf. PA4	31	L11
Gibson St. G12	34	T11
Gibson St. G40	36	X13
Giffnock Pk. Av. (Giff.) G46	62	T18
Gifford Dr. G52	32	P13
Gifford Wynd, Pais. PA2	45	G15
Gilbert St. G3	34	T12
Gilbertfield Pl. G33	38	BB11
Gilbertfield Rd. (Camb.) G72	67	CC18
Gilbertfield St. G33	38	BB11
Gilfillan Way, Pais. PA2	45	G16
Gilhill St. G20	20	T8
Gilia St. (Camb.) G72	66	AA17
Gillies La. (Bail.) G69	56	FF14
Bredisholm Rd.		
Gilmerton St. G32	54	BB14
Gilmour Av., Clyde. G81	5	L5
Gilmour Cres. (Ruther.) G73	52	X16
Gilmour Pl. G5	52	W14
Gilmour St., Clyde. G81	5	M6
Gilmour St., Pais. PA1	30	K13
Girthon St. G32	55	CC14
Girvan St. G33	37	Z11
Gladney Av. G13	18	N8
Gladsmuir Rd. G52	32	P13
Gladstone Av. (Barr.) G78	59	L19
Gladstone Av., John. PA5	43	C16
Gladstone St. G4	35	V11
Gladstone St., Clyde. G81	4	K7
Glaive Rd. G13	7	Q7
Glamis Av. (Elder.), John. PA5	44	E15
Glamis Gdns. (Bishop.) G64	11	Y6
Glamis Pl. G31	53	Z14
Glamis Rd.		
Glamis Rd. G31	53	Z14
Glanderston Av. (Barr.) G78	60	N19
Glanderston Dr. G13	18	P8
Glaselune St. G34	40	FF12
Lochdochart Rd.		
Glasgow Airport (Abbots.), Pais. PA3	30	J11
Glasgow Bri. G1	35	V13
Glasgow Bri. G5	35	V13
Glasgow Grn. G1	36	W13
Glasgow Grn. G40	36	W13
Glasgow Rd. G53	60	N18
Glasgow Rd. (Cumb.) G67	70	MM4
Glasgow Rd. (Cumb.V.) G67	71	PP2
Glasgow Rd. (Bail.) G69	55	DD14
Glasgow Rd. (Udd.) G71	56	FF16
Glasgow Rd. (Blan.) G72	68	FF19
Glasgow Rd. (Camb.) G72	54	AA16
Glasgow Rd. (Turnlaw) G72	66	AA19
Glasgow Rd. (Ruther.) G73	52	X15
Glasgow Rd. (Barr.) G78	59	M18
Glasgow Rd., Clyde. G81	17	L8
Glasgow Rd. (Hardgate), Clyde. G81	5	L5
Glasgow Rd., Pais. PA1	31	L13
Glasgow Rd., Renf. PA4	18	N10
Glasgow St. G12	21	U10
Glassel Rd. G34	40	FF11
Glasserton Pl. G43	63	U17
Glasserton Rd. G43	63	U17
Glassford St. G1	36	W12
Glaudhall Av. (Gart.) G69	27	GG8
Glebe Av. (Both.) G71	69	HH19
Glebe Av. (Both.) G71	69	HH19
Green St.		
Glebe Ct. G4	36	W12
Glebe Hollow (Both.) G71	69	HH19
Glebe Wynd		
Glebe Pl. (Camb.) G72	66	BB17
Glebe Pl. (Ruther.) G73	52	X16
Glebe St. G4	36	W11
Glebe St., Renf. PA4	17	M10
Glebe Wynd (Both.) G71	69	HH19
Gleddoch Rd. G52	32	N13
Glen Affric Dr. G53	61	Q18
Glen Alby Pl. G53	61	Q18
Glen Av. G32	38	BB13
Glen Av. (Chry.) G69	15	GG7
Glen Clova Dr. (Cumb.) G68	70	MM2
Glen Clunie Av. G53	61	Q18
Glen Clunie Dr. G53	61	Q18
Glen Clunie Pl. G53	61	Q18
Glen Cona Dr. G53	61	Q18
Glen Cres. G13	18	N8
Glen Douglas Dr. (Cumb.) G68	70	MM2
Glen Esk Cres. G53	61	Q18
Glen Esk Dr. G53	61	Q18
Glen Esk Pl. G53	61	Q18
Glen Etive Pl. (Ruther.) G73	66	AA19
Glen Fyne Rd. (Cumb.) G68	70	LL2
Glen Gdns. (Elder.), John. PA5	44	F14
Glen La., Pais. PA3	30	K13
Glen Lednock Dr. (Cumb.) G68	70	LL2
Glen Livet Pl. G53	61	Q18
Glen Loy Pl. G53	61	Q18
Glen Luss Gdns. (Cumb.) G68	70	MM2
Glen Markie Dr. G53	61	Q18
Glen Moriston Rd. G53	61	Q18
Glen Moriston Rd. (Cumb.) G68	70	LL2
Glen Nevis Pl. (Ruther.) G73	65	Z19
Glen Ogle St. G32	55	CC14
Glen Orchy Ct. (Cumb.) G68	70	MM1
Glen Orchy Dr. G53	61	Q18
Glen Orchy Dr. (Cumb.) G68	70	LL2
Glen Orchy Pl. G53	61	Q18
Glen Orchy Pl. (Cumb.) G68	70	LL2
Glen Rd. G32	38	BB12
Glen Rosa Gdns. (Cumb.) G68	70	LL2
Glen Sannox Dr. (Cumb.) G68	70	LL2
Glen Sannox Vw. (Cumb.) G68	70	LL2
Glen Sax Dr., Renf. PA4	32	N11
Glen St. (Camb.) G72	67	CC18
Glen St. (Barr.) G78	59	M18
Glen St., Pais. PA3	30	J13
Glen Vw. (Cumb.) G67	71	QQ2
Glenacre Cres. (Udd.) G71	57	GG16
Glenacre Dr. G45	64	W18
Glenacre Rd. (Cumb.) G67	70	NN4
Glenacre St. G45	64	W18
Glenacre Ter. G45	64	W18
Glenallan Way, Pais. PA2	45	G16
Glenalmond Rd. (Ruther.) G73	65	Z18
Glenalmond St. G32	54	BB14
Glenapp Av., Pais. PA2	47	L15
Glenapp Pl. (Mood.) G69	15	GG6
Whithorn Cres.		
Glenapp Rd., Pais. PA2	47	L15
Glenapp St. G41	51	U14
Glenarklet Dr., Pais. PA2	47	L15
Glenartney Row (Chry.) G69	14	FF7
Glenashdale Way, Pais. PA2	47	L15
Glenbrittle Dr.		
Glenavon Av. (Ruther.) G73	65	Z18
Glenavon Rd. G20	20	T8
Thornton St.		
Glenavon Ter. G11	34	S11
Crow Rd.		
Glenbank Av. (Lenzie) G66	13	CC6
Glenbank Ct. (Thorn.) G46	61	R19
Glenbank Dr.		
Glenbank Dr. (Thorn.) G46	61	R19
Glenbank Rd. (Lenzie) G66	13	CC6
Glenbarr St. G21	36	X11
Glenbervie Cres. (Cumb.) G68	70	NN2
Glenbervie Pl. G23	8	T7
Glenbrittle Dr., Pais. PA2	47	L15
Glenbrittle Way, Pais. PA2	47	L15
Glenbuck Av. G33	24	AA9
Glenbuck Dr. G33	24	AA9
Glenburn Av. (Bail.) G69	40	FF13
Glenburn Av. (Chry.) G69	15	GG7
Glenburn Av. (Camb.) G72	65	Z17
Glenburn Cres., Pais. PA2	46	J16
Glenburn Gdns. (Bishop.) G64	10	X7
Glenburn Rd. (Giff.) G46	62	S19
Glenburn Rd. (Bears.) G61	7	Q5
Glenburn Rd., Pais. PA2	45	H16
Glenburn St. G20	21	U8
Glenburnie Pl. G34	40	EE12
Glencairn Dr. G41	50	T15
Glencairn Dr. (Chry.) G69	15	GG7

Entry	No.	Grid
Glencairn Dr. (Ruther.) G73	52	X16
Glencairn Gdns. G41	51	U15
Glencairn Dr.		
Glencairn Gdns. (Camb.) G72	67	CC17
Glencairn La. G41	51	U15
Shields Rd.		
Glencairn Rd. (Cumb.) G67	71	QQ3
Glencairn Rd., Pais. PA3	31	L12
Glencally Av., Pais. PA2	47	L15
Glencart Gro. (Mill.Pk.), John. PA10	43	C15
Milliken Pk. Rd.		
Glenclora Dr., Pais. PA2	47	L15
Glencloy St. G20	20	T8
Glencoats Cres., Pais. PA3	29	H13
Glencoats Dr., Pais. PA3	29	H13
Glencoe Pl. G13	19	R8
Glencoe Rd. (Ruther.) G73	65	Z18
Glencoe St. G13	19	R8
Glencorse Rd., Pais. PA2	46	J15
Glencorse St. G32	38	AA12
Glencroft Av. (Udd.) G71	57	GG16
Glencroft Rd. G44	64	W17
Glencryan Rd. (Cumb.) G67	71	PP4
Glendale Cres. (Bishop.) G64	23	Z8
Glendale Dr. (Bishop.) G64	23	Z8
Glendale Pl. G31	37	Y13
Glendale St.		
Glendale Pl. (Bishop.) G64	23	Z8
Glendale St. G31	37	Y13
Glendaruel Av. (Bears.) G61	8	S6
Glendaruel Rd. (Ruther.) G73	66	AA19
Glendarvel Gdns. G22	22	W10
Glendee Gdns., Renf. PA4	31	M11
Glendee Rd., Renf. PA4	31	M11
Glendevon Pl., Clyde. G81	4	K6
Glendevon Sq. G33	38	BB11
Glendinning Rd. G13	7	R7
Glendore St. G14	33	R11
Glendower Way, Pais. PA2	45	G16
Spencer Dr.		
Glenduffhill Rd. (Bail.) G69	39	DD13
Gleneagles Av. (Cumb.) G67	71	PP1
Gleneagles Cotts. G14	19	Q10
Dumbarton Rd.		
Gleneagles Dr. (Bishop.) G64	11	Y6
Gleneagles Gdns. (Bishop.) G64	11	Y6
Gleneagles La. N. G14	19	Q10
Dunglass Av.		
Gleneagles La. S. G14	19	Q10
Harland St.		
Gleneagles Pk. (Both.) G71	69	GG19
Gleneagles Ter. G14	19	Q10
Dumbarton Rd.		
Glenelg Quad. G34	40	FF11
Glenfarg Cres. (Bears.) G61	8	S6
Glenfarg Rd. (Ruther.) G73	65	Y18
Glenfarg St. G20	35	V11
Glenfield Cres., Pais. PA2	58	J17
Glenfield Gdns., Pais. PA2	58	J17
Glenfield Rd., Pais. PA2	46	J16
Glenfinnan Dr. G20	20	T9
Glenfinnan Dr. (Bears.) G61	8	T6
Glenfinnan Pl. G20	20	T9
Glenfinnan Rd. G20	20	T9
Glenfruin Cres., Pais. PA2	47	L15
Glengarry Dr. G52	33	Q13
Glengavel Cres. G33	24	AA9
Glengyre St. G34	40	FF11
Glenhead Cres. G22	22	W9
Glenhead Rd. (Lenzie) G66	13	CC6
Glenhead Rd., Clyde. G81	5	L5
Glenhead St. G22	22	W9
Glenholme Av., Pais. PA2	45	H15
Glenhove Rd. (Cumb.) G67	71	PP3
Gleniffer Av. G13	18	P9
Gleniffer Cres. (Elder.), John. PA5	44	F15
Gleniffer Dr. (Barr.) G78	59	L17
Gleniffer Rd., Pais. PA2	45	H16
Gleniffer Rd., Renf. PA4	31	L11
Gleniffer Vw., Clyde. G81	5	M6
Kirkoswald Dr.		
Glenisla Av. (Mood.) G69	15	HH6
Glenisla St. G31	53	Z14
Glenkirk Dr. G15	6	P7
Glenlee Cres. G52	48	N14
Glenlora Dr. G53	48	P16
Glenlora Ter. G53	48	P16
Glenluce Dr. G32	55	CC14
Glenluce Gdns. (Mood.) G69	15	HH6
Brady Cres.		
Glenlui Av. (Ruther.) G73	65	Y17
Glenlyon Pl. (Ruther.) G73	65	Z18
Glenmalloch Pl. (Elder.), John. PA5	44	F14
Glenmanor Av. (Chry.) G69	15	GG7
Glenmavis St. G4	35	V11
Maitland St.		
Glenmore Av. G42	52	X16
Glenmuir Dr. G53	60	P17
Glenpark Av. (Thorn.) G46	61	R19
Glenpark Rd. G31	37	Y13
Glenpark St. G31	37	Y13
Glenpark Ter. (Camb.) G72	54	AA16
Glenpatrick Bldgs. (Elder.), John. PA5	44	F15
Glenpatrick Rd. (Elder.), John. PA5	44	F15
Glenraith Rd. G33	24	BB10
Glenraith Sq. G33	24	BB10
Glenraith Wk. G33	25	CC10
Glenshee Ct. G31	53	Z14
Glenshee Gdns. G31	54	AA14
Glenshee St. G31	53	Z14
Glenshiel Av., Pais. PA2	47	L15
Glenshira Av., Pais. PA2	47	L15
Glenside Av. G53	48	P15
Glenside Dr. (Ruther.) G73	65	Z17
Glenspean Pl. G43	62	T17
Glenspean St.		
Glenspean St. G43	62	T17
Glentanar Dr. (Mood.) G69	15	HH7
Glentanar Pl. G22	21	V8
Glentanar Rd. G22	21	V8
Glentarbert Rd. (Ruther.) G73	65	Z18
Glentrool Gdns. G22	22	W10
Glenturret St. G32	54	BB14
Glentyan Av. (Kilb.), John. PA10	42	B14
Glentyan Dr. G53	60	P17
Glentyan Ter. G53	48	P16
Glenview Cres. (Chry.) G69	15	GG6
Glenview Pl. (Blan.) G72	68	FF19
Glenville Av. (Giff.) G46	62	S18
Glenwood Ct. (Kirk.) G66	12	BB5
Glenwood Dr. (Thorn.) G46	61	R19
Glenwood Gdns. (Kirk.) G66	12	BB5
Glenwood Path G45	64	X18
Glenwood Pl. G45	64	X18
Glenwood Pl. (Kirk.) G66	12	BB5
Glenwood Rd. (Kirk.) G66	12	BB5
Gloucester Av. (Ruther.) G73	65	Z17
Gloucester St. G5	35	V13
Gockston Rd., Pais. PA3	30	J12
Gogar Pl. G33	38	AA12
Gogar St. G33	38	AA12
Goldberry Av. G14	18	P9
Goldie Rd. (Udd.) G71	69	HH18
Golf Ct. G44	63	U19
Golf Dr. G15	6	N7
Golf Dr., Pais. PA1	47	M14
Golf Rd. (Ruther.) G73	65	Y18
Golf Vw. (Bears.) G61	6	P5
Golf Vw., Clyde. G81	4	K6
Golfhill Dr. G31	37	Y12
Golfhill La. G31	37	Y12
Whitehill St.		
Golfhill Ter. G31	36	X12
Firpark St.		
Golspie St. G51	34	S12
Goosedubbs G1	36	W13
Stockwell St.		
Gopher Av. (Udd.) G71	57	HH16
Gorbals Cross G5	36	W13
Gorbals La. G5	35	V13
Oxford St.		
Gorbals St. G5	35	V13
Gordon Av. G44	63	U19
Gordon Av. (Bail.) G69	39	DD13
Gordon Dr. G44	63	U18
Gordon La. G1	35	V12
Gordon St.		
Gordon Rd. G44	63	U19
Gordon St. G1	35	V12
Gordon St., Pais. PA1	46	K14
Gordon Ter. (Blan.) G72	68	FF19
Gorebridge St. G32	38	AA12
Gorget Av. G13	7	Q7
Gorget Pl. G13	7	Q7
Gorget Quad. G13	6	P7
Gorget Av.		
Gorse Dr. (Barr.) G78	59	L18
Gorse Pl. (Udd.) G71	57	HH16
Gorsewood (Bishop.) G64	10	X7
Gorstan Pl. G20	20	T9
Wyndford Rd.		
Gorstan St. G23	20	T8
Gosford La. G14	18	P10
Dumbarton Rd.		
Goudie St., Pais. PA3	30	J12
Gough St. G33	37	Z12
Gourlay Path G21	22	W10
Endrick St.		
Gourlay St. G21	22	X10
Crichton St.		
Gourock St. G5	51	V14
Govan Cross G51	34	S12
Govan Rd. G51	33	R12
Govanhill St. G42	51	V15
Gowan Brae (Kirk.) G66	13	CC5
Marguerite Av.		
Gowanbank Gdns., John. PA5	43	D15
Floors St.		
Gowanlea Av. G15	6	P7
Gowanlea Dr. (Giff.) G46	62	T18
Gowanlea Ter. (Udd.) G71	57	HH16
Gower La. G51	34	T13
North Gower St.		
Gower St. G41	50	T14
Gower Ter. G41	34	T13
Goyle Av. G15	7	Q6
Grace Av. (Bail.) G69	41	GG13
Grace St. G3	35	U12
Graffham Av. (Giff.) G46	62	T18
Grafton Pl. G1	36	W12
Graham Av. (Camb.) G72	67	CC17
Graham Av., Clyde. G81	5	L6
Graham Sq. G31	36	X13
Graham St. (Barr.) G78	59	L18
Graham St., John. PA5	43	D15
Graham Ter. (Bishop.) G64	23	Y8
Grahamston Ct., Pais. PA2	47	M16
Grahamston Cres., Pais. PA2	47	M16
Grahamston Pk. (Barr.) G78	59	L17
Grahamston Pl., Pais. PA2	47	M16
Grahamston Rd.		
Grahamston Rd. (Barr.) G78	59	L17
Grahamston Rd., Pais. PA2	47	M16
Grainger Rd. (Bishop.) G64	11	Z7
Grampian Av., Pais. PA2	46	J16
Grampian Cres. G32	54	BB14
Grampian Pl. G32	54	BB14
Grampian St. G32	54	BB14
Grampian Way (Barr.) G78	59	M19
Gran St., Clyde. G81	18	N8
Granby La. G12	20	T10
Great George St.		
Granby Pl. G12	20	T10
Great George St.		
Grandtully Dr. G12	20	T9
Grange Gdns. (Both.) G71	69	HH19
Blairston Av.		
Grange Rd. G42	51	V16
Grange Rd. (Bears.) G61	7	R5
Grangeneuk Gdns. (Cumb.) G68	70	MM3
Grant St. G3	35	U11
Grantlea Gro. G32	55	CC14
Grantlea Ter. G32	55	CC14
Grantley Gdns. G41	50	T16
Grantley St. G41	50	T16
Granton St. G5	52	X15
Grants Av., Pais. PA2	46	J15
Grants Way, Pais. PA2	46	J15
Granville St. G3	35	U12
Granville St., Clyde. G81	5	L6
Gray Dr. (Bears.) G61	7	R6
Gray St. G3	34	T11
Great Dovehill G1	36	W13
Great George St. G12	20	T10
Great George St.		
Great George St. G12	20	T10
Great Hamilton St., Pais. PA2	46	K15
Great Kelvin La. G12	21	U10
Glasgow St.		
Great Western Rd. G4	20	S9
Great Western Rd. G12	20	T10
Great Western Rd. G13	6	P7
Great Western Rd. G15	6	P7

Great Western Rd., Clyde. G81	4	J5
Great Western Ter. G12	20	T10
Green, The G40	36	X13
Green Lo. Ter. G40	52	X14
Greenhead St.		
Green Pk. (Both.) G71	69	HH19
Green St.		
Green Rd. (Ruther.) G73	53	Y16
Green Rd., Pais. PA2	45	G14
Green St. G40	36	X13
Green St. (Both.) G71	69	HH19
Green St., Clyde. G81	5	L6
Greenan Av. G42	52	X16
Greenbank Dr., Pais. PA2	46	J16
Greenbank Rd. (Cumb.) G68	70	MM3
Greenbank St. (Ruther.) G73	53	Y16
Greendyke St. G1	36	W13
Greenend Av., John. PA5	43	C15
Greenend Pl. G32	39	CC12
Greenfarm Rd. (Linw.), Pais. PA3	28	E13
Greenfaulds Cres. (Cumb.) G67	71	PP4
Greenfaulds Rd. (Cumb.) G67	70	NN4
Greenfield Av. G32	38	BB12
Greenfield Pl. G32	38	BB13
Budhill Av.		
Greenfield Rd. G32	39	CC13
Greenfield St. G51	33	R12
Greengairs Av. G51	33	Q12
Greenhead Rd. (Bears.) G61	7	R6
Greenhead Rd. (Inch.), Renf. PA4	16	J8
Greenhead St. G40	52	X14
Greenhill (Bishop.) G64	11	Y7
Greenhill Av. (Giff.) G46	62	S19
Greenhill Av. (Gart.) G69	27	GG8
Greenhill Ct. (Ruther.) G73	53	Y16
Greenhill Cres. (Elder.), John. PA5	44	F15
Greenhill Cres. (Linw.), Pais. PA3	28	E13
Greenhill Dr. (Linw.), Pais. PA3	28	F13
Greenhill Rd. (Ruther.) G73	53	Y16
Greenhill Rd., Pais. PA3	30	J13
Greenhill St. (Ruther.) G73	53	Y16
Greenholm Av. (Udd.) G71	57	GG16
Greenholme St. G44	63	V17
Greenknowe Rd. G43	62	S17
Greenlaw Av., Pais. PA1	31	L13
Greenlaw Cres., Pais. PA1	31	L13
Greenlaw Dr., Pais. PA1	31	L13
Greenlaw Rd. G14	17	M9
Greenlaw Ter., Pais. PA1	31	L13
Greenlaw Av.		
Greenlea Rd. (Chry.) G69	26	EE8
Greenlea St. G13	19	R9
Greenlees Gdns. (Camb.) G72	66	AA18
Greenlees Pk. (Camb.) G72	66	BB18
Greenlees Rd. (Camb.) G72	66	BB17
Greenloan Av. G51	33	Q12
Greenmount G22	21	V8
Greenock Av. G44	63	V17
Greenock Rd., Pais. PA3	30	J12
Greenock Rd. (Inch.), Renf. PA4	16	J9
Greenrig St. G33	23	Z10
Greenrig St. (Udd.) G71	69	GG17
Greenrigg (Udd.) G71	69	GG17
Greenrigg Rd. (Cumb.) G67	71	PP3
Greenshields Rd. (Bail.) G69	40	EE13
Greenside Cres. G33	24	AA10
Greenside St. G33	24	AA10
Greentree Dr. (Bail.) G69	55	DD14
Greenview St. G43	50	T16
Greenways Av., Pais. PA2	45	H15
Greenways Ct., Pais. PA2	45	H15
Greenwell Pl. G51	34	S12
Greenwell St. G51	34	S12
Govan Rd.		
Greenwood Av. (Chry.) G69	15	GG7
Greenwood Av. (Camb.) G72	67	DD17
Greenwood Dr. (Bears.) G61	8	S6
Greenwood Rd., John. PA5	43	C16
Greenwood Quad., Clyde. G81	5	M7
Greer Quad., Clyde. G81	5	L6
Grenville Dr. (Camb.) G72	66	AA18
Gretna St. G40	53	Y14
Greyfriars Rd. (Udd.) G71	56	FF16

Greyfriars St. G32	38	AA12
Greystone Av. (Ruther.) G73	65	Z17
Greywood St. G13	19	R8
Grierson La. G33	37	Z12
Lomax St.		
Grierson St. G33	37	Z12
Grieve Cft. (Both.) G71	69	HH19
Grieve Rd. (Cumb.) G67	71	PP2
Griqua Ter. (Both.) G71	69	HH19
Grogarry Rd. G15	6	P6
Springside Pl.		
Grosvenor Cres. G12	20	T10
Observatory Rd.		
Grosvenor Cres. La. G12	20	T10
Byres Rd.		
Grosvenor La. G12	20	T10
Byres Rd.		
Grosvenor Mans. G12	20	T10
Observatory Rd.		
Grosvenor Ter. G12	20	T10
Grove, The (Kilb.), John. PA10	42	B14
Grove Pk. (Lenzie) G66	13	CC6
Groveburn Av. (Thorn.) G46	62	S18
Grovepark Ct. G20	35	V11
Grovepark Gdns. G20	35	V11
Grovepark Pl. G20	21	V10
Grovepark St. G20	21	V10
Groves, The (Bishop.) G64	23	Z8
Woodhill Rd.		
Grudie St. G34	40	EE12
Gryffe Av., Renf. PA4	17	L9
Gryffe Cres., Pais. PA2	45	G15
Gryffe St. G44	63	V17
Guildford St. G33	39	CC11
Gullane Cres. (Cumb.) G68	70	NN1
Gullane St. G11	34	S11
Purdon St.		
Guthrie Dr. (Udd.) G71	57	HH15
Guthrie St. G20	20	T9

H

Haberlea Av. G53	61	Q18
Haberlea Gdns. G53	61	Q19
Haddow Gro. (Udd.) G71	57	HH16
Hagg Cres., John. PA5	43	D14
Hagg Pl., John. PA5	43	D14
Hagg Rd., John. PA5	43	D15
Haggs Rd. G41	50	T15
Haggswood Av. G41	50	S15
Haghill Rd. G31	37	Z12
Haig Dr. (Bail.) G69	55	DD14
Haig St. G21	23	Y10
Hailes Av. G32	39	CC13
Haining, The, Renf. PA4	31	M11
Haining Rd., Renf. PA4	17	M10
Hairmyres St. G42	51	V15
Govanhill St.		
Hairst St., Renf. PA4	17	M10
Halbeath Av. G15	6	N6
Halbert St. G41	51	U15
Haldane La. G14	19	Q10
Haldane St.		
Haldane St. G14	19	Q10
Halgreen Av. G15	5	M6
Halifax Way, Renf. PA4	31	M11
Britannia Way		
Hall St., Clyde. G81	5	L7
Hallbrae St. G33	38	AA11
Halley Dr. G13	18	N8
Halley Pl. G13	18	N9
Halley Sq. G13	18	N8
Halley St. G13	18	N8
Hallforest St. G33	38	BB11
Gartloch Rd.		
Hallhill Cres. G33	39	DD13
Hallhill Rd. G32	38	BB13
Hallhill Rd. G33	39	DD13
Hallhill Rd., John. PA5	43	C16
Halliburton Cres. G34	40	EE12
Ware Rd.		
Hallidale Cres., Renf. PA4	32	N11
Hallrule Dr. G52	33	Q13
Hallside Av. (Camb.) G72	67	DD17
Hallside Boul. (Camb.) G72	67	DD18
Hallside Cres. (Camb.) G72	67	DD17
Hallside Dr. (Camb.) G72	67	DD17
Hallside Pl. G5	52	W14
Hallside Rd. (Camb.) G72	67	DD18
Hallside St. G5	52	W14

Hallydown Dr. G13	19	Q9
Halton Gdns. (Bail.) G69	55	DD14
Hamilton Av. G41	50	S14
Hamilton Cres. (Camb.) G72	67	CC18
Hamilton Cres., Renf. PA4	17	M9
Hamilton Dr. G12	21	U10
Hamilton Dr. (Giff.) G46	62	T19
Hamilton Dr. (Both.) G71	69	HH19
Hamilton Dr. (Camb.) G72	66	BB17
Hamilton Pk. Av. G12	21	U10
Hamilton Rd. G32	55	CC15
Hamilton Rd. (Both.) G71	69	HH19
Hamilton Rd. (Camb.) G72	66	BB17
Hamilton Rd. (Ruther.) G73	53	Y16
Hamilton St. G42	52	W15
Hamilton St., Clyde. G81	17	M8
Hamilton St., Pais. PA3	30	K13
Hamilton Ter., Clyde. G81	17	M8
Hamilton Vw. (Udd.) G71	57	HH16
Hamiltonhill Cres. G22	21	V10
Hamiltonhill Rd.		
Hamiltonhill Rd. G22	21	V10
Hampden Dr. G42	51	V16
Cathcart Rd.		
Hampden La. G42	51	V16
Cathcart Rd.		
Hampden Ter. G42	51	V16
Cathcart Rd.		
Hampden Way, Renf. PA4	31	M11
Lewis Av.		
Hangingshaw Pl. G42	52	W16
Hanover Clo. G42	51	V16
Battlefield Gdns.		
Hanover Ct., Pais. PA1	31	L13
Kelburne Gdns.		
Hanover Gdns., Pais. PA1	46	J14
Broomlands St.		
Hanover St. G1	36	W12
Hanson St. G31	36	X12
Hapland Av. G53	49	Q15
Hapland Rd. G53	49	Q15
Harbour La., Pais. PA3	30	K13
Harbour Rd., Pais. PA3	30	K12
Harburn Pl. G23	9	U7
Harbury Pl. G14	18	N9
Harcourt Dr. G31	37	Y12
Roebank St.		
Hardgate Dr. G51	33	Q12
Hardgate Gdns. G51	33	Q12
Hardgate Pl. G51	33	Q12
Hardgate Rd. G51	33	Q12
Hardie Av. (Ruther.) G73	53	Z16
Hardridge Av. G52	49	Q15
Hardridge Rd.		
Hardridge Pl. G52	49	R15
Hardridge Rd. G52	49	Q15
Harefield Dr. G14	18	P9
Harelaw Av. G44	63	U18
Harelaw Av. (Barr.) G78	59	M19
Harelaw Cres., Pais. PA2	46	J16
Harhill St. G51	33	R12
Harland Cotts. G14	33	Q11
South St.		
Harland St. G14	19	Q10
Harlaw Gdns. (Bishop.) G64	11	Z7
Harley St. G51	34	T13
Harmetray St. G22	22	W9
Harmony Ct. G52	34	S12
Helen St.		
Harmony Pl. G51	34	S12
Harmony Row G51	34	S12
Harmony Sq. G51	34	S12
Harmsworth St. G11	33	R11
Harport St. (Thorn.) G46	61	R18
Harriet Pl. G43	62	S17
Harriet St. (Ruther.) G73	53	Y16
Harris Rd. G23	9	U7
Harris Rd. (Old Kil.) G60	4	J5
Harrison Dr. G51	34	S13
Harrow Ct. G15	6	N6
Linkwood Dr.		
Harrow Pl. G15	6	N6
Hart St. G31	38	AA13
Hart St. (Linw.), Pais. PA3	28	E13
Hartfield Ter., Pais. PA2	47	L15
Hartlaw Cres. G52	32	P13
Hartree Av. G13	18	N8
Hartstone Pl. G53	48	P16
Hartstone Rd. G53	48	P16
Hartstone Ter. G53	48	P16
Harvey St. G4	36	W11
Harvie St. G51	34	T13

Name	Page	Grid
Harwood Gdns. (Mood.) G69	15	HH6
Dryburgh Wk.		
Harwood St. G32	38	AA12
Hastie St. G3	34	T11
Old Dumbarton Rd.		
Hatfield Dr. G12	19	R9
Hathaway Dr. (Giff.) G46	62	S19
Hathaway La. G20	21	U9
Avenuepark St.		
Hathaway St. G20	21	U9
Hathersage Av. (Bail.) G69	40	EE13
Hathersage Dr. (Bail.) G69	40	EE13
Hathersage Gdns. (Bail.) G69	40	EE13
Hatters Row G40	52	X14
Dalmarnock Rd.		
Hatton Dr. G52	48	P14
Hatton Gdns. G52	48	P14
Haugh Rd. G3	34	T12
Haughburn Pl. G53	48	P16
Haughburn Rd. G53	48	P16
Haughburn Ter. G53	49	Q16
Havelock La. G11	34	T11
Dowanhill St.		
Havelock St. G11	34	T11
Hawick Av., Pais. PA2	45	H15
Hawick St. G13	18	N8
Hawkhead Av., Pais. PA2	47	L15
Hawkhead Rd., Pais. PA1	47	L14
Hawkhead Rd., Pais. PA2	47	L14
Hawthorn Av. (Bishop.) G64	23	Y8
Hawthorn Av. (Lenzie) G66	13	CC5
Hawthorn Av., Ersk. PA8	16	K8
Hawthorn Av., John. PA5	44	E15
Hawthorn Cres., Ersk. PA8	4	K7
Hawthorn Gdns. (Camb.) G72	67	DD18
Elder Cres.		
Hawthorn Quad. G22	22	W9
Hawthorn Rd., Ersk. PA8	16	K8
Hawthorn St. G22	22	W9
Hawthorn St., Clyde. G81	5	L6
Hawthorn Ter. (Udd.) G71	57	HH16
Douglas St.		
Hawthorn Wk. (Bishop.) G64	23	Z8
Letham Dr.		
Hawthorn Wk. (Camb.) G72	65	Z17
Hawthornden Gdns. G23	9	U7
Hay Dr., John. PA5	44	E14
Hayburn Cres. G11	20	S10
Hayburn Gate G11	34	S11
Fortrose St.		
Hayburn La. G11	20	S10
Queensborough Gdns.		
Hayburn St. G11	34	S11
Hayfield St. G5	52	W14
Hayhill Cotts. (Gart.) G69	27	HH9
Hayle Gdns. (Chry.) G69	15	GG6
Haylynn St. G14	33	R11
Haymarket St. G32	38	AA12
Haystack Pl. (Lenzie) G66	13	CC6
Hayston Cres. G22	21	V9
Hayston Rd. (Cumb.) G68	70	NN2
Hayston St. G22	21	V9
Haywood St. G22	21	V9
Hazel Av. G44	63	U18
Clarkston Rd.		
Hazel Av. (Lenzie) G66	13	CC5
Hazel Av., John. PA5	44	E15
Hazel Dene (Bishop.) G64	11	Y7
Hazel Gro. (Kirk.) G66	13	CC5
Hazel Rd. (Cumb.) G67	71	QQ2
Hazel Ter. (Udd.) G71	57	HH16
Douglas St.		
Hazelden Gdns. G44	63	U18
Hazellea Dr. (Giff.) G46	62	T18
Hazelwood Av., Pais. PA2	45	G16
Hazelwood Gdns. (Ruther.) G73	65	Z18
Hazelwood Rd. G41	50	T14
Hazlitt Gdns. G20	21	V9
Bilsland Dr.		
Hazlitt Pl. G20	21	V9
Bilsland Dr.		
Hazlitt St. G20	21	V9
Heath Av. (Bishop.) G64	23	Y8
Heath Av. (Lenzie) G66	13	CC6
Heathcliff Av. (Blan.) G72	68	FF19
Heathcot Av. G15	6	N7
Heathcot Pl. G15	6	N7
Heathcot Av.		
Heather Av. (Barr.) G78	59	L17
Heather Dr. (Kirk.) G66	12	BB6
Heather Gdns. (Kirk.) G66	12	BB6
Heather Pl. (Kirk.) G66	12	BB5
Heather Pl., John. PA5	44	E15
Heather St. G41	35	U13
Scotland St.		
Heatherbrae (Bishop.) G64	10	X7
Heatheryknowe Rd. (Bail.) G69	41	GG12
Heathfield Av. (Mood.) G69	15	GG7
Heathfield St. G33	39	CC12
Heathfield Ter. G21	22	X9
Broomfield Rd.		
Heathside Rd. (Giff.) G46	62	T18
Heathwood Dr. (Thorn.) G46	62	S18
Hecla Av. G15	6	N6
Hecla Pl. G15	6	N6
Hecla Sq. G15	6	N7
Hector Rd. G41	50	T16
Heddle Pl. G2	35	V12
Cadogan St.		
Heggie Ter. G14	19	Q10
Dumbarton Rd.		
Helen St. G51	34	S12
Helen St. G52	33	R13
Helensburgh Dr. G13	19	Q9
Helenslea (Camb.) G72	67	CC18
Helenvale Ct. G31	37	Z13
Helenvale St. G31	53	Z14
Helmsdale Av. (Blan.) G72	68	FF18
Helmsdale Ct. (Camb.) G72	67	CC17
Helmsdale Dr., Pais. PA2	45	G15
Hemlock St. G13	19	R8
Henderland Dr. (Bears.) G61	7	R7
Henderland Rd. (Bears.) G61	7	R7
Henderson Av. (Camb.) G72	67	CC17
Henderson St. G20	21	U10
Henderson St., Clyde. G81	18	N8
Henderson St., Pais. PA1	30	J13
Henrietta St. G14	19	Q10
Henry St. (Barr.) G78	59	L18
Hepburn Rd. G52	32	P12
Herald Av. G13	7	Q7
Herald Way, Renf. PA4	31	M11
Viscount Av.		
Herbert St. G20	21	U10
Herbertson Gro. (Blan.) G72	68	FF19
Herbertson St. G5	35	V13
Eglinton St.		
Hercla Av. G15	6	N6
Hercla Pl. G15	6	N6
Hercla Sq. G15	6	N7
Hercules Way, Renf. PA4	31	M11
Friendship Way		
Heriot Av., Pais. PA2	45	G16
Heriot Cres. (Bishop.) G64	11	Y6
Heriot Rd. (Lenzie) G66	13	CC6
Herma St. G23	21	U8
Hermiston Av. G32	39	CC13
Hermiston Pl. G32	39	CC13
Hermiston Rd. G32	38	BB12
Hermitage Av. G13	19	Q9
Heron Ct., Clyde. G81	5	L5
Heron Pl., John. PA5	43	C16
Heron Way, Renf. PA4	31	M11
Britannia Way		
Herries Rd. G41	50	T15
Herriet St. G41	51	U14
Herschell St. G13	19	R9
Hertford Av. G12	20	S9
Hexham Gdns. G41	50	T15
Heys St. (Barr.) G78	59	M19
Hickman St. G42	51	V15
Hickman Ter. G42	52	W15
Hickory St. G22	22	X9
High Barholm (Kilb.), John. PA10	42	B14
High Calside, Pais. PA2	46	J14
High Craighall Rd. G4	35	V11
High Parksail, Ersk. PA8	16	J8
High Rd. (Castlehead), Pais. PA2	46	J14
High St. G1	36	W13
High St. G4	36	W13
High St. (Ruther.) G73	53	Y16
High St., John. PA5	43	D14
High St., Pais. PA1	46	J14
High St., Renf. PA4	17	M10
Highburgh Dr. (Ruther.) G73	65	Y17
Highburgh Rd. G12	34	T11
Highburgh Ter. G12	34	T11
Highburgh Rd.		
Highcraig Av., John. PA5	43	C15
Highcroft Av. G44	64	W17
Highfield Av., Pais. PA2	46	J16
Highfield Cres., Pais. PA2	46	J16
Highfield Dr. G12	20	S9
Highfield Dr. (Ruther.) G73	65	Z18
Highfield Pl. G12	20	S9
Highkirk Vw., John. PA5	43	D15
Highland La. G51	34	T12
Hilary Av. (Ruther.) G73	65	Z17
Hilary Dr. (Bail.) G69	39	DD13
Hilda Cres. G33	24	AA10
Hill Pk., Clyde. G81	5	L5
Hill Path G52	32	P13
Hill Pl. G52	32	P13
Hill Rd. (Cumb.) G67	70	NN3
Hill St. G3	35	V11
Hillcrest (Chry.) G69	26	FF8
Hillcrest Av. G32	54	BB16
Hillcrest Av. G44	63	U18
Hillcrest Av. (Cumb.) G67	70	NN3
Hillcrest Av., Pais. PA2	58	J17
Hillcrest Ct. (Cumb.) G67	70	NN3
Hillcrest Rd. G32	55	CC16
Hillcrest Rd. (Bears.) G61	7	R6
Hillcrest Rd. (Udd.) G71	57	HH16
Hillcrest Ter. (Both.) G71	69	HH18
Churchill Cres.		
Hillcroft Ter. (Bishop.) G64	22	X8
Hillend Cres., Clyde. G81	4	K5
Hillend Rd. G22	21	V8
Hillend Rd. (Ruther.) G73	65	Y17
Hillfoot Av. (Bears.) G61	7	R5
Hillfoot Av. (Ruther.) G73	53	Y16
Hillfoot Dr. (Bears.) G61	7	R5
Hillfoot Gdns. (Udd.) G71	57	GG16
Hillfoot St. G31	37	Y12
Hillfoot Ter. (Bears.) G61	8	S5
Milngavie Rd.		
Hillhead Av. (Chry.) G69	15	GG7
Hillhead Av. (Ruther.) G73	65	Y18
Hillhead Gdns. G12	34	T11
Hillhead St.		
Hillhead Pl. G12	35	U11
Bank St.		
Hillhead Rd. G21	23	Z8
Hillhead St. G12	34	T11
Hillhouse St. G21	23	Y10
Hillington Gdns. G52	49	Q14
Hillington Ind. Est. G52	32	N12
Hillington Pk. Circ. G52	33	Q13
Hillington Quad. G52	32	P13
Hillington Rd. G52	32	N11
Hillington Rd. S. G52	32	P13
Hillington Ter. G52	32	P13
Hillkirk Pl. G21	22	X10
Hillkirk St. G21	22	X10
Hillkirk St. La. G21	22	X10
Hillkirk St.		
Hillneuk Av. (Bears.) G61	7	R5
Hillneuk Dr. (Bears.) G61	8	S5
Hillpark Av., Pais. PA2	46	J15
Hillpark Dr. G43	62	S17
Hillsborough Rd. (Bail.) G69	39	DD13
Hillsborough Sq. G12	34	T11
Hillhead St.		
Hillsborough Ter. G12	21	U10
Bower St.		
Hillside Av. (Bears.) G61	7	R5
Hillside Ct. (Thorn.) G46	61	R18
Hillside Dr. (Bears.) G61	8	S5
Hillside Dr. (Bishop.) G64	11	Y7
Hillside Dr. (Barr.) G78	59	L18
Hillside Gdns. G11	20	S10
Turnberry Rd.		
Hillside Gdns. La. G11	20	S10
North Gardner St.		
Hillside Gro. (Bishop.) G64	23	Z8
Hillside Gro. (Barr.) G78	59	L19
Hillside Quad. G43	62	S17
Hillside Rd. G43	62	S17
Hillside Rd. (Barr.) G78	59	L18
Hillside Rd., Pais. PA2	47	L15
Hillswick Cres. G22	21	V8
Hilltop Rd. (Chry.) G69	15	GG7
Eastwood Rd.		
Hillview Cres. (Udd.) G71	57	GG16
Hillview Dr. (Blan.) G72	68	FF19
Hillview Rd. (Elder), John. PA5	44	F15
Hillview St. G32	38	AA13
Hilton Dr. (Bishop.) G64	10	X6
Hilton Gdns. G13	19	R8

Invercanny Pl. G15	6	P6
Inverclyde Gdns. G11	19	R10
Broomhill Dr.		
Inverclyde Gdns. (Ruther.) G73	66	AA18
Inveresk Quad. G32	38	BB13
Inveresk St. G32	38	BB13
Inverewe Av. (Thorn.) G46	61	Q18
Inverewe Dr. (Thorn.) G46	61	Q19
Inverewe Gdns. (Thorn.) G46	61	Q19
Inverewe Pl. (Thorn.) G46	61	Q18
Invergarry Av. (Thorn.) G46	61	Q19
Invergarry Ct. (Thorn.) G46	61	R19
Invergarry Dr. (Thorn.) G46	61	Q19
Invergarry Gdns. (Thorn.) G46	61	Q19
Invergarry Gro. (Thorn.) G46	61	Q19
Invergarry Pl. (Thorn.) G46	61	Q19
Invergarry Quad. (Thorn.) G46	61	R19
Invergarry Vw. (Thorn.) G46	61	R19
Inverglas Av., Renf. PA4	32	N11
Morriston Cres.		
Invergordon Av. G43	51	U16
Invergyle Dr. G52	32	P13
Inverkar Dr., Pais. PA2	45	H15
Inverkip St. G5	36	W13
Inverlair Av. G43	63	U17
Inverlair Av. G44	63	U17
Inverleith St. G32	37	Z13
Inverlochy St. G33	39	CC11
Inverness St. G51	33	Q13
Inveroran Dr. (Bears.) G61	8	S6
Invershiel Rd. G23	8	T7
Invershin Dr. G20	20	T9
Wyndford Rd.		
Inverurie St. G21	22	W10
Inzievar Ter. G32	54	BB15
Iona Cres. (Old Kil.) G60	4	J5
Iona Dr. (Old Kil.) G60	4	J5
Iona Dr., Pais. PA2	46	J16
Iona Gdns. (Old Kil.) G60	4	J5
Iona La. (Chry.) G69	15	HH7
Heathfield Av.		
Iona Pl. (Old Kil.) G60	4	J5
Iona Rd. (Ruther.) G73	66	AA18
Iona Rd., Renf. PA4	31	M11
Iona St. G51	34	S12
Iona Way (Stepps) G33	25	CC10
Iris Av. G45	65	Y18
Irongray St. G31	37	Z12
Irvine Dr. (Linw.), Pais. PA3	28	E13
Irvine St. G40	53	Y14
Irving Av., Clyde. G81	5	L5
Stewart Dr.		
Irving Quad., Clyde. G81	5	L5
Stewart Dr.		
Iser La. G41	51	U16
Island Rd. (Cumb.) G67	70	MM4
Islay Av. (Ruther.) G73	66	AA18
Islay Cres. (Old Kil.) G60	4	J5
Islay Cres., Pais. PA2	46	J16
Islay Dr. (Old Kil.) G60	4	J5
Ivanhoe Rd. G13	19	Q8
Ivanhoe Rd. (Cumb.) G67	70	NN4
Ivanhoe Rd., Pais. PA2	45	G15
Ivanhoe Way, Pais. PA2	45	G15
Ivanhoe Rd.		
Ivybank Av. (Camb.) G72	67	CC18

J

Jacks Rd. (Udd.) G71	69	HH17
Jagger Gdns. (Bail.) G69	55	DD14
Jamaica St. G1	35	V13
James Dunlop Gdns. (Bishop.) G64	23	Y8
Graham Ter.		
James Gray St. G41	51	U16
James Morrison St. G1	36	W13
St. Andrews Sq.		
James Nisbet St. G21	36	X11
James St. G40	52	X14
James Watt La. G2	35	V12
James Watt St.		
James Watt St. G2	35	V12
Jamieson Ct. G42	51	V15
Jamieson Path G42	51	V15
Jamieson St.		
Jamieson St. G42	51	V15
Janebank Av. (Camb.) G72	67	CC18
Janefield Av., John. PA5	43	D15

Janefield St. G31	37	Y13
Janes Brae (Cumb.) G67	70	NN4
Janetta St., Clyde. G81	5	L6
Jardine St. G20	21	U10
Jardine Ter. (Gart.) G69	27	GG9
Jasgray St. G42	51	U15
Jean Armour Dr., Clyde. G81	5	M6
Jean Maclean Pl. (Bishop.) G64	11	Y5
Jedburgh Av. (Ruther.) G73	53	Y16
Jedburgh Dr., Pais. PA2	45	H15
Jedburgh Gdns. G20	21	U10
Jedworth Av. G15	6	P6
Jedworth Pl. G15	6	P6
Tallant Rd.		
Jedworth Rd. G15	6	P6
Jellicoe St., Clyde. G81	4	K6
Jenny's Well Ct., Pais. PA2	47	L15
Jenny's Well Rd.		
Jenny's Well Rd., Pais. PA2	47	L15
Jerviston Rd. G33	39	CC11
Jessie St. G42	52	W15
Jessiman Sq., Renf. PA4	31	L11
Jocelyn Sq. G1	36	W13
John Brown Pl. (Chry.) G69	26	FF8
John Hendry Rd. (Udd.) G71	69	HH18
John Knox La. G4	36	X12
Drygate		
John Knox St. G4	36	X12
John Knox St., Clyde. G81	17	M8
John Lang St., John. PA5	44	E14
John Marshall Dr. (Bishop.) G64	22	X8
John Smith Gate (Barr.) G78	59	M18
John St. G1	36	W12
John St. (Barr.) G78	59	L18
John St., Pais. PA1	46	J14
Johnsburn Dr. G53	60	P17
Johnsburn Rd. G53	60	P17
Johnshaven St. G43	50	T16
Shawbridge St.		
Johnston Av. G52	32	P13
Johnston Rd. (Gart.) G69	27	HH9
Johnston St., Pais. PA1	46	K14
Gordon St.		
Johnstone Av. G52	32	P13
Johnstone Dr. (Camb.) G72	66	BB17
Johnstone Dr. (Ruther.) G73	53	Y16
Joppa St. G33	38	AA12
Jordan St. G14	33	Q11
Jordanhill Cres. G13	19	Q9
Jordanhill Dr. G13	19	Q9
Jordanhill La. G13	19	R9
Austen Rd.		
Jordanvale Av. G14	33	Q11
Jowitt Av., Clyde. G81	5	M7
Jubilee Bk. (Kirk.) G66	13	CC6
Heriot Rd.		
Jubilee Ct. G52	32	N12
Jubilee Path (Bears.) G61	7	R6
Jubilee Ter., John. PA5	43	C15
Julian Av. G12	20	T10
Julian La. G12	20	T10
Julian Av.		
Juniper Ct. (Kirk.) G66	12	BB5
Juniper Pl. G32	55	DD14
Juniper Pl., John. PA5	44	E16
Juniper Ter. G32	55	DD14
Jura Av., Renf. PA4	31	M11
Jura Ct. G52	33	R13
Jura Dr. (Old Kil.) G60	4	J5
Jura Rd.		
Jura Dr. (Blan.) G72	68	FF18
Jura Gdns. (Old Kil.) G60	4	J5
Jura Rd.		
Jura Pl. (Old Kil.) G60	4	J5
Jura Rd.		
Jura Rd. (Old Kil.) G60	4	J5
Jura Rd., Pais. PA2	46	J16
Jura St. G52	33	R13

K

Kaim Dr. G53	61	Q17
Karol Path G4	35	V11
St. Peters St.		
Katewell Av. G15	6	N6
Katewell Pl. G15	6	N6
Katrine Av. (Bishop.) G64	11	Y7
Katrine Dr., Pais. PA2	45	G15
Katrine Pl. (Camb.) G72	66	BB17
Kay St. G21	22	X10

Kaystone Rd. G15	6	P7
Keal Av. G15	18	P8
Keal Cres. G15	18	P8
Keal Dr. G15	18	P8
Keal Pl. G15	18	P8
Kearn Av. G15	6	P7
Kearn Pl. G15	6	P7
Keats Pk. (Both.) G71	69	HH18
Keir Dr. (Bishop.) G64	10	X7
Keir St. G41	51	U14
Keirhill Rd. (Cumb.) G68	70	MM3
Woodburn Way		
Keirs Wk. (Camb.) G72	66	BB17
Keith Av. (Giff.) G46	62	T18
Keith Ct. G11	34	T11
Keith St.		
Keith St. G11	34	T11
Kelbourne St. G20	21	U10
Kelburn St. (Barr.) G78	59	L19
Kelburne Dr., Pais. PA1	31	L13
Kelburne Gdns. (Bail.) G69	56	EE14
Kelburne Gdns., Pais. PA1	31	L13
Kelburne Oval, Pais. PA1	31	L13
Kelhead Av. G52	32	N13
Kelhead Dr. G52	32	N13
Kelhead Path G52	32	P13
Kelhead Pl. G52	32	N13
Kellas St. G51	34	S13
Kells Pl. G15	6	N6
Kelso Av. (Ruther.) G73	53	Y16
Kelso Av., Pais. PA2	45	H15
Kelso Gdns. (Mood.) G69	15	GG6
Whithorn Cres.		
Kelso Pl. G14	18	N9
Kelso St. G13	18	N9
Kelso St. G14	18	N9
Kelton St. G32	54	BB14
Kelty Pl. G5	35	V13
Bedford St.		
Kelty St. G5	51	V14
Eglinton St.		
Kelvin Av. G52	32	N11
Kelvin Ct. G12	19	R9
Kelvin Cres. (Bears.) G61	7	R7
Kelvin Dr. G20	20	T10
Kelvin Dr. (Bishop.) G64	11	Y7
Kelvin Dr. (Chry.) G69	15	GG7
Kelvin Dr. (Barr.) G78	59	M19
Kelvin Rd. (Cumb.) G67	71	PP4
Kelvin Rd. (Udd.) G71	57	GG16
Kelvin Way G3	34	T11
Kelvin Way (Both.) G71	69	HH18
Bracken Ter.		
Kelvindale Bldgs. G12	20	T9
Kelvindale Rd.		
Kelvindale Cotts. G12	20	T9
Kelvindale Rd.		
Kelvindale Gdns. G20	20	T9
Kelvindale Glen G12	20	T9
Kelvindale Rd.		
Kelvindale Pl. G20	20	T9
Kelvindale Rd. G12	20	T9
Kelvindale Rd. G20	20	T9
Kelvingrove St. G3	35	U12
Kelvingrove Ter. G3	35	U12
Kelvingrove St.		
Kelvinhaugh Pl. G3	34	T12
Kelvinhaugh St.		
Kelvinhaugh St. G3	34	T12
Kelvinside Av. G20	21	U10
Queen Margaret Dr.		
Kelvinside Dr. G20	21	U10
Kelvinside Gdns. G20	21	U10
Kelvinside Gdns. E. G20	21	U10
Kelvinside Gdns. La. G20	21	U10
Kelvinside Gdns.		
Kelvinside Ter. S. G20	21	U10
Kelvinside Ter. W. G20	21	U10
Kemp Av., Pais. PA3	31	L11
Kemp St. G21	22	X10
Kempock St. G31	53	Z14
Kempsthorn Cres. G53	48	P15
Kempsthorn Path G53	48	P15
Kempsthorn Rd. G53	48	P15
Kendal Av. G12	20	S9
Kendal Av. (Giff.) G46	62	T18
Kendal Dr. G12	20	S9
Kendal Ter. G12	20	S9
Kendoon Av. G15	6	N6
Kenilworth Av. G41	50	T16
Kenilworth Cres. (Bears.) G61	7	Q5
Kenilworth Way, Pais. PA2	45	G16

119

Kingsborough Ter. G12	20	S10
Hyndland Rd.		
Kingsbrae Av. G44	52	W16
Kingsbridge Cres. G44	64	W17
Kingsbridge Dr. G44	64	W17
Kingsbridge Dr. (Ruther.) G73	64	W17
Kingsburgh Dr., Pais. PA1	31	L13
Kingsburn Dr. (Ruther.) G73	65	Y17
Kingsburn Gro. (Ruther.) G73	65	Y17
Kingscliffe Av. G44	64	W17
Kingscourt Av. G44	64	W17
Kingsdale Av. G44	52	W16
Kingsdyke Av. G44	52	W16
Kingsford Av. G44	63	U18
Kingsheath Av. (Ruther.) G73	64	X17
Kingshill Dr. G44	64	W17
Kingshouse Av. G44	64	W17
Kingshurst Av. G44	52	W16
Kingsknowe Dr. (Ruther.) G73	64	X17
Kingsland Cres. G52	32	P13
Kingsland Dr. G52	32	P13
Kingsland La. G52	33	Q13
Berryknowes Rd.		
Kingsley Av. G42	51	V15
Kingsley Ct. (Udd.) G71	57	HH16
Kingslynn Dr. G44	64	W17
Kingslynn La. G44	64	W17
Kingslynn Dr.		
Kingsmuir Dr. (Ruther.) G73	64	X17
Kingston Av. (Udd.) G71	57	HH16
Kingston Bri. G3	35	U13
Kingston Bri. G5	35	U13
Kingston Pl., Clyde. G81	4	J6
Kingston St. G5	35	V13
Kingsway G14	18	P9
Kingsway Ct. G14	18	P9
Kingswood Dr. G44	64	W17
Kingussie Dr. G44	64	W17
Kiniver Dr. G15	6	P7
Kinloch Av. (Camb.) G72	66	BB18
Kinloch Av. (Linw.), Pais. PA3	28	E13
Pentland Av.		
Kinloch Rd., Renf. PA4	31	L11
Kinloch St. G40	53	Z14
Kinmount Av. G44	51	V16
Kinmount La. G44	51	V16
Kinmount Av.		
Kinnaird Cres. (Bears.) G61	8	S6
Kinnaird Dr. (Linw.), Pais. PA3	28	E13
Kinnaird Pl. (Bishop.) G64	23	Y8
Kinnear Rd. G40	53	Y14
Kinnell Av. G52	49	Q14
Kinnell Cres. G52	49	Q14
Kinnell Path G52	49	Q14
Kinnell Cres.		
Kinnell Pl. G52	49	R15
Mosspark Dr.		
Kinnell Sq. G52	49	Q14
Kinning St. G5	35	U13
Kinnoul La. G12	20	T10
Dowanhill St.		
Kinpurnie Rd., Pais. PA1	31	M13
Kinross Av. G52	48	P14
Kinsail Dr. G52	32	N13
Kinstone Av. G14	18	P9
Kintessack Pl. (Bishop.) G64	11	Z7
Kintillo Dr. G13	18	P9
Kintore Rd. G43	63	U17
Kintra St. G51	34	S13
Kintyre Av. (Linw.), Pais. PA3	28	E13
Kintyre St. G21	37	Y11
Kippen St. G22	22	W9
Kippford St. G32	55	CC14
Kirk La. G43	50	T16
Riverbank St.		
Kirk Pl. (Udd.) G71	69	GG17
Kirk Rd. (Bears.) G61	7	R5
Kirkaig Av., Renf. PA4	32	N11
Kirkbean Av. (Ruther.) G73	65	Y18
Kirkburn Av. (Camb.) G72	66	BB18
Kirkcaldy Rd. G41	50	T15
Kirkconnel Av. G13	18	N9
Kirkconnel Dr. (Ruther.) G73	64	X17
Kirkdale Dr. G52	49	R14
Kirkfield Rd. (Both.) G71	69	HH18
Kirkford Rd. (Chry.) G69	15	GG7
Bridgeburn Dr.		
Kirkhill Av. (Camb.) G72	66	BB18
Kirkhill Dr. G20	20	T9
Kirkhill Gdns. (Camb.) G72	66	BB18
Kirkhill Gro. (Camb.) G72	66	BB18
Kirkhill Pl. G20	20	T9
Kirkhill Rd. (Gart.) G69	27	GG9
Kirkhill Rd. (Udd.) G71	57	GG16
Kirkhill Ter. (Camb.) G72	66	BB18
Kirkhope Dr. G15	6	P7
Kirkinner Rd. G32	55	CC14
Kirkintilloch Rd. (Bishop.) G64	22	X8
Kirkintilloch Rd. (Kirk.) G66	13	CC5
Kirkland Gro., John. PA5	43	D14
Kirkland St. G20	21	U10
Kirklandneuk Cres., Renf. PA4	17	L10
Kirklandneuk Rd.		
Kirklandneuk Rd., Renf. PA4	17	L10
Kirklands Cres. (Both.) G71	69	HH18
Kirklea Av., Pais. PA3	29	H13
Kirklee Circ. G12	20	T10
Kirklee Gdns. G12	20	T9
Bellshaugh Rd.		
Kirklee Gdns. La. G12	20	T9
Bellshaugh Rd.		
Kirklee Pl. G12	20	T10
Kirklee Quad. G12	20	T10
Kirklee Quad. La. G12	20	T10
Kirklee Quad.		
Kirklee Rd. G12	20	T10
Kirklee Ter. G12	20	T10
Kirklee Ter. La. G12	20	T10
Kirklee Ter.		
Kirkles Gdns., Pais. PA3	29	H13
Kirkliston St. G32	38	AA13
Kirkmichael Gdns. G11	20	S10
Blairatholl Av.		
Kirkmuir Dr. (Ruther.) G73	65	Y18
Kirknewton St. G32	38	BB13
Kirkoswald Dr., Clyde. G81	5	M6
Kirkoswald Rd. G43	62	T17
Kirkpatrick St. G40	37	Y13
Kirkriggs Av. (Ruther.) G73	65	Y17
Kirkriggs Gdns. (Ruther.) G73	65	Y17
Kirkriggs Way (Ruther.) G73	65	Y17
Kirkstall Gdns. (Bishop.) G64	11	Y6
Kirkton Av. G13	18	P9
Kirkton Av. (Barr.) G78	59	L19
Kirkton Cres. G13	18	P9
Kirkton Rd. (Camb.) G72	66	BB17
Kirktonside (Barr.) G78	59	L19
Kirkview Gdns. (Udd.) G71	57	GG16
Glencroft Av.		
Kirkville Pl. G15	6	P7
Kirkwall (Cumb.) G67	71	PP1
Kirkwall Av. (Blan.) G72	68	FF18
Kirkwell Rd. G44	63	V17
Kirkwood Av., Clyde. G81	5	M7
Kirkwood Quad., Clyde. G81	5	M7
Kirkwood Av.		
Kirkwood Rd. (Udd.) G71	57	GG15
Newlands Rd.		
Kirkwood St. G51	34	T13
Kirkwood St. (Ruther.) G73	53	Y16
Kirn St. G20	20	T8
Kirriemuir Av. G52	49	Q14
Kirriemuir Gdns. (Bishop.) G64	11	Z7
Kirriemuir Pl. G52	49	Q14
Kirriemuir Rd. (Bishop.) G64	11	Z7
Kirtle Dr., Renf. PA4	32	N11
Kishorn Pl. G33	39	CC11
Knapdale St. G22	21	V8
Knights Gate (Both.) G71	69	GG17
Knight's Gate (Udd.) G71	69	GG17
Knightsbridge Rd. G13	19	Q9
Knightsbridge St. G13	19	Q9
Knightscliffe Av. G13	19	Q8
Knightswood Ct. G13	19	Q9
Knightswood Cross G13	19	Q8
Knightswood Rd. G13	7	Q7
Knightswood Ter. (Blan.) G72	69	GG19
Knock Way, Pais. PA3	31	L12
Knockburnie Rd. (Both.) G71	69	HH18
Knockhall St. G33	39	CC11
Knockhill Dr. G44	51	V16
Knockhill La. G44	51	V16
Mount Annan Dr.		
Knockhill Rd., Renf. PA4	31	L11
Knockside Av., Pais. PA2	46	J16
Knowe Rd. (Chry.) G69	26	FF8
Knowe Rd., Pais. PA3	31	L12
Knowe Ter. G22	21	V8
Hillend Rd.		
Knowehead Dr. (Udd.) G71	69	GG17
Knowehead Gdns. G41	51	U14
Knowehead Ter.		
Knowehead Gdns. (Udd.) G71	69	GG17
Knowehead Ter. G41	51	U14
Knowetap St. G20	21	U8
Knox St., Pais. PA1	45	H14
Kyle Dr. (Giff.) G46	62	T18
Kyle Rd. (Cumb.) G67	71	PP2
Kyle Sq. (Ruther.) G73	65	Y17
Kyle St. G4	36	W11
Kyleaken Gdns. (Blan.) G72	68	EE19
Kyleakin Rd. (Thorn.) G46	61	Q18
Kyleakin Ter. (Thorn.) G46	61	Q18
Kylepark Av. (Udd.) G71	68	FF17
Kylepark Cres. (Udd.) G71	56	FF16
Kylepark Dr. (Udd.) G71	56	FF16
Kylerhea Rd. (Thorn.) G46	61	Q18

L

La Belle Allee G3	35	U11
Clifton St.		
La Belle Pl. G3	35	U11
La Crosse Ter. G12	21	U10
Laburnum Gdns. (Kirk.) G66	12	BB5
Laburnum Gro.		
Laburnum Gro. (Kirk.) G66	12	BB5
Laburnum Pl., John. PA5	44	E16
Laburnum Rd. G41	50	T14
Gower St.		
Lacy St., Pais. PA1	31	L13
Lade Ter. G52	48	P14
Ladeside Dr., John. PA5	43	C15
Ladhope Pl. G13	18	N8
Lady Anne St. G14	18	N9
Lady Isle Cres. (Udd.) G71	69	GG17
Lady Jane Gate (Both.) G71	69	GG18
Lady La., Pais. PA1	46	J14
Ladyacres (Inch.), Renf. PA4	16	J9
Ladyacres (Inch.), Renf. PA4	16	J9
Ladybank Dr. G52	49	R14
Ladyburn St., Pais. PA1	47	L14
Ladyhill Dr. (Bail.) G69	56	EE14
Ladykirk Cres. G52	32	P13
Ladykirk Cres., Pais. PA2	46	K14
Ladykirk Dr. G52	32	P13
Ladyloan Av. G15	6	N6
Ladyloan Ct. G15	6	N6
Ladyloan Gdns. G15	6	N6
Ladyloan Pl. G15	6	N6
Ladymuir Cres. G53	49	Q15
Ladysmith Av. (Mill.Pk.), John. PA10	42	B15
Ladywell St. G4	36	X12
Laggan Rd. G43	63	U17
Laggan Rd. (Bishop.) G64	11	Y7
Laggan Ter., Renf. PA4	17	L10
Laidlaw Gdns. (Udd.) G71	57	GG15
Laidlaw St. G5	35	V13
Laigh Kirk La., Pais. PA1	46	K14
Causeyside St.		
Laigh Possil Rd. G23	21	V8
Balmore Rd.		
Laighcartside St., John. PA5	44	E14
Laighlands Rd. (Both.) G71	69	HH19
Laighmuir St. (Udd.) G71	69	GG17
Laighpark Harbour, Pais. PA3	30	K12
Laighpark Vw., Pais. PA3	30	K12
Lainshaw Dr. G45	63	V19
Laird Gro. (Udd.) G71	57	HH16
Laird Pl. G40	52	X14
Lairds Gate (Udd.) G71	69	GG17
Lairds Hill (Cumb.) G67	70	NN3
Lairg Dr. (Blan.) G72	68	FF19
Lamb St. G22	21	V9
Lamberton Dr. G52	32	P13
Lambhill St. G41	34	T13
Lamerton Rd. (Cumb.) G67	71	QQ3
Lamington Rd. G52	48	P14
Lamlash Cres. G33	38	BB12
Lammermoor Av. G52	49	Q14
Lammermoor Dr. (Cumb.) G67	70	NN4

Lammermuir Ct., Pais. PA2	46	K16
Lammermuir Dr., Pais. PA2	46	J15
Lamont Rd. G21	23	Y9
Lanark St. G1	36	W13
Lancaster Cres. G12	20	T10
Lancaster Cres. La. G12	20	S9
Cleveden Rd.		
Lancaster Rd. (Bishop.) G64	11	Y6
Lancaster Ter. G12	20	T10
Westbourne Gdns. W.		
Lancaster Ter. La. G12	20	T10
Westbourne Gdns. W.		
Lancefield Quay G3	35	U12
Lancefield St. G3	35	U12
Landemer Dr. (Ruther.) G73	64	X17
Landressy Pl. G40	52	X14
Landressy St. G40	52	X14
Lane Gdns. G11	20	S10
North Gardner St.		
Lanfine Rd., Pais. PA1	47	L14
Lang Av., Renf. PA4	31	M11
Lang Pl., John. PA5	43	D14
Lang St., Pais. PA1	47	L14
Langa St. G20	21	U8
Langbank St. G5	51	V14
Eglinton St.		
Langbar Cres. G33	39	DD12
Langbar Path G33	39	CC12
Langcraigs Dr., Pais. PA2	58	J17
Langcraigs Ter., Pais. PA2	58	J17
Langcroft Dr. (Camb.) G72	67	CC18
Langcroft Pl. G51	33	Q12
Langcroft Rd. G51	33	Q12
Langcroft Ter. G51	33	Q12
Langdale Av. G33	24	AA10
Langdale Rd. (Chry.) G69	15	GG7
Langdale St. G33	24	AA10
Langdale's Av. (Cumb.) G68	70	MM3
Langford Av. G53	60	P18
Langford Dr. G53	60	P18
Langford Pl. G53	60	P18
Langford Dr.		
Langhaul Rd. G53	48	N15
Langhill Dr. (Cumb.) G68	70	MM2
Langholm Ct. (Chry.) G69	15	HH7
Heathfield Av.		
Langholm Dr. (Linw.), Pais. PA3	28	F13
Langlands Av. G51	33	Q12
Langlands Dr. G51	33	Q12
Langlands Rd. G51	33	Q12
Langlea Av. (Camb.) G72	65	Z18
Langlea Ct. (Camb.) G72	66	AA18
Langlea Dr. (Camb.) G72	66	AA17
Langlea Gdns. (Camb.) G72	66	AA17
Langlea Gro. (Camb.) G72	66	AA18
Langlea Rd. (Camb.) G72	66	AA18
Langlea Way (Camb.) G72	66	AA17
Langley Av. G13	18	P8
Langmuir Rd. (Bail.) G69	41	HH13
Langmuir Way (Bail.) G69	41	HH13
Langmuirhead Rd. (Kirk.) G66	24	BB8
Langness Rd. G33	38	BB12
Langrig Rd. G21	23	Y10
Langshot St. G51	34	T13
Langside Av. G41	51	U15
Langside Dr. G43	63	U17
Langside Dr. (Kilb.), John. PA10	42	B15
Langside Gdns. G42	51	V16
Langside La. G42	51	V15
Langside Pk. (Kilb.), John. PA10	42	B15
Langside Pl. G41	51	U16
Langside Rd. G42	51	V16
Langside Rd. (Both.) G71	69	HH19
Langside St., Clyde. G81	5	M5
Langstile Pl. G52	32	N13
Langstile Rd. G52	32	N13
Langton Cres. G53	49	Q15
Langton Cres. (Barr.) G78	59	M19
Langton Gdns. (Bail.) G69	55	DD14
Langton Rd. G53	49	Q15
Langtree Av. (Giff.) G46	62	S19
Lanrig Pl. (Chry.) G69	26	FF8
Lanrig Rd. (Chry.) G69	26	FF8
Lansbury Gdns., Pais. PA3	30	J12
Lansdowne Cres. G20	35	U11
Lansdowne Cres. La. G20	35	U11
Napiershall St.		
Lansdowne Dr. (Cumb.) G68	70	NN2
Lanton Dr. G52	32	P13
Lanton Rd. G43	63	U17
Lappin St., Clyde. G81	17	M8
Larbert St. G4	35	V11
Milton St.		
Larch Av. (Bishop.) G64	23	Y8
Larch Av. (Lenzie) G66	13	CC5
Larch Ct. (Cumb.) G67	71	QQ2
Larch Cres. (Kirk.) G66	13	CC5
Larch Gro. (Cumb.) G67	71	RR2
Larch Pl., John. PA5	44	E16
Larch Rd. G41	50	S14
Larch Rd. (Cumb.) G67	71	QQ2
Larches, The (Mood.) G69	15	HH6
Larchfield Av. G14	18	P10
Larchfield Dr. (Ruther.) G73	65	Y18
Larchfield Pl. G14	18	P10
Larchfield Rd. (Bears.) G61	7	R7
Larchfield Rd. (Chry.) G69	15	GG7
Larchgrove Av. G32	39	CC13
Larchgrove Pl. G32	39	CC12
Larchgrove Rd.		
Larchgrove Rd. G32	39	CC12
Larchwood Ter. (Barr.) G78	60	N19
Largie Rd. G43	63	U17
Largo Pl. G51	33	R12
Largs St. G31	37	Y12
Larkfield Rd. (Lenzie) G66	13	DD5
Larkfield St. G42	51	V14
Inglefield St.		
Larkin Gdns., Pais. PA3	30	J12
Lasswade St. G14	17	M9
Latherton Dr. G20	20	T9
Latherton Pl. G20	20	T9
Latherton Dr.		
Latimer Gdns. G52	48	P14
Laudedale La. G12	20	S10
Clarence Dr.		
Lauder Dr. (Ruther.) G73	65	Z17
Lauder Dr. (Linw.), Pais. PA3	28	E13
Lauder Gdns. (Blan.) G72	68	FF19
Lauder St. G5	51	V14
Eglinton St.		
Lauderdale Gdns. G12	20	S10
Laundry La. G33	25	CC9
Laurel Av. (Lenzie) G66	13	CC5
Laurel Av., Clyde. G81	4	J6
Laurel Bk. Rd. (Chry.) G69	26	EE8
Laurel Gdns. (Udd.) G71	57	GG16
Laurel Pk. Gdns. G13	19	Q9
Laurel Pl. G11	34	S11
Laurel St. G11	34	S11
Laurel Wk. (Ruther.) G73	65	Z18
Laurel Way (Barr.) G78	59	L18
Laurence Dr. (Bears.) G61	7	Q5
Laurie Ct. (Udd.) G71	57	HH16
Hillcrest Rd.		
Laurieston La. G51	34	T13
Paisley Rd. W.		
Laurieston Rd. G5	36	W13
Laurieston Way (Ruther.) G73	65	Y18
Lauriston Rd. G5	51	V14
Laverock Ter. (Chry.) G69	15	GG7
Laverockhall St. G21	22	X10
Law St. G40	37	Y13
Lawers Dr. (Bears.) G61	7	Q5
Lawers Rd. G43	62	S17
Lawers Rd., Renf. PA4	31	M11
Lawhill Av. G44	64	W18
Lawmoor Av. G5	52	W14
Lawmoor La. G5	36	W13
Ballater St.		
Lawmoor Pl. G5	52	W15
Lawmoor Av.		
Lawmoor Rd. G5	52	W14
Lawmoor St. G5	52	W14
Lawn St., Pais. PA1	30	K13
Lawrence Av. (Giff.) G46	62	T19
Lawrence St. G11	34	T11
Lawrie St. G11	34	S11
Lawside Dr. G53	49	Q16
Laxford Av. G44	63	V18
Laxton Dr. (Lenzie) G66	13	DD6
Leabank Av., Pais. PA2	46	K16
Leadburn Rd. G21	23	Z10
Rye Rd.		
Leadburn St. G32	38	AA12
Leader St. G33	37	Z11
Leander Cres., Renf. PA4	32	N11
Leckethill St. G21	22	X10
Springburn Rd.		
Leckie St. G43	50	T16
Ledaig Pl. G31	37	Z12
Ledaig St. G31	37	Z12
Ledard Rd. G42	51	U16
Ledcameroch Cres. (Bears.) G61	7	Q6
Ledcameroch Pk. (Bears.) G61	7	Q6
Ledcameroch Rd.		
Ledcameroch Rd. (Bears.) G61	7	Q6
Ledgowan Pl. G20	20	T8
Ledi Dr. (Bears.) G61	7	Q5
Ledi Rd. G43	62	T17
Ledmore Dr. G15	6	N6
Lednock Rd. (Stepps) G33	25	CC9
Lednock Rd. G52	32	P13
Lee Av. G33	38	AA11
Lee Cres. (Bishop.) G64	22	X8
Leebank Dr. G44	63	U19
Leefield Dr. G44	63	U19
Leehill Rd. G21	22	X8
Leeside Rd. G21	22	X8
Leesland (Udd.) G71	57	HH16
Leewood Dr. G44	63	U19
Leggatston Rd. G53	61	Q19
Leglen Wd. Cres. G21	23	Z9
Leglen Wd. Dr. G21	23	Z9
Leglen Wd. Pl. G21	24	AA9
Leglen Wd. Rd. G21	23	Z9
Leicester Av. G12	20	S9
Leighton St. G20	21	U9
Leitchland Rd. (Elder.), John. PA5	44	F16
Leitchland Rd., Pais. PA2	44	F16
Leitchs Ct. G1	36	W13
Trongate		
Leith St. G33	37	Z12
Leithland Av. G53	48	P16
Leithland Rd. G53	48	P15
Lendale La. (Bishop.) G64	11	Y6
Lendel Pl. G51	35	U13
Paisley Rd. W.		
Lenihall Dr. G45	64	X19
Lenihall Ter. G45	64	X19
Lennox Av. G14	19	Q10
Lennox Cres. (Bishop.) G64	22	X8
Lennox Dr. (Bears.) G61	7	R5
Lennox Gdns. G14	19	Q10
Lennox La. W. G14	19	Q10
Lennox Av.		
Lennox Pl. G14	19	Q10
Scotstoun St.		
Lennox Pl., Clyde. G81	4	K6
Swindon St.		
Lennox Rd. (Cumb.) G67	70	NN3
Lennox St. G20	20	T8
Maryhill Rd.		
Lennox Ter., Pais. PA3	31	L12
Lennox Vw., Clyde. G81	5	L6
Granville St.		
Lentran St. G34	40	FF12
Leny St. G20	21	V10
Lenzie Pl. G21	22	X9
Lenzie Rd. (Stepps) G33	25	CC9
Lenzie St. G21	22	X9
Lenzie Ter. G21	22	X9
Lenzie Way G21	22	X9
Lenziemill Rd. (Cumb.) G67	71	PP4
Lerwick St. G4	35	V11
Dobbies Ln.		
Leslie Rd. G41	51	U15
Leslie St. G41	51	U14
Lesmuir Dr. G14	18	P9
Lesmuir Pl. G14	18	N9
Letham Ct. G43	63	U17
Letham Dr. G43	63	U17
Letham Dr. (Bishop.) G64	23	Z8
Letham Gra. (Cumb.) G68	70	NN2
Lethamhill Cres. G33	38	AA11
Lethamhill Pl. G33	38	AA11
Lethamhill Rd. G33	38	AA11
Letherby Dr. G42	51	V16
Letherby Dr. G44	51	V16
Lethington Av. G41	51	U16
Lethington Pl. G41	51	U16
Letterfearn Dr. G23	9	U7
Letterickhills Cres. (Camb.) G72	67	DD18
Lettoch St. G51	34	S13

Name	Page	Grid
Leven Av. (Bishop.) G64	11	Y7
Leven Ct. (Barr.) G78	59	L17
Leven Dr. (Bears.) G61	7	R6
Leven Sq., Renf. PA4	17	L10
Leven St. G41	51	U14
Leven Vw., Clyde. G81	5	L6
Radnor St.		
Leven Way, Pais. PA2	45	G15
Levern Cres. (Barr.) G78	59	L19
Levern Gdns. (Barr.) G78	59	L18
Leverndale Rd. G53	48	N15
Levernside Av. (Barr.) G78	59	L19
Levernside Cres. G53	48	P15
Levernside Rd. G53	48	P15
Lewis Av., Renf. PA4	31	M11
Lewis Cres. (Old Kil.) G60	4	J5
Lewis Cres. (Mill.Pk.), John. PA10	42	B15
Lewis Gdns. (Old Kil.) G60	4	J5
Lewis Cres.		
Lewis Gdns. (Bears.) G61	6	P5
Lewis Gro. (Old Kil.) G60	4	J5
Lewiston Dr. G23	8	T7
Lewiston Rd.		
Lewiston Pl. G23	8	T7
Lewiston Rd.		
Lewiston Rd. G23	8	T7
Lexwell Av. (Elder.), John. PA5	44	F14
Leyden Ct. G20	21	U9
Leyden St.		
Leyden Gdns. G20	21	U9
Leyden St.		
Leyden St. G20	21	U9
Leys, The (Bishop.) G64	11	Y7
Liberton St. G33	37	Z12
Liberty Av. (Bail.) G69	41	HH13
Libo Av. G53	49	Q15
Library Gdns. (Camb.) G72	66	AA17
Liddel Rd. (Cumb.) G67	70	NN3
Liddell St. G32	55	CC15
Liddesdale Av., Pais. PA2	44	F16
Liddesdale Pl. G22	22	W8
Liddesdale Sq.		
Liddesdale Rd. G22	22	W8
Liddesdale Sq. G22	22	W8
Liddesdale Ter. G22	22	X8
Liddoch Way (Ruther.) G73	52	X16
Liff Gdns. (Bishop.) G64	23	Z8
Liff Pl. G34	40	FF11
Lightburn Pl. G32	38	BB12
Lightburn Rd. G31	37	Z13
Duke St.		
Lightburn Rd. (Camb.) G72	67	CC18
Lilac Av., Clyde. G81	4	J6
Lilac Cres. (Udd.) G71	57	HH16
Lilac Gdns. (Bishop.) G64	23	Y8
Lilac Wynd (Camb.) G72	67	DD18
Lillyburn Pl. G15	6	N5
Lily St. G40	53	Y14
Lilybank Av. (Muir.) G69	26	FF8
Lilybank Av. (Camb.) G72	67	CC18
Lilybank Gdns. G12	34	T11
Lilybank Gdns. La. G12	20	T10
Great George St.		
Lilybank La. G12	34	T11
Lilybank Gdns.		
Lilybank Ter. G12	20	T10
Great George St.		
Lilybank Ter. La. G12	20	T10
Great George St.		
Lime Gro. (Lenzie) G66	13	CC5
Lime Gro. (Blan.) G72	68	FF19
Lime La. G14	19	Q10
Lime St.		
Lime St. G14	19	Q10
Limecraigs Cres., Pais. PA2	46	J16
Limecraigs Rd., Pais. PA2	45	H16
Limeside Av. (Ruther.) G73	53	Y16
Limeside Gdns. (Ruther.) G73	53	Z16
Calderwood Rd.		
Limetree Av. (Udd.) G71	57	HH16
Limetree Dr., Clyde. G81	5	L6
Limeview Av., Pais. PA2	45	H16
Limeview Cres., Pais. PA2	45	H16
Limeview Rd., Pais. PA2	45	H16
Limeview Av.		
Limeview Way, Pais. PA2	45	H16
Limeview Av.		
Linacre Dr. G32	39	CC13
Linacre Gdns. G32	39	CC13
Linburn Pl. G52	32	P12
Linburn Rd. G52	32	N12
Linclive Link Rd. (Linw.), Pais. PA3	28	F13
Linclive Ter. (Linw.), Pais. PA3	28	F13
Lincluden Path G41	51	U14
McCulloch St.		
Lincoln Av. G13	18	P9
Lincoln Av. (Udd.) G71	57	GG15
Lindams (Udd.) G71	69	GG17
Linden Dr., Clyde. G81	5	L5
Linden Pl. G13	19	R8
Linden St. G13	19	R8
Lindores Av. (Ruther.) G73	53	Y16
Lindores St. G42	51	V16
Somerville Dr.		
Lindrick Dr. G23	9	U7
Lindsay Dr. G12	20	S9
Lindsay Pl. G12	20	S9
Lindsay Pl. (Lenzie) G66	13	CC6
Lindsay Pl., John. PA5	44	E14
Thorn Brae		
Lindsaybeg Rd. (Lenzie) G66	13	DD6
Lindsaybeg Rd. (Chry.) G69	14	EE7
Linfern Rd. G12	20	T10
Links Rd. G32	55	CC14
Links Rd. G44	64	W18
Linkwood Av. G15	6	N6
Kinfauns Dr.		
Linkwood Cres. G15	6	N6
Linkwood Dr. G15	6	N6
Linkwood Gdns. G15	6	P6
Linkwood Pl. G15	6	N6
Kinfauns Dr.		
Linlithgow Gdns. G32	39	CC13
Linn Brae, John. PA5	43	D15
Linn Cres., Pais. PA2	46	J16
Linn Dr. G44	63	U18
Linn Pk. G44	63	V18
Linn Pk. Gdns., John. PA5	44	E15
Linn Valley Vw. G45	64	W18
Linnet Av., John. PA5	43	C16
Linnet Pl. G13	18	N8
Linnhe Av. G44	63	V18
Linnhe Av. (Bishop.) G64	11	Y7
Linnhe Dr. (Barr.) G78	59	L17
Linnhe Pl. (Blan.) G72	68	FF19
Linnhead Dr. G53	60	P17
Linnhead Pl. G14	18	P10
Linnpark Av. G44	63	U19
Linnpark Ct. G44	63	U19
Bowling Grn. Rd.		
Linnwell Cres., Pais. PA2	46	J16
Linwood Ct. G44	63	V17
Bowling Grn. Rd.		
Linwood Moss Rd. (Linw.), Pais. PA3	28	F13
Linwood Rd., Pais. PA1	28	F13
Linwood Rd. (Linw.), Pais. PA3	28	F13
Linwood Ter. G12	21	U10
Glasgow St.		
Lismore Av., Renf. PA4	31	M11
Lismore Dr., Pais. PA2	46	J16
Lismore Gdns. (Mill.Pk.), John. PA10	43	C15
Tandlehill Rd.		
Lismore Pl. (Chry.) G69	15	HH6
Altnacreag Gdns.		
Lismore Rd. G12	20	S10
Lister Rd. G52	32	P12
Lister St. G4	36	W11
Lithgow Cres., Pais. PA2	47	L15
Little Dovehill G1	36	W13
Little Mill Gdns. G53	48	P16
Dalmellington Rd.		
Little St. G3	35	U12
Littlehill St. G21	22	X10
Edgefauld Rd.		
Littleholm, Clyde. G81	4	K6
Littlemill Cres. G53	48	P16
Littlemill Dr. G53	48	P16
Littleton Dr. G23	8	T7
Rothes Dr.		
Littleton St. G23	8	T7
Rothes Dr.		
Livingstone Av. G52	32	P12
Livingstone Cres. (Blan.) G72	68	FF19
Livingstone St. G21	22	W10
Keppochhill Rd.		
Livingstone St., Clyde. G81	5	M7
Lloyd Av. G32	54	BB15
Lloyd St. G31	37	Y12
Lloyd St. (Ruther.) G73	53	Y15
Loanbank Quad. G51	34	S12
Loancroft Av. (Bail.) G69	56	FF14
Loancroft Gdns. (Udd.) G71	69	GG17
Loancroft Gate (Udd.) G71	69	GG17
Loancroft Pl. (Bail.) G69	56	EE14
Loanend Cotts. (Camb.) G72	67	DD19
Loanfoot Av. G13	18	P8
Loanhead Av. (Linw.), Pais. PA3	28	E13
Loanhead Av., Renf. PA4	17	M10
Loanhead La. (Linw.), Pais. PA3	28	E13
Loanhead Rd.		
Loanhead Rd. (Linw.), Pais. PA3	28	E13
Loanhead St. G32	38	AA12
Lobnitz Av., Renf. PA4	17	M10
Loch Achray St. G32	55	CC14
Loch Katrine St. G32	55	CC14
Loch Laidon St. G32	55	CC14
Loch Rd. (Stepps) G33	25	CC9
Loch Voil St. G32	55	CC14
Lochaber Dr. (Ruther.) G73	65	Z18
Lochaber Rd. (Bears.) G61	8	S7
Lochaline Av., Pais. PA2	45	H15
Lochaline Dr. G44	63	V18
Lochalsh Dr., Pais. PA2	45	G15
Lochalsh Pl. (Blan.) G72	68	EE19
Lochar Cres. G53	49	Q15
Lochard Dr., Pais. PA2	45	H15
Lochay St. G32	55	CC14
Lochbrae Dr. (Ruther.) G73	65	Z18
Lochbridge Rd. G34	40	EE12
Lochbroom Dr., Pais. PA2	45	H15
Lochburn Cres. G20	21	U8
Lochburn Gro. G20	21	U8
Cadder Rd.		
Lochburn Pas. G20	21	U8
Lochburn Rd. G20	20	T9
Lochdochart Path G34	40	FF12
Lochdochart Rd.		
Lochdochart Rd. G34	40	FF12
Lochearn Cres., Pais. PA2	45	H15
Lochearnhead Rd. G33	25	CC9
Lochend Av. (Gart.) G69	27	GG8
Lochend Cres. (Bears.) G61	7	Q6
Lochend Dr. (Bears.) G61	7	Q6
Lochend Rd. G34	40	EE11
Lochend Rd. (Bears.) G61	7	R6
Lochend Rd. (Gart.) G69	27	GG8
Locher Rd. (Kilb.), John. PA10	42	A14
Lochfauld Rd. G23	9	V7
Lochfield Cres., Pais. PA2	46	K15
Lochfield Dr., Pais. PA2	47	L15
Lochfield Gdns. G34	40	FF11
Lochfield Rd., Pais. PA2	46	K15
Lochgilp St. G20	20	T8
Lochgoin Av. G15	6	N6
Lochgreen St. G33	23	Z10
Lochhead Av. (Linw.), Pais. PA3	28	E13
Lochiel La. (Ruther.) G73	65	Z18
Lochiel Rd. (Thorn.) G46	61	R18
Lochinver Cres., Pais. PA2	45	H15
Lochinver Dr. G44	63	V18
Lochinver Gro. (Camb.) G72	67	CC17
Andrew Sillars Av.		
Lochlea Av., Clyde. G81	5	M6
Lochlea Rd. G43	62	T17
Lochlea Rd. (Cumb.) G67	71	QQ2
Lochlea Rd. (Ruther.) G73	64	X17
Lochleven La. G42	51	V16
Battlefield Rd.		
Lochleven Rd. G42	51	V16
Lochlibo Av. G13	18	N9
Lochlibo Cres. (Barr.) G78	59	L19

Lochlibo Rd. (Barr.) G78 59 L19
Lochlibo Ter. (Barr.) G78 59 L19
Lochmaben Rd. G52 48 N14
Lochmaddy Av. G44 63 V18
Lochore Av., Pais. PA3 31 L12
Lochside (Bears.) G61 7 R6
Drymen Rd.
Lochside (Gart.) G69 27 GG9
Lochside St. G41 51 U15
Minard Rd.
Lochview Cotts. (Gart.) 27 GG10
G69
Lochview Cres. G33 24 AA10
Lochview Dr. G33 24 AA10
Lochview Gdns. G33 24 AA10
Lochview Pl. G33 24 AA10
Lochview Rd. (Bears.) G61 7 R6
Lochview Ter. (Gart.) G69 27 GG9
Lochwood Ln. (Mood.) G69 15 HH6
Lochwood St. G33 38 AA11
Lochy Av., Renf. PA4 32 N11
Lochy Gdns. (Bishop.) G64 11 Y7
Lockerbie Av. G43 63 U17
Lockhart Av. (Camb.) G72 67 CC17
Lockhart Dr. (Camb.) G72 67 CC17
Lockhart St. G21 37 Y11
Locksley Av. G13 19 Q8
Locksley Rd., Pais. PA2 45 G15
Logan Dr. (Cumb.) G68 70 MM2
Logan Dr., Pais. PA3 30 J13
Logan St. G5 52 W15
Logan Twr. (Camb.) G72 67 DD18
Claude Av.
Loganswell Dr. (Thorn.) G46 61 Q19
Loganswell Gdns. (Thorn.) 61 R19
G46
Loganswell Pl. (Thorn.) G46 61 R19
Loganswell Rd. (Thorn.) G46 61 R19
Lomax St. G33 37 Z12
Lomond Av., Renf. PA4 31 L11
Lomond Ct. (Barr.) G78 59 M19
Lomond Cres., Pais. PA2 46 J16
Lomond Dr. (Both.) G71 69 HH18
Lomond Dr. (Barr.) G78 59 L18
Lomond Gdns. (Elder.), John. 44 F15
PA5
Lomond Pl. (Stepps) G33 25 CC10
Lomond Rd. (Bears.) G61 7 R7
Lomond Rd. (Bishop.) G64 10 X6
Lomond Rd. (Lenzie) G66 13 CC5
Lomond Rd. (Udd.) G71 57 GG15
Lomond St. G22 21 V9
Lomond Vw., Clyde. G81 5 L6
Granville St.
London Arc. G1 36 W13
London Rd.
London La. G1 36 W13
London Rd.
London Rd. G1 36 W13
London Rd. G31 53 Z14
London Rd. G32 54 BB15
London Rd. G40 52 X14
London St., Renf. PA4 17 M9
Lonend, Pais. PA1 46 K14
Long Row (Bail.) G69 40 FF13
Longay Pl. G22 22 W8
Longay St. G22 22 W8
Longcroft Dr., Renf. PA4 17 M10
Longden St., Clyde. G81 17 M8
Longford St. G33 37 Z12
Longlee (Bail.) G69 56 EE14
Longmeadow, John. PA5 43 C15
Longstone Rd. G33 38 BB12
Longwill Ter. (Cumb.) G67 71 PP2
Lonmay Rd. G33 39 CC12
Lonsdale Av. (Giff.) G46 62 T18
Loom St. G40 36 X13
Stevenson St.
Loom Wk. (Kilb.), John. 42 B14
PA10
Shuttle St.
Lora Dr. G52 49 R14
Lord Way (Bail.) G69 41 GG13
Dukes Rd.
Loretto Pl. G33 38 AA12
Loretto St. G33 38 AA12
Lorn Av. (Chry.) G69 26 FF8
Lorne Cres. (Bishop.) G64 11 Z7
Lorne Dr. (Linw.), Pais. PA3 28 E13
Lorne Rd. G52 32 N12
Lorne St. G51 34 T13
Lorne Ter. (Camb.) G72 66 AA18

Lorraine Gdns. G12 20 T10
Kensington Rd.
Lorraine Rd. G12 20 T10
Loskin Dr. G22 21 V8
Lossie Cres., Renf. PA4 32 N11
Lossie St. G33 37 Z11
Lothian Cres., Pais. PA2 46 J15
Lothian Gdns. G20 21 U10
Lothian St. G52 32 N12
Louden Hill Dr. G21 24 AA9
Louden Hill Gdns. G21 24 AA9
Louden Hill Pl. G21 24 AA9
Louden Hill Rd. G21 24 AA9
Louden Hill Way G21 24 AA9
Loudon Gdns., John. PA5 44 E14
Loudon Rd. G33 24 BB9
Loudon Ter. G12 20 T10
Observatory Rd.
Lounsdale Av., Pais. PA2 45 H14
Lounsdale Cres., Pais. PA2 45 H15
Lounsdale Dr., Pais. PA2 45 H15
Lounsdale Gro., Pais. PA2 45 H15
Lounsdale Ho., Pais. PA2 45 H15
Gallacher Av.
Lounsdale Pl. G14 18 P10
Lounsdale Rd., Pais. PA2 45 H15
Lounsdale Way, Pais. PA2 45 H14
Lourdes Av. G52 49 Q14
Lourdes Ct. G52 49 Q14
Lourdes Av.
Lovat Pl. (Ruther.) G73 65 Z18
Lovat St. G4 36 W11
Love St., Pais. PA3 30 K13
Low Barholm (Kilb.), John. 42 B15
PA10
Low Cres., Clyde. G81 18 N8
Low Parksail, Ersk. PA8 16 J8
Low Rd. (Castlehead), Pais. 46 J14
PA2
Lower Bourtree Dr. (Ruther.) 65 Z18
G73
Lower English Bldgs. G42 51 V14
Lower Millgate (Udd.) G71 57 GG16
Lowndes La., Pais. PA3 30 K13
New Sneddon St.
Lowndes St. (Barr.) G78 59 M19
Lowther Ter. G12 20 T10
Loyne Dr., Renf. PA4 32 N11
Morriston Cres.
Luath St. G51 34 S12
Lubas Av. G42 52 W16
Lubas Pl. G42 52 W16
Lubnaig Rd. G43 63 U17
Luckingsford Av. (Inch.), 16 J8
Renf. PA4
Luckingsford Dr. (Inch.), 16 J8
Renf. PA4
Luckingsford Rd. (Inch.), 16 J8
Renf. PA4
Lucy Brae (Udd.) G71 57 GG16
Ludovic Sq., John. PA5 43 D14
Luffness Gdns. G32 54 BB15
Lugar Dr. G52 49 R14
Lugar Pl. G44 64 X17
Luggiebank Pl. (Bail.) G69 57 HH14
Luing Rd. G52 33 R13
Luma Gdns. G51 33 Q12
Lumloch St. G21 23 Y10
Lumsden La. G3 34 T12
Lumsden St.
Lumsden St. G3 34 T12
Lunan Dr. (Bishop.) G64 23 Z8
Lunan Pl. G51 33 R12
Luncarty Pl. G32 54 BB14
Luncarty St. G32 54 BB14
Lunderston Dr. G53 48 P16
Lundie Gdns. (Bishop.) G64 23 Z8
Lundie St. G32 54 AA14
Luss Rd. G51 33 R12
Lusset Vw., Clyde. G81 5 L6
Radnor St.
Lusshill Ter. (Udd.) G71 56 EE15
Lyall Pl. G21 22 W10
Keppochhill Rd.
Lyall St. G21 22 W10
Lybster Cres. (Ruther.) G73 65 Z18
Lye Brae (Cumb.) G67 71 PP3
Lyle Pl., Pais. PA2 46 K15
Lylesland Ct., Pais. PA2 46 K15
Lymburn St. G3 34 T12
Lyndale Pl. G20 20 T8
Lyndale Rd. G20 20 T8

Lyndhurst Gdns. G20 21 U10
Lyndhurst Gdns. La. G20 21 U10
Melrose Gdns.
Lyne Cft. (Bishop.) G64 11 Y6
Lyne Dr. G23 9 U7
Lynedoch Cres. G3 35 U11
Lynedoch Cres. La. G3 35 U11
Woodlands Rd.
Lynedoch Pl. G3 35 U11
Lynedoch St. G3 35 U11
Lynedoch Ter. G3 35 U11
Lynn Gdns. G12 20 T10
Great George St.
Lynn Wk. (Udd.) G71 69 HH17
Flax Rd.
Lynnhurst (Udd.) G71 57 GG16
Lynton Av. (Giff.) G46 62 S19
Lyon Rd., Pais. PA2 45 G15
Lyon Rd. (Linw.), Pais. PA3 44 E14
Lyoncross Av. (Barr.) G78 59 M19
Lyoncross Rd. (Barr.) G78 59 M18
Lyoncross Rd. G53 48 P15
Lytham Dr. G23 9 U7
Lytham Meadows (Both.) 69 GG19
G71

M

Macarthur Wynd (Camb.) 67 CC17
G72
Macbeth Pl. G31 53 Z14
Macbeth St.
Macbeth St. G31 53 Z14
Maccallum Dr. (Camb.) G72 67 CC17
Macdonald St. (Ruther.) G73 53 Y16
Greenhill Rd.
Macdougall Dr. (Camb.) G72 67 CC17
Macdougall St. G43 50 T16
Macdowall St., John. PA5 43 D14
Macdowall St., Pais. PA3 30 J13
Macduff Pl. G31 53 Z14
Macduff St. G31 53 Z14
Mace Rd. G13 7 Q7
Macfarlane Cres. (Camb.) 67 CC17
G72
Macfarlane Rd. (Bears.) G61 7 R6
Macgregor Ct. (Camb.) G72 67 CC17
Machrie Dr. G45 64 X18
Machrie Rd. G45 64 X18
Machrie St. G45 64 X18
Mackean St., Pais. PA3 30 J13
Mackechnie St. G51 34 S12
Mackeith St. G40 52 X14
Mackenzie Dr. (Mill.Pk.), 42 B15
John. PA10
Mackie St. G4 22 W10
Borron St.
Mackiesmill Rd. (Elder.), 44 F16
John. PA5
Mackinlay St. G5 51 V14
Maclay Av. (Kilb.), John. 42 B15
PA10
Maclean St. G51 34 T13
Maclean St., Clyde. G81 18 N8
Wood Quad.
Maclehose Rd. (Cumb.) G67 71 QQ2
Maclellan St. G41 34 T13
Macleod Way (Camb.) G72 67 CC17
Macarthur Wynd
Macmillan Gdns. (Udd.) G71 57 HH16
Madison Av. G44 63 V17
Madison La. G44 63 V17
Carmunnock Rd.
Madras Pl. G40 52 X14
Madras St.
Madras St. G40 52 X14
Mafeking St. G51 34 S13
Magdalen Way, Pais. PA2 44 F16
Magnolia Dr. (Camb.) G72 67 DD18
Magnus Cres. G44 63 V18
Mahon Ct. (Mood.) G69 15 GG7
Maidland Rd. G53 49 Q16
Mailerbeg Gdns. (Chry.) G69 15 GG6
Mailing Av. (Bishop.) G64 11 Y7
Main Rd. (Elder.), John. PA5 44 F14
Main Rd. (Millarston), Pais. 44 F14
PA1
Main Rd. (Castlehead), Pais. 46 J14
PA2
Main St. G40 52 X14
Main St. (Thorn.) G46 61 R18
Main St. (Cumb.) G67 71 PP1

123

Main St. (Bail.) G69   56 EE14
Main St. (Chry.) G69   26 FF8
Main St. (Both.) G71   69 HH19
Main St. (Udd.) G71   69 GG17
Main St. (Camb.) G72   66 BB17
Main St. (Ruther.) G73   53 Y16
Main St. (Barr.) G78   59 L19
Mainhead Ter. (Cumb.) G67   71 PP1
  Roadside
Mainhill Av. (Bail.) G69   40 FF13
Mainhill Dr. (Bail.) G69   40 FF13
Mainhill Pl. (Bail.) G69   40 FF13
Mainhill Rd. (Bail.) G69   41 GG13
Mains Av. (Giff.) G46   62 S19
Mains Dr., Ersk. PA8   4 J7
Mains Hill, Ersk. PA8   4 J7
Mains River, Ersk. PA8   4 J7
Mains Wd., Ersk. PA8   4 J7
Mainscroft, Ersk. PA8   4 J7
Mair St. G51   35 U13
Maitland Pl., Renf. PA4   31 L11
Maitland St. G4   35 V11
Malcolm St. G31   37 Z13
Malin Pl. G33   38 AA12
Mallaig Path G51   33 Q12
Mallaig Pl. G51   33 Q12
Mallaig Rd. G51   33 Q12
Mallard Rd., Clyde. G81   5 L5
Malloch Cres. (Elder.), John.   44 E15
  PA5
Malloch St. G20   21 U9
Maltbarns St. G20   21 V10
Malvern Ct. G31   37 Y13
Malvern Way, Pais. PA3   30 J12
Mambeg Dr. G51   33 R12
Mamore Pl. G43   62 T17
Mamore St. G43   62 T17
Manchester Dr. G12   20 S9
Manitoba Pl. G31   37 Y13
  Janefield St.
Mannering Ct. G41   50 T16
  Pollokshaws Rd.
Mannering Rd. G41   50 T16
Mannering Rd., Pais. PA2   45 G16
Mannofield (Bears.) G61   7 Q6
  Chesters Rd.
Manor Rd. G14   19 R10
Manor Rd. G15   6 N7
Manor Rd. (Gart.) G69   27 GG9
Manor Rd., Pais. PA2   45 G15
Manor Way (Ruther.) G73   65 Y18
Manresa Pl. G4   35 V11
  Braid Sq.
Manse Av. (Bears.) G61   7 R5
Manse Av. (Both.) G71   69 HH19
Manse Brae G44   63 V17
Manse Ct. (Barr.) G78   59 M18
Manse Gdns. G32   55 CC14
Manse Rd. G32   55 CC14
Manse Rd. (Bears.) G61   7 R5
Manse Rd. (Bail.) G69   41 GG13
Manse St., Renf. PA4   17 M10
Mansefield Av. (Camb.) G72   66 BB18
Mansefield Dr. (Udd.) G71   69 GG17
Mansel St. G21   22 X9
Mansewood Rd. G43   62 S17
Mansfield Rd. G52   32 N12
Mansfield St. G11   34 T11
Mansion Ct. (Camb.) G72   66 BB17
Mansion St. G22   22 W9
Mansion St. (Camb.) G72   66 BB17
Mansionhouse Av. G32   55 CC16
Mansionhouse Dr. G32   39 CC13
Mansionhouse Gdns. G41   51 U16
  Mansionhouse Rd.
Mansionhouse Gro. G32   55 DD14
Mansionhouse Rd. G32   55 DD14
Mansionhouse Rd. G41   51 U16
Mansionhouse Rd. G42   51 U16
Mansionhouse Rd., Pais.   31 L13
  PA1
Manus Duddy Ct. (Blan.)   68 FF19
  G72
Maple Cres. (Camb.) G72   67 DD18
Maple Dr. (Kirk.) G66   12 BB5
Maple Dr. (Barr.) G78   59 M19
Maple Dr., Clyde. G81   4 K5
Maple Dr., John. PA5   44 E16
Maple Rd. G41   50 S14
Mar Gdns. (Ruther.) G73   65 Z18
March La. G41   51 U15
  Nithsdale Dr.

March St. G41   51 U15
Marchbank Gdns., Pais. PA1   47 M14
Marchfield (Bishop.) G64   10 X6
Marchfield Av., Pais. PA3   30 J12
Marchglen Pl. G51   33 Q12
  Mallaig Rd.
Marchmont Gdns. (Bishop.)   10 X6
  G64
Marchmont Ter. G12   20 T10
  Observatory Rd.
Maree Dr. G52   49 R14
Maree Gdns. (Bishop.) G64   11 Y7
Maree Rd., Pais. PA2   45 H15
Marfield St. G32   38 AA13
Margaret St. G1   36 W12
  Martha St.
Margaretta Bldgs. G44   63 V17
  Clarkston Rd.
Marguerite Av. (Lenzie) G66   13 CC5
Marguerite Dr. (Kirk.) G66   13 CC5
Marguerite Gdns. (Kirk.) G66   13 CC5
Marguerite Gdns. (Both.)   69 HH18
  G71
Marguerite Gro. (Kirk.) G66   13 CC5
Marine Cres. G51   35 U13
Marine Gdns. G51   35 U13
  Mavisbank Gdns.
Mariscat Rd. G41   51 U15
Marjory Dr., Pais. PA3   31 L12
Marjory Rd., Renf. PA4   31 L11
Markdown Av. G53   48 P15
Market St. G40   36 X13
Markinch St. G5   35 V13
  West St.
Marlach Pl. G53   48 P16
Marlborough Av. G11   19 R10
Marlborough La. N. G11   19 R10
  Marlborough Av.
Marlborough La. S. G11   19 R10
  Marlborough Av.
Marldon La. G11   19 R10
  Marlborough Av.
Marlow St. G41   51 U14
Marlow Ter. G41   35 U13
  Seaward St.
Marmion Pl. (Cumb.) G67   70 NN4
Marmion Rd. (Cumb.) G67   70 NN4
Marmion Rd., Pais. PA2   45 G16
Marmion St. G20   21 U10
Marne St. G31   37 Y12
Marnock Ter., Pais. PA2   47 L15
Marnock Way (Chry.) G69   15 GG7
  Braeside Av.
Marquis Gate (Udd.) G71   69 GG17
Marshall's La., Pais. PA1   46 K14
Mart St. G1   36 W13
Martha St. G1   36 W12
Martin Cres. (Bail.) G69   40 FF13
Martin St. G40   52 X14
Martlet Dr., John. PA5   43 C16
Marwick St. G31   37 Y12
Mary Sq. (Bail.) G69   41 GG13
Mary St. G4   35 V11
Mary St., John. PA5   44 E14
Mary St., Pais. PA2   46 K15
Maryhill Rd. G20   20 S8
Maryhill Rd. (Bears.) G61   8 S7
Maryland Dr. G52   33 R13
Maryland Gdns. G52   33 R13
Marys La., Renf. PA4   17 M10
Maryston Pl. G33   37 Z11
Maryston St. G33   37 Z11
Maryview Gdns. (Udd.) G71   56 FF15
  Old Edinburgh Rd.
Maryville Av. (Giff.) G46   62 T19
Maryville Gdns. (Giff.) G46   62 S19
Maryville Vw. (Udd.) G71   56 FF15
Marywood Sq. G41   51 U15
Masonfield Av. (Cumb.) G68   70 MM3
Masterton St. G21   22 W10
Mathieson La. G5   52 W14
  Mathieson St.
Mathieson Rd. (Ruther.) G73   53 Z15
Mathieson St. G5   52 W14
Mathieson St., Pais. PA1   31 L13
Matilda Rd. G41   51 U14
Mauchline St. G5   51 V14
Maukinfauld Ct. G32   54 AA14
Maukinfauld Rd. G32   54 AA14
Mauldslie St. G40   53 Y14
Maule Dr. G11   34 S11

Mavis Bk. (Bishop.) G64   22 X8
Mavisbank Gdns. G51   35 U13
Mavisbank Rd. G51   34 S12
  Govan Rd.
Mavisbank Ter., Pais. PA1   46 K14
Maxton Av. (Barr.) G78   59 L18
Maxton Gro. (Barr.) G78   59 L18
Maxton Ter. (Camb.) G72   66 AA18
Maxwell Av. G41   51 U14
Maxwell Av. (Bears.) G61   7 R7
Maxwell Av. (Bail.) G69   56 EE14
Maxwell Dr. G41   50 T14
Maxwell Dr. (Bail.) G69   40 EE13
Maxwell Gdns. G41   50 T14
Maxwell Gro. G41   50 T14
Maxwell La. G41   51 U14
Maxwell Oval G41   51 U14
Maxwell Pl. G41   51 V14
Maxwell Pl. (Udd.) G71   69 HH17
  North British Road
Maxwell Rd. G41   51 U14
Maxwell Sq. G41   51 U14
Maxwell St. G1   36 W13
Maxwell St. (Bail.) G69   56 EE14
Maxwell St., Clyde. G81   4 K6
Maxwell St., Pais. PA3   30 K13
  Old Sneddon St.
Maxwellton Rd., Pais. PA1   45 H14
Maxwellton St., Pais. PA1   46 J14
Maxwellton Trd. Est., Pais.   45 H14
  PA1
Maxwelton Rd. G33   37 Z11
May Rd., Pais. PA2   46 K16
May Ter. G42   51 V16
  Prospecthill Rd.
May Ter. (Giff.) G46   62 T18
Maybank La. G42   51 V15
  Victoria Rd.
Maybank St. G42   51 V15
Mayberry Cres. G32   39 CC13
Mayberry Gdns. G32   39 CC13
Mayberry Gro. G32   39 CC13
Maybole St. G53   60 N17
Mayfield St. G20   21 U9
McAlpine St. G2   35 V13
McArthur St. G43   50 T16
  Pleasance St.
McAslin Ct. G4   36 W12
McAslin St. G4   36 X12
McCallum Av. (Ruther.) G73   53 Y16
McClue Av., Renf. PA4   17 L10
McClue Rd., Renf. PA4   17 L10
McCracken Av., Renf. PA4   31 L11
McCreery St., Clyde. G81   17 M8
McCulloch St. G41   51 U14
McDonald Av., John. PA5   43 D15
McDonald Cres., Clyde. G81   17 M8
McFarlane St. G4   36 X13
McFarlane St., Pais. PA3   30 J12
McGhee St., Clyde. G81   5 L6
McGown St., Pais. PA3   30 J13
McGregor Av., Renf. PA4   31 L11
  Porterfield Rd.
McGregor Rd. (Cumb.) G67   70 NN3
McGregor St. G51   33 R13
McGregor St., Clyde. G81   17 M8
McIntosh Ct. G31   36 X12
  McIntosh St.
McIntosh St. G31   36 X12
McIntyre Pl., Pais. PA2   46 K15
McIntyre St. G3   35 U12
McIntyre Ter. (Camb.) G72   66 BB17
McIver St. (Camb.) G72   67 CC17
McKay Cres., John. PA5   44 E15
McKenzie Av., Clyde. G81   5 L6
McKenzie St., Pais. PA3   29 H13
McKerrell St., Pais. PA1   31 L13
McLaren Av., Renf. PA4   31 M11
  Newmains Rd.
McLaren Ct. (Giff.) G46   62 S19
  Fenwick Pl.
McLaren Cres. G20   21 U8
McLaren Gdns. G20   21 U8
McLaurin Cres., John. PA5   43 C15
McLean Pl., Pais. PA3   30 J12
McLean Sq. G51   34 T13
McLennan St. G42   51 V16
McLeod St. G4   36 X12
McNair St. G32   38 BB13
McNeil St. G5   52 W14
McNeill Av., Clyde. G81   6 N7
McPhail St. G40   52 X14

McPhater St. G4　35　V11
Dunblane St.
McPherson Dr. (Both.) G71　69　HH18
Wordsworth Way
McPherson St. G1　36　W13
High St.
McTaggart Rd. (Cumb.) G67　70　NN4
Meadow La., Renf. PA4　17　M9
Meadow Rd. G11　34　S11
Meadow Vw. (Cumb.) G67　71　QQ2
Meadowbank La. (Udd.) G71　68　FF17
Meadowburn (Bishop.) G64　11　Y6
Meadowburn Av. (Lenzie) G66　13　DD5
Meadowhead Av. (Chry.) G69　15　GG7
Meadowpark St. G31　37　Y12
Meadowside Av. (Elder.), John. PA5　44　F15
Meadowside Quay G11　33　R11
Meadowside St. G11　34　S11
Meadowside St., Renf. PA4　17　M9
Meadowwell St. G32　38　BB13
Meadside Av. (Kilb.), John. PA10　42　B14
Meadside Rd. (Kilb.), John. PA10　42　B14
Mearns Way (Bishop.) G64　11　Z7
Medlar Ct. (Camb.) G72　67　DD18
Maple Cres.
Medlar Rd. (Cumb.) G67　71　QQ3
Medwin St. (Camb.) G72　67　DD17
Mill Rd.
Medwyn St. G14　19　Q10
Meek Pl. (Camb.) G72　66　BB17
Meetinghouse La., Pais. PA1　30　K13
Moss St.
Megan Gate G40　52　X14
Megan St.
Megan St. G40　52　X14
Meikle Av., Renf. PA4　31　M11
Meikle Rd. G53　49　Q16
Meiklerig Cres. G53　49　Q15
Meikleriggs Dr., Pais. PA2　45　H15
Meiklewood Rd. G51　33　Q13
Melbourne Av., Clyde. G81　4　J5
Melbourne Ct. (Giff.) G46　62　T18
Melbourne St. G31　36　X13
Meldon Pl. G51　33　R12
Meldrum Gdns. G41　50　T15
Meldrum St., Clyde. G81　18　N8
Melford Av. (Giff.) G46　62　T19
Melford Way, Pais. PA3　31　L12
Knock Way
Melfort Av. G41　50　S14
Melfort Av., Clyde. G81　5　L6
Melfort Gdns. (Mill.Pk.), John. PA10　43　C15
Milliken Pk. Rd.
Mellerstain Dr. G14　18　N9
Melness Pl. G51　33　Q12
Mallaig Rd.
Melrose Av. (Bail.) G69　41　GG13
Melrose Av. (Ruther.) G73　53　Y16
Melrose Av., Pais. PA2　45　H15
Melrose Av. (Linw.), Pais. PA3　28　E13
Melrose Ct. (Ruther.) G73　53　Y16
Dunard Rd.
Melrose Gdns. G20　21　U10
Melrose Gdns. (Udd.) G71　57　GG15
Lincoln Av.
Melrose Pl. (Blan.) G72　68　FF19
Melrose St. G4　35　V11
Queens Cres.
Melvaig Pl. G20　20　T9
Melvick Pl. G51　33　Q12
Mallaig Rd.
Melville Ct. G1　36　W12
Brunswick St.
Melville Gdns. (Bishop.) G64　11　Y7
Melville St. G41　51　U14
Memel St. G21　22　X9
Memus Av. G52　49　Q14
Mennock Dr. (Bishop.) G64　11　Y6
Menock Rd. G44　63　V17
Menteith Av. (Bishop.) G64　11　Y7
Menteith Dr. (Ruther.) G73　65　Z19
Menteith Pl. (Ruther.) G73　65　Z19
Menzies Dr. G21　23　Y9
Menzies Pl. G21　23　Y9

Menzies Rd. G21　23　Y9
Merchant La. G1　36　W13
Clyde St.
Merchants Clo. (Kilb.), John. PA10　42　B14
Church St.
Merchiston St. G32　38　AA12
Merkland Ct. G11　34　S11
Vine St.
Merkland St. G11　34　S11
Merksworth Way, Pais. PA3　30　J12
Mosslands Rd.
Merlewood Av. (Both.) G71　69　HH18
Merlin Way, Pais. PA3　31　L12
Merlinford Av., Renf. PA4　18　N10
Merlinford Cres., Renf. PA4　18　N10
Merlinford Dr., Renf. PA4　18　N10
Merlinford Way, Renf. PA4　18　N10
Merrick Gdns. G51　34　S13
Merrick Ter. (Udd.) G71　57　HH16
Merrick Way (Ruther.) G73　65　Y18
Merryburn Av. (Giff.) G46　62　T17
Merrycrest Av. (Giff.) G46　62　T18
Merrycroft Av. (Giff.) G46　62　T18
Merryland Pl. G51　34　T12
Merryland St. G51　34　S12
Merrylee Cres. (Giff.) G46　62　T17
Merrylee Pk. Av. (Giff.) G46　62　T18
Merrylee Pk. La. (Giff.) G46　62　T18
Merrylee Pk. Ms. (Giff.) G46　62　T18
Merrylee Rd. G43　62　T17
Merrylee Rd. G44　62　T17
Merryton Av. G15　6　P6
Merryton Av. (Giff.) G46　62　T18
Merryton Pl. G15　6　P6
Merryvale Av. (Giff.) G46　62　T18
Merryvale Pl. (Giff.) G46　62　T17
Merton Dr. G52　32　P13
Meryon Gdns. G32　55　CC15
Meryon Rd. G32　55　CC15
Methil St. G14　19　Q10
Methuen Rd., Pais. PA3　31　L11
Methven Av. (Bears.) G61　8　S6
Methven St. G31　53　Z14
Methven St., Clyde. G81　4　K6
Metropole La. G1　35　V13
Howard St.
Mews La., Pais. PA3　30　K12
Renfrew Rd.
Mickelhouse Oval (Bail.) G69　40　EE13
Mickelhouse Rd.
Mickelhouse Pl. (Bail.) G69　40　EE13
Mickelhouse Rd.
Mickelhouse Rd. (Bail.) G69　40　EE13
Mickelhouse Wynd (Bail.) G69　40　EE13
Mickelhouse Rd.
Mid Cotts. (Gart.) G69　26　FF10
Midcroft (Bishop.) G64　10　X6
Midcroft Av. G44　64　W17
Middle Pk., Pais. PA2　46　J15
Middlemuir Av. (Kirk.) G66　13　CC5
Middlemuir Rd. (Lenzie) G66　13　CC5
Middlerigg Rd. (Cumb.) G68　70　MM3
Middlesex Gdns. G41　35　U13
Middlesex St. G41　35　U13
Middleton Cres., Pais. PA3　30　J13
Middleton Rd., Pais. PA3　28　F13
Middleton St. G51　34　T13
Midfaulds Av., Renf. PA4　32　N11
King George Pk. Av.
Midland St. G1　35　V13
Midlem Dr. G52　33　Q13
Midlem Oval G52　33　Q13
Midlock St. G51　34　T13
Midlothian Dr. G41　50　T15
Midton Cotts. (Mood.) G69　15　HH7
Midton St. G21　22　X10
Midwharf St. G4　36　W11
Migvie Pl. G20　20　T9
Wyndford Rd.
Milan St. G41　51　V14
Milford St. G33　38　BB12
Mill Ct. (Ruther.) G73　53　Y16
Mill Cres. G40　52　X14
Mill Pl. (Linw.), Pais. PA3　28　E13
Mill Ri. (Lenzie) G66　13　CC6
Mill Rd. (Both.) G71　69　HH19
Mill Rd. (Camb.) G72　67　CC18
Mill Rd., Clyde. G81　17　M8
Mill St. G40　52　X14
Mill St. (Ruther.) G73　53　Y16

Mill St., Pais. PA1　46　K14
Mill Vennel, Renf. PA4　18　N10
High St.
Millands Av. (Blan.) G72　68　FF19
Millar St., Pais. PA1　30　K13
Millar Ter. (Ruther.) G73　53　Y15
Millarbank St. G21　22　X10
Millarston Av., Pais. PA1　45　H14
Millarston Dr., Pais. PA1　45　H14
Millbeg Cres. G33　39　DD13
Millbeg Pl. G33　39　DD13
Millbrae Ct. G42　51　U16
Millbrae Rd.
Millbrae Cres. G42　51　U16
Millbrae Cres., Clyde. G81　17　M8
Millbrae Gdns. G42　51　U16
Millbrae Rd.
Millbrae Rd. G42　51　U16
Millbrix Av. G14　18　P9
Millburn Av. (Ruther.) G73　65　Y17
Millburn Av., Clyde. G81　18　N8
Millburn Av., Renf. PA4　17　M10
Millburn Dr., Renf. PA4　18　N10
Millburn Rd., Renf. PA4　17　M10
Millburn St. G21　37　Y11
Millburn Way, Renf. PA4　18　N10
Millcroft Rd. (Cumb.) G67　71　PP3
Millcroft Rd. (Ruther.) G73　52　X15
Millennium Gdns. G34　40　FF12
Miller St. G1　36　W12
Miller St. (Bail.) G69　56　EE14
Miller St., Clyde. G81　5　L7
Miller St., John. PA5　44　E14
Millerfield Pl. G40　53　Y14
Millerfield Rd. G40　53　Y14
Millers Pl. (Lenzie) G66　13　CC6
Millersneuk Av. (Lenzie) G66　13　CC6
Millersneuk Cres. G33　24　BB9
Millersneuk Dr. (Lenzie) G66　13　CC6
Millerston St. G31　37　Y13
Millford Dr. (Linw.), Pais. PA3　28　E13
Millgate (Udd.) G71　57　GG16
Millgate Av. (Udd.) G71　57　GG16
Millgate Ct. (Udd.) G71　57　GG16
Millholm Rd. G44　63　V18
Millhouse Cres. G20　20　T8
Millhouse Dr. G20　20　T8
Millichen Rd. G23　8　T5
Milliken Dr. (Mill.Pk.), John. PA10　43　C15
Milliken Pk. Rd. (Mill.Pk.), John. PA10　43　C15
Milliken Rd. (Mill.Pk.), John. PA10　43　C15
Millpond Dr. G40　36　X13
Millport Av. G44　52　W16
Millroad Dr. G40　36　X13
Millroad Gdns. G40　36　X13
Millroad St. G40　36　X13
Millview (Barr.) G78　59　M18
Millview Pl. G53　60　P18
Millwood St. G41　51　U16
Milnbank St. G31　37　Y12
Milncroft Rd. G33　38　BB11
Milner La. G13　19　R9
Southbrae Dr.
Milner Rd. G13　19　R9
Milngavie Rd. (Bears.) G61　7　R6
Milnpark Gdns. G41　35　U13
Milnpark St. G41　35　U13
Milovaig Av. G23　8　T7
Milovaig St. G23　8　T7
Milrig Rd. (Ruther.) G73　52　X16
Milton Av. (Camb.) G72　66　AA17
Milton Douglas Rd., Clyde. G81　5　L5
Milton Dr. (Bishop.) G64　22　X8
Milton Gdns. (Udd.) G71　57　GG16
Milton Mains Rd., Clyde. G81　5　L5
Milton St. G4　35　V11
Milverton Av. (Bears.) G61　7　Q5
Milverton Rd. (Giff.) G46　62　S19
Minard Rd. G41　51　U15
Minard Way (Udd.) G71　57　HH16
Newton Dr.
Minerva St. G3　35　U12
Minerva Way G3　35　U12
Mingarry La. G20　20　T10
Clouston St.
Mingarry St. G20　21　U10
Mingulay Cres. G22　22　W8

Mingulay Pl. G22	22	X8
Mingulay St. G22	22	W8
Minister Wk. (Bail.) G69	41	GG13
Dukes Rd.		
Minmoir Rd. G53	48	N16
Minstrel Rd. G13	7	Q7
Minto Av. (Ruther.) G73	65	Z18
Minto Cres. G52	33	R13
Minto St. G52	33	R13
Mireton St. G22	21	V9
Mirrlees Dr. G12	20	T10
Mirrlees La. G12	20	T10
Redlands Rd.		
Mitchell Av. (Camb.) G72	67	DD17
Mitchell Av., Renf. PA4	31	L11
Mitchell Dr. (Ruther.) G73	65	Y17
Mitchell La. G1	35	V12
Buchanan St.		
Mitchell Rd. (Cumb.) G67	71	PP3
Mitchell St. G1	35	V12
Mitchell St., Coat. ML5	57	HH14
Mitchellhill Rd. G45	64	X19
Mitchison Rd. (Cumb.) G67	71	PP2
Mitre Ct. G11	19	R10
Mitre Rd.		
Mitre La. G14	19	R10
Mitre La. W. G14	19	R10
Mitre La.		
Mitre Rd. G11	19	R10
Mitre Rd. G14	19	R10
Moat Av. G13	19	Q8
Mochrum Rd. G43	63	U17
Moffat Pl. (Blan.) G72	68	FF19
Moffat St. G5	52	W14
Mogarth Av., Pais. PA2	45	H16
Amochrie Rd.		
Moidart Av., Renf. PA4	17	L10
Moidart Ct. (Barr.) G78	59	L18
Moidart Cres. G52	33	R13
Moidart Rd.		
Moidart Pl. G52	33	R13
Moidart Rd.		
Moidart Rd. G52	33	R13
Moir La. G1	36	W13
Moir St.		
Moir St. G1	36	W13
Molendinar St. G1	36	W13
Mollinsburn St. G21	22	X10
Monach Rd. G33	39	CC12
Monachie Gdns. (Bishop.) G64	11	Z7
Muirhead Way		
Monar Dr. G22	21	V10
Monar Pl. G22	21	V10
Monar St. G22	21	V10
Monart Pl. G20	21	U10
Caithness St.		
Moncrieff Av. (Lenzie) G66	13	CC5
Moncrieff Gdns. (Kirk.) G66	13	CC5
Moncrieff Av.		
Moncrieff Pl. G4	35	V11
North Woodside Rd.		
Moncrieff St. G4	35	V11
Braid Sq.		
Moncur St. G40	36	X13
Moness Dr. G52	49	R14
Monifieth Av. G52	49	Q14
Monikie Gdns. (Bishop.) G64	11	Z7
Muirhead Way		
Monkcastle Dr. (Camb.) G72	66	BB17
Monkland Av. (Kirk.) G66	13	CC5
Monkland Vw. (Udd.) G71	57	HH15
Lincoln Av.		
Monkland Vw. Cres. (Bail.) G69	41	HH13
Monksbridge Av. G13	7	Q7
Monkscroft Av. G11	20	S10
Monkscroft Ct. G11	34	S11
Monkscroft Gdns. G11	20	S10
Monkscroft Av.		
Monkton Dr. G15	6	P7
Monmouth Av. G12	20	S9
Monreith Av. (Bears.) G61	7	Q7
Monreith Rd. G43	62	T17
Monreith Rd. E. G44	63	V17
Monroe Dr. (Udd.) G71	57	GG15
Monroe Pl. (Udd.) G71	57	GG15
Montague La. G12	20	S10
Montague St. G4	35	U11
Montague Ter. G12	20	S10
Hyndland Rd.		
Montclair Pl. (Linw.), Pais. PA3	28	E13
Monteith Dr. (Clark.) G76	63	V19
Monteith Pl. G40	36	X13
Monteith Row G40	36	X13
Monteith Row La. G40	36	X13
Monteith Pl.		
Montford Av. G44	52	W16
Montford Av. (Ruther.) G73	52	W16
Montgomerie Gdns. G14	19	Q10
Lennox Av.		
Montgomery Av., Pais. PA3	31	L12
Montgomery Dr. (Giff.) G46	62	T19
Montgomery Dr. (Kilb.), John. PA10	42	B14
Meadside Av.		
Montgomery La. G42	51	V16
Somerville Dr.		
Montgomery Pl. (Camb.) G72	68	EE17
Newton Fm. Rd.		
Montgomery Rd., Pais. PA3	31	L12
Montgomery St. G40	52	X14
London Rd.		
Montgomery St. (Camb.) G72	67	DD17
Mill Rd.		
Montrave St. G52	49	Q14
Montrave St. (Ruther.) G73	53	Z15
Montreal Ho., Clyde. G81	4	J5
Perth Cres.		
Montrose Av. G32	54	BB15
Montrose Av. G52	32	N12
Montrose Gdns. (Blan.) G72	68	FF19
Montrose Pl. (Linw.), Pais. PA3	28	E13
Montrose Rd., Pais. PA2	45	G16
Montrose St. G1	36	W12
Montrose St. G4	36	W12
Montrose St., Clyde. G81	5	L7
Montrose Ter. (Bishop.) G64	23	Z8
Monument Dr. G33	24	AA9
Monymusk Gdns. (Bishop.) G64	11	Z7
Monymusk Pl. G15	6	N5
Moodies Ct. G1	36	W13
Osborne St.		
Moodiesburn St. G33	37	Z11
Moorburn Av. (Giff.) G46	62	S18
Moore Dr. (Bears.) G61	7	R6
Moore St. G31	37	Y13
Gallowgate		
Moorfoot (Bishop.) G64	11	Z7
Moorfoot Av. (Thorn.) G46	62	S18
Moorfoot Av., Pais. PA2	46	J15
Moorfoot St. G32	38	AA13
Moorhouse Av. G13	18	N9
Moorhouse Av., Pais. PA2	45	H15
Moorhouse St. (Barr.) G78	59	M19
Moorings, The, Pais. PA2	45	H14
Moorpark Av. G52	32	N13
Moorpark Av. (Muir.) G69	26	FF8
Cumbernauld Rd.		
Moorpark Dr. G52	32	P13
Moorpark Pl. G52	32	N13
Moorpark Sq., Renf. PA4	31	L11
Morag Av. (Blan.) G72	68	FF19
Moraine Av. G15	6	P7
Moraine Circ. G15	6	P7
Moraine Dr. G15	6	P7
Moraine Pl. G15	6	P7
Moraine Dr.		
Morar Av., Clyde. G81	5	L6
Morar Ct. (Cumb.) G67	70	LL4
Morar Ct., Clyde. G81	5	L6
Morar Cres. (Bishop.) G64	10	X7
Morar Cres., Clyde. G81	5	L6
Morar Dr. (Bears.) G61	8	S6
Morar Dr. (Cumb.) G67	70	LL4
Morar Dr. (Ruther.) G73	65	Y18
Morar Dr., Clyde. G81	5	L6
Morar Dr., Pais. PA2	45	G15
Morar Dr. (Linw.), Pais. PA3	28	E13
Morar Pl., Clyde. G81	5	L6
Morar Pl., Renf. PA4	17	L10
Morar Rd. G52	33	R13
Morar Rd., Clyde. G81	5	L6
Morar Ter. (Udd.) G71	57	HH16
Morar Ter. (Ruther.) G73	65	Z18
Moravia Av. (Both.) G71	69	HH18
Moray Ct. (Ruther.) G73	53	Y16
Moray Gdns. (Cumb.) G68	71	PP1
Moray Gdns. (Udd.) G71	57	GG16
Moray Gate (Both.) G71	69	GG18
Moray Pl. G41	51	U15
Moray Pl. (Bishop.) G64	11	Z7
Moray Pl. (Linw.), Pais. PA3	28	E13
Mordaunt St. G40	53	Y14
Moredun Cres. G32	39	CC12
Moredun Dr., Pais. PA2	45	H15
Moredun Rd., Pais. PA2	45	H15
Moredun St. G32	39	CC12
Morefield Rd. G51	33	Q12
Morgan Ms. G42	51	V14
Morina Gdns. G53	61	Q19
Morion Rd. G13	19	Q8
Morley St. G42	51	V16
Morna Pl. G14	33	R11
Victoria Pk. Dr. S.		
Morningside St. G33	37	Z12
Morrin Path G21	22	X10
Crichton St.		
Morrin Sq. G4	36	X12
Collins St.		
Morrin St. G21	22	X10
Morris Pl. G40	36	X13
Morrison Quad., Clyde. G81	6	N7
Morrison St. G5	35	V13
Morrison St., Clyde. G81	4	K5
Morrisons Ct. G2	35	V12
Argyle St.		
Morriston Cres., Renf. PA4	32	N11
Morriston Pk. Dr. (Camb.) G72	54	BB16
Morriston St. (Camb.) G72	66	BB17
Mortimer St. G20	21	U10
Hotspur St.		
Morton Gdns. G41	50	T15
Morven Av. (Bishop.) G64	11	Z7
Morven Av. (Blan.) G72	68	FF19
Morven Av., Pais. PA2	46	J16
Morven Dr. (Linw.), Pais. PA3	28	E13
Morven Gdns. (Udd.) G71	57	GG16
Morven Rd. (Bears.) G61	7	R5
Morven Rd. (Camb.) G72	66	AA18
Morven St. G52	33	R13
Mosesfield St. G21	22	X9
Mosesfield Ter. G21	22	X9
Balgrayhill Rd.		
Moss Av. (Linw.), Pais. PA3	28	E13
Moss Dr. (Barr.) G78	59	L17
Moss Hts. Av. G52	33	Q13
Moss Knowe (Cumb.) G67	71	QQ3
Moss Path (Bail.) G69	55	DD14
Castle St.		
Moss Rd. G51	33	Q12
Moss Rd. (Kirk.) G66	13	CC5
Moss Rd. (Cumb.) G67	71	RR2
Moss Rd. (Muir.) G69	26	FF8
Moss St., Pais. PA1	30	K13
Moss-side Rd. G41	50	T15
Mossbank Av. G33	24	AA10
Mossbank Dr. G33	24	AA10
Mosscastle Rd. G33	39	CC11
Mossend La. G33	39	CC12
Mossend Rd., Pais. PA3	30	J12
Mosslands Rd.		
Mossend St. G33	39	CC12
Mossgiel Av. (Ruther.) G73	65	Y17
Mossgiel Dr., Clyde. G81	5	M6
Mossgiel Gdns. (Udd.) G71	57	GG16
Mossgiel Pl. (Ruther.) G73	65	Y17
Mossgiel Rd. G43	62	T17
Mossgiel Rd. (Cumb.) G67	71	PP3
Mossgiel Ter. (Blan.) G72	68	FF19
Mossland Rd. G52	32	N12
Mosslands Rd., Pais. PA3	30	J12
Mossneuk Dr., Pais. PA2	46	J16
Mosspark Av. G52	49	R14
Mosspark Boul. G52	49	R14
Mosspark Dr. G52	49	Q14
Mosspark La. G52	49	R15
Mosspark Dr.		
Mosspark Oval G52	49	R14
Mosspark Sq. G52	49	R14
Mossvale Cres. G33	39	CC11
Mossvale La., Pais. PA3	30	J13
Mossvale Path G33	25	CC10
Mossvale Rd. G33	24	BB10
Mossvale Sq. G33	39	CC11
Mossvale Sq., Pais. PA3	30	J13
Mossvale St., Pais. PA3	30	J12
Mossvale Ter. (Chry.) G69	15	HH6

Name	Page	Grid
Mossvale Wk. G33	39	CC11
Mossvale Way G33	39	CC11
Mossview Cotts. (Muir.) G69	26	FF9
Mossview Quad. G52	33	Q13
Mossview Rd. G33	25	DD9
Mote Hill Rd., Pais. PA3	31	L13
Moulin Circ. G52	48	P14
Moulin Pl. G52	48	P14
Moulin Rd. G52	48	P14
Moulin Ter. G52	48	P14
Mount Annan Dr. G44	51	V16
Mount Harriet Av. (Stepps) G33	25	DD9
Mount Harriet Dr. (Stepps) G33	25	CC9
Mount Lockhart (Udd.) G71	56	EE15
Mount Lockhart Gdns. (Udd.) G71	56	EE15
Mount Lockhart		
Mount Lockhart Pl. (Udd.) G71	56	EE15
Mount Lockhart		
Mount St. G20	21	U10
Mount Stuart St. G41	51	U16
Mount Vernon Av. G32	55	DD14
Mountainblue St. G31	37	Y13
Mountblow Ho., Clyde. G81	4	J5
Melbourne Av.		
Mountblow Rd., Clyde. G81	4	K5
Mountgarrie Path G51	33	Q12
Mountgarrie Rd.		
Mountgarrie Rd. G51	33	Q12
Mowbray Av. (Gart.) G69	27	GG9
Mowcraigs Ct., Clyde. G81	17	M8
Yokerburn Ter.		
Moy St. G11	34	T11
Church St.		
Moyne Rd. G53	48	P15
Muckcroft Rd. (Chry.) G69	14	EE6
Muir Pk. Ter. (Bishop.) G64	22	X8
Muir St. G21	22	X10
Muir St. (Bishop.) G64	11	Y7
Muir St., Renf. PA4	17	M10
Muir Ter., Pais. PA3	31	L12
Muirbank Av. (Ruther.) G73	52	X16
Muirbank Gdns. (Ruther.) G73	52	X16
Muirbrae Rd. (Ruther.) G73	65	Y18
Muirbrae Way (Ruther.) G73	65	Y18
Muirburn Av. G44	63	U18
Muirdrum Av. G52	49	Q14
Muirdykes Av. G52	32	P13
Muirdykes Cres., Pais. PA3	29	H13
Muirdykes Rd. G52	32	P13
Muirdykes Rd., Pais. PA3	29	H13
Muiredge Ct. (Udd.) G71	69	GG17
Watson St.		
Muiredge Ter. (Bail.) G69	56	EE14
Muirend Av. G44	63	U18
Muirend Rd. G44	63	U18
Muirfield Ct. G44	63	U18
Muirend Rd.		
Muirfield Cres. G23	9	U7
Muirfield Meadows (Both.) G71	69	GG19
Muirfield Rd. (Cumb.) G68	71	PP1
Muirhead Ct. (Bail.) G69	56	FF14
Muirhead Dr. (Linw.), Pais. PA3	28	E13
Muirhead Gdns. (Bail.) G69	56	FF14
Muirhead Gate (Udd.) G71	57	HH16
Muirhead Gro. (Bail.) G69	56	FF14
Muirhead Rd. (Bail.) G69	56	FF14
Muirhead Rd. (Udd.) G71	56	EE14
Muirhead St. G11	34	S11
Purdon St.		
Muirhead Way (Bishop.) G64	11	Z7
Muirhill Av. G44	63	U18
Muirhill Cres. G13	18	P8
Muirhouse St. G41	51	U15
Pollokshaws Rd.		
Muirkirk Dr. G13	19	R8
Muirpark Av., Renf. PA4	31	M11
Muirpark Dr. (Bishop.) G64	23	Y8
Muirpark St. G11	34	S11
Muirpark Ter. (Bishop.) G64	22	X8
Crowhill Rd.		
Muirshiel Av. G53	61	Q17
Muirshiel Cres. G53	61	Q17
Muirside Av. G32	55	DD14
Muirside Rd. (Bail.) G69	56	EE14
Muirside Rd., Pais. PA3	29	H12
Muirside St. (Bail.) G69	56	EE14
Muirskeith Cres. G43	63	U17
Muirskeith Pl. G43	63	U17
Muirskeith Rd. G43	63	U17
Muirton Dr. (Bishop.) G64	10	X6
Muirton Gdns. (Bishop.) G64	10	X6
Muiryfauld Dr. G31	54	AA14
Mulben Cres. G53	48	N16
Mulben Pl. G53	48	N16
Mulben Ter. G53	48	N16
Mulberry Rd. G43	62	T17
Mulberry Wynd (Camb.) G72	67	DD18
Mull Av., Pais. PA2	46	J16
Mull Av., Renf. PA4	31	M11
Mull St. G21	37	Y11
Mullardoch St. G23	8	T7
Rothes Dr.		
Mungo Pl. (Udd.) G71	57	HH15
Lincoln Av.		
Munlochy Rd. G51	33	Q12
Gentle Row		
Munro Ct., Clyde. G81	4	K5
Munro La. G13	19	R9
Munro Pl. G13	19	R9
Munro Pl. (Udd.) G71	57	HH15
Newlands Rd.		
Munro Rd. G13	19	R9
Munro Vw. (Udd.) G71	57	HH15
Newlands Rd.		
Murano St. G20	21	U10
Murchison G12	20	S9
Murdoch St. G21	22	X9
Lenzie St.		
Muriel St. (Barr.) G78	59	M18
Murray Path (Udd.) G71	69	GG17
Easter Av.		
Murray Pl. (Barr.) G78	59	M18
Murray Rd. (Both.) G71	69	HH18
Murray St., Pais. PA3	30	J13
Murray St., Renf. PA4	17	M10
Murrayfield (Bishop.) G64	11	Y6
Ashfield		
Murrayfield Dr. (Bears.) G61	7	R7
Murrayfield St. G32	38	AA12
Murrin Av. (Bishop.) G64	11	Z7
Murroes Rd. G51	33	Q12
Muslin St. G40	52	X14
Mybster Pl. G51	33	Q12
Mybster Rd. G51	33	Q12
Myers Cres. (Udd.) G71	69	HH17
Myres Rd. G53	49	Q16
Myreside Pl. G32	37	Z13
Myreside St. G32	37	Z13
Myrie Gdns. (Bishop.) G64	11	Y7
Myroch Pl. G34	40	FF11
Myrtle Av. (Lenzie) G66	13	CC5
Myrtle Hill La. G42	52	W16
Myrtle Pk. G42	52	W15
Myrtle Pl. G42	52	W16
Myrtle Rd. (Udd.) G71	57	HH16
Myrtle Rd., Clyde. G81	4	J6
Myrtle Sq. (Bishop.) G64	23	Y8
Myrtle St. (Blan.) G72	68	FF19
Myrtle Wk. (Camb.) G72	66	AA17

N

Name	Page	Grid
Naburn Gate G5	52	W14
Naburn St. G5	52	W14
Nairn Av. (Blan.) G72	68	FF19
Nairn Pl., Clyde. G81	4	K6
Dumbarton Rd.		
Nairn St. G3	34	T11
Nairn St., Clyde. G81	4	K6
Nairn Way (Cumb.) G68	71	PP1
Nairnside Rd. G21	23	Z8
Naismith St. G32	55	CC16
Nansen St. G20	21	V10
Napier Ct. (Old Kil.) G60	4	J5
Freelands Rd.		
Napier Dr. G51	34	S12
Napier Gdns. (Linw.), Pais. PA3	28	F13
Napier Pl. G51	34	S12
Napier Pl. (Old Kil.) G60	4	J5
Old Dalnottar Rd.		
Napier Rd. G51	34	S12
Napier Rd. G52	32	N11
Napier St. G51	34	T12
Napier St., Clyde. G81	17	M8
Napier St., John. PA5	43	D14
Barrochan Rd.		
Napier St. (Linw.), Pais. PA3	28	F13
Napier Ter. G51	34	S12
Napiershall La. G20	35	U11
Napiershall St.		
Napiershall Pl. G20	35	U11
Napiershall St.		
Napiershall St. G20	35	U11
Naseby Av. G11	19	R10
Nasmyth Pl. G52	32	P12
Nasmyth Rd. G52	32	P12
Nasmyth Rd. N. G52	32	P12
Nasmyth Rd. S. G52	32	P12
National Bk. La. G2	35	V12
St. Vincent St.		
Navar Pl., Pais. PA2	47	L15
Naver St. G33	38	AA11
Neil St., Pais. PA1	46	J14
Neil St., Renf. PA4	17	M9
Neilsland Oval G53	49	Q16
Neilsland Sq. G53	49	Q15
Neilston Av. G53	61	Q17
Neilston Rd. (Barr.) G78	59	L19
Neilston Rd., Pais. PA2	46	K14
Neilvaig Dr. (Ruther.) G73	65	Z18
Neistpoint Dr. G33	38	BB12
Nelson Mandela Pl. G2	36	W12
West George St.		
Nelson Pl. (Bail.) G69	56	EE14
Nelson St. G5	35	V13
Nelson St. (Bail.) G69	56	EE14
Nelson Ter. G12	21	U10
Glasgow St.		
Neptune St. G51	34	S12
Nerston Av. G53	49	Q16
Ness Av., John. PA5	43	C16
Ness Dr. (Blan.) G72	69	GG19
Ness Gdns. (Bishop.) G64	11	Y7
Ness Rd., Renf. PA4	17	L10
Ness St. G33	38	AA11
Nethan St. G51	34	S12
Nether Auldhouse Rd. G43	62	S17
Netherburn Av. G44	63	U19
Netherby Dr. G41	50	T14
Nethercairn Rd. G43	62	T18
Nethercliffe Av. G44	63	U19
Nethercommon Harbour, Pais. PA3	30	K12
Nethercraig Cotts., Pais. PA2	58	J17
Glenfield Rd.		
Nethercraigs Dr., Pais. PA2	46	J16
Nethercraigs Rd., Pais. PA2	45	H16
Netherdale Dr., Pais. PA1	48	N14
Netherfield St. G31	37	Z13
Nethergreen Cres., Renf. PA4	17	L10
Nethergreen Rd., Renf. PA4	17	L10
Nethergreen Wynd, Renf. PA4	17	L10
Netherhill Av. G44	63	U19
Netherhill Cotts., Pais. PA3	31	L12
Netherhill Rd.		
Netherhill Cres., Pais. PA3	31	L13
Netherhill Rd. (Chry.) G69	15	GG7
Netherhill Rd., Pais. PA3	30	K13
Netherhouse Av. (Lenzie) G66	13	DD6
Netherhouse Pl. G34	41	GG12
Netherhouse Rd. (Bail.) G69	40	FF12
Netherlee Rd. G44	63	U18
Netherpark Av. G44	63	U19
Netherplace Cres. G53	48	P16
Netherplace Rd.		
Netherplace Rd. G53	48	P16
Netherton Ct. G45	64	X19
Netherton Dr. (Barr.) G78	60	N19
Netherton Rd. G13	19	R8
Netherton St. G13	19	R8
Crow Rd.		
Nethervale Av. G44	63	U19
Netherview Rd. G44	63	U19
Netherway G44	63	U19
Nethy Rd., Renf. PA4	32	N11
Teith Av.		
Neuk Av. (Muir.) G69	26	FF8
Station Rd.		
Neuk Way G32	55	CC16
Nevis Rd. G43	62	S17
Nevis Rd. (Bears.) G61	6	P5

Nevis Rd. (Abbots.), Pais. PA3	30	K11
Nevis Rd., Renf. PA4	31	L11
New City Rd. G4	35	V11
New Edinburgh Rd. (Udd.) G71	57	GG16
New Inchinnan Rd., Pais. PA3	30	K12
New Kirk Pl. (Bears.) G61	7	R5
New Kirk Rd.		
New Kirk Rd. (Bears.) G61	7	R5
New Loop Av. (Barr.) G78	59	M18
Stewart St.		
New Rd. (Camb.) G72	67	DD18
New Sneddon St., Pais. PA3	30	K13
New St., Clyde. G81	4	K5
New St. (Kilb.), John. PA10	42	B14
New St., Pais. PA1	46	K14
New Wynd G1	36	W13
Newall Rd., Pais. PA3	30	K12
Newark Dr. G41	50	T14
Newark Dr., Pais. PA2	46	J16
Newbattle Ct. G32	54	BB15
Newbattle Gdns. G32	54	BB15
Newbattle Pl. G32	54	BB15
Newbattle Rd. G32	54	BB15
Newbold Av. G21	22	X8
Newburgh St. G43	50	T16
Newcastleton Dr. G23	9	U7
Newcroft Dr. G44	64	W17
Newfield Pl. (Thorn.) G46	61	R19
Newfield Pl. (Ruther.) G73	52	X16
Newfield Sq. G53	60	P17
Newgrove Gdns. (Camb.) G72	66	BB17
Newhall St. G40	52	X14
Newhaven Rd. G33	38	BB12
Newhaven St. G32	38	BB12
Newhills Rd. G33	39	DD12
Newington St. G32	38	AA13
Newlands Gdns. (Elder.), John. PA5	44	F15
Renshaw Rd.		
Newlands Rd. G43	63	U17
Newlands Rd. G44	63	V17
Newlands Rd. (Udd.) G71	57	GG16
Newlandsfield Rd. G43	50	T16
Newluce Dr. G32	55	CC14
Newmains Rd., Renf. PA4	31	L11
Newmill Rd. G21	23	Z9
Newnham Rd., Pais. PA1	48	N14
Newpark Cres. (Camb.) G72	54	BB16
Newshot Ct., Clyde. G81	17	M8
Clydeholm Ter.		
Newshot Dr., Ersk. PA8	4	J7
Newstead Gdns. G23	9	U7
Newton Av. (Camb.) G72	67	CC17
Newton Av. (Barr.) G78	59	M19
Newton Av. (Elder.), John. PA5	45	G14
Newton Brae (Camb.) G72	67	DD17
Newton Dr. (Udd.) G71	57	HH16
Newton Dr. (Elder.), John. PA5	45	G14
Newton Fm. Rd. (Camb.) G72	55	DD16
Newton Pl. G3	35	U11
Newton Rd. (Lenzie) G66	13	DD6
Newton Sta. Rd. (Camb.) G72	67	DD17
Newton St. G3	35	U13
Anderston Quay		
Newton St., Pais. PA1	46	J14
Newton Ter. G3	35	U12
Sauchiehall St.		
Newton Ter. La. G3	35	U11
Elderslie St.		
Newtongrange Av. G32	54	BB15
Newtongrange Gdns. G32	54	BB15
Newtyle Dr. G53	48	N15
Newtyle Pl. G53	48	N15
Langhaul Rd.		
Newtyle Pl. (Bishop.) G64	11	Z7
Newtyle Rd., Pais. PA1	47	L14
Nicholas St. G1	36	W12
Nicholson La. G5	35	V13
Nicholson St.		
Nicholson St. G5	35	V13
Nicolson Ct. (Stepps) G33	25	CC9
Niddrie Rd. G42	51	U15
Niddrie Sq. G42	51	U15
Niddry St., Pais. PA3	30	K13

Nigel Gdns. G41	50	T15
Nigg Pl. G34	40	EE12
Nightingale Pl., John. PA5	43	C16
Nimmo Dr. G51	33	R12
Nisbet St. G31	37	Z13
Nith Dr., Renf. PA4	32	N11
Nith Pl., John. PA5	43	C16
Nith St. G33	37	Z11
Nithsdale Cres. (Bears.) G61	7	Q5
Nithsdale Dr. G41	51	U15
Nithsdale Pl. G41	51	U14
Nithsdale Rd.		
Nithsdale Rd. G41	50	S14
Nithsdale St. G41	51	U15
Nitshill Rd. (Thorn.) G46	61	Q18
Nitshill Rd. G53	60	N17
Niven St. G20	20	T9
Noldrum Av. G32	55	CC16
Noldrum Gdns. G32	55	CC16
Norbreck Dr. (Giff.) G46	62	T18
Norby Rd. G11	19	R10
Norfield Dr. G44	51	V16
Norfolk Ct. G5	35	V13
Norfolk Cres. (Bishop.) G64	10	X6
Norfolk La. G5	35	V13
Norfolk St.		
Norfolk St. G5	35	V13
Norham St. G41	51	U15
Norman St. G40	52	X14
Norse La. N. G14	19	Q10
Ormiston Av.		
Norse La. S. G14	19	Q10
Verona Av.		
Norse Pl. G14	19	Q10
Norse Rd. G14	19	Q10
North Av. (Camb.) G72	66	AA17
North Av., Clyde. G81	5	L7
North Bk. Pl., Clyde. G81	17	M8
North Bk. St.		
North Bk. St., Clyde. G81	17	M8
North Berwick Av. (Cumb.) G68	70	NN1
North Berwick Gdns. (Cumb.) G68	70	NN1
North Brae Pl. G13	18	P8
North British Rd. (Udd.) G71	69	GG17
North Calder Gro. (Udd.) G71	56	EE15
North Calder Pl. (Udd.) G71	56	EE15
North Canal Bk. G4	36	W11
North Canal Bk. St. G4	36	W11
North Carbrain Rd. (Cumb.) G67	70	NN4
North Claremont St. G3	35	U11
North Corsebar Rd., Pais. PA2	46	J15
North Ct. La. G1	36	W12
Buchanan St.		
North Cft. St., Pais. PA3	30	K13
North Dean Pk. Av. (Both.) G71	69	HH18
North Douglas St., Clyde. G81	17	M8
North Dr. G1	36	W13
North Dr. (Linw.), Pais. PA3	28	E13
North Elgin St., Clyde. G81	17	M8
North Erskine Pk. (Bears.) G61	7	Q5
North Frederick St. G1	36	W12
North Gardner St. G11	20	S10
North Gower St. G51	34	T13
North Gra. Rd. (Bears.) G61	7	R5
North Hanover Pl. G4	36	W11
North Hanover St. G1	36	W12
North Iverton Pk. Rd., John. PA5	44	E14
North La. (Linw.), Pais. PA3	28	F13
Napier St.		
North Lo. Rd., Renf. PA4	17	M10
North Moraine La. G15	7	Q7
Moraine Av.		
North Pk. Av. (Thorn.) G46	61	R18
North Pk. Av. (Barr.) G78	59	L18
North Pl. G3	35	U12
North St.		
North Portland St. G1	36	W12
North Queen St. G2	36	W12
George Sq.		
North Rd., John. PA5	43	D15
North Spiers Wf. G4	35	V11
North St. G3	35	U12
North St., Clyde. G81	5	L7
Dumbarton Rd.		

North St., Pais. PA3	30	K13
North Vw. (Bears.) G61	7	Q7
North Wallace St. G4	36	W11
North Woodside Rd. G20	21	U10
Northampton Dr. G12	20	S9
Northampton La. G12	20	S9
Northampton Dr.		
Northbank Av. (Camb.) G72	67	CC17
Northbank St. (Camb.) G72	67	CC17
Northcroft Rd. G21	22	X10
Northcroft Rd. (Chry.) G69	15	GG7
Northgate Quad. G21	23	Z8
Northgate Rd. G21	23	Z8
Northinch St. G14	33	Q11
Northland Av. G14	19	Q9
Northland Dr. G14	19	Q9
Northland Gdns. G14	19	Q9
Northland La. G14	19	Q10
Upland Rd.		
Northmuir Rd. G15	6	P6
Northpark St. G20	21	U10
Northpark Ter. G12	21	U10
Hamilton Dr.		
Northumberland St. G20	21	U10
Northway (Blan.) G72	68	FF19
Norval St. G11	34	S11
Norwich Dr. G12	20	S9
Norwood Dr. (Giff.) G46	62	S19
Norwood Pk. (Bears.) G61	7	R6
Norwood Ter. G12	35	U11
Southpark Av.		
Norwood Ter. (Udd.) G71	57	HH16
Nottingham Av. G12	20	S9
Nottingham La. G12	20	S9
Northampton Dr.		
Novar Dr. G12	20	S10
Novar Gdns. (Bishop.) G64	10	X7
Numrow Ct., Clyde. G81	4	K5
Nuneaton St. G40	53	Y14
Nurseries Rd. (Bail.) G69	39	DD13
Nursery La. G41	51	U15
Nursery St. G41	51	U15
Nursery St. La. G41	51	U15
Nithsdale Dr.		
Nutberry Ct. G42	51	V15

O

Oak Cres. (Bail.) G69	56	EE14
Oak Dr. (Kirk.) G66	12	BB5
Oak Dr. (Camb.) G72	67	CC18
Oak Pk. (Bishop.) G64	11	Y7
Oak Rd., Clyde. G81	4	K5
Oak Rd., Pais. PA2	47	L15
Oak St. G2	35	V12
Cadogan St.		
Oak Wynd (Camb.) G72	67	DD18
Oakbank Dr. (Barr.) G78	60	N19
Oakbank La. G20	21	V10
Oakbank Ter. G20	21	V10
Oakdene Av. (Udd.) G71	57	HH16
Oakfield Av. G12	35	U11
Oakfield La. G12	35	U11
Gibson St.		
Oakfield Ter. G12	35	U11
Oakfield Av.		
Oakhill Av. (Bail.) G69	55	DD14
Oakley Dr. G44	63	U18
Oakley Ter. G31	36	X12
Oaks, The, John. PA5	43	D15
Oakshaw Sch. Brae, Pais. PA1	30	J13
Oakshaw St. E., Pais. PA1	30	K13
Oakshaw St. W., Pais. PA1	30	J13
Oakshawhead, Pais. PA1	30	J13
Oaktree Gdns. G45	64	X18
Oakwood Av., Pais. PA2	45	H15
Oakwood Cres. G34	40	FF11
Oakwood Dr. G34	40	FF11
Oatfield St. G21	23	Y10
Oban Ct. G20	21	U10
Oban Dr. G20	21	U10
Oban La. G20	21	U10
Oban Dr.		
Observatory La. G12	20	T10
Observatory Rd.		
Observatory Rd. G12	20	T10
Ochil Dr. (Barr.) G78	59	M19
Ochil Dr., Pais. PA2	46	K16
Ochil Pl. G32	54	BB14
Ochil Rd. (Bishop.) G64	11	Z7
Ochil Rd., Renf. PA4	31	L11

Parkvale Pl., Ersk. PA8 16 J8
Parkvale Av.
Parkvale Way, Ersk. PA8 16 J8
Parkvale Av.
Parkview Av. (Kirk.) G66 13 CC5
Parkview Ct. (Kirk.) G66 13 CC5
Parkview Dr. (Stepps) G33 25 DD9
Parnie St. G1 36 W13
Parson St. G4 36 X12
Parsonage Row G1 36 W12
Parsonage Sq. G4 36 W12
Partick Bri. St. G11 34 T11
Partickhill Av. G11 20 S10
Partickhill Ct. G11 20 S10
Partickhill Av.
Partickhill Rd. G11 20 S10
Paterson St. G5 35 V13
Pathead Gdns. G33 24 AA9
Patna St. G40 53 Y14
Paton St. G31 37 Y12
Patrick St., Pais. PA2 46 K14
Patterton Dr. (Barr.) G78 59 M19
Pattison St., Clyde. G81 4 K6
Payne St. G4 36 W11
Peacock Av., Pais. PA2 45 G15
Peacock Dr.
Peacock Dr., Pais. PA2 45 G14
Pearce La. G51 34 S12
Pearce St.
Pearce St. G51 34 S12
Pearson Dr., Renf. PA4 31 M11
Pearson Pl. (Linw.), Pais. PA3 28 E13
Peat Pl. G53 60 P17
Peat Rd. G53 60 P17
Peathill Av. (Chry.) G69 26 EE8
Peathill St. G21 22 W10
Peebles Dr. (Ruther.) G73 53 Z16
Peel Glen Gdns. G15 6 P5
Peel Glen Rd. G15 6 P6
Peel Glen Rd. (Bears.) G61 6 N5
Peel La. G11 34 S11
Burgh Hall St.
Peel Pl. (Both.) G71 69 HH18
Peel St. G11 34 S11
Peel Vw., Clyde. G81 5 M6
Kirkoswald Dr.
Pembroke St. G3 35 U12
Pencaitland Dr. G32 54 BB14
Falside Rd.
Pencaitland Gro. G32 54 BB14
Falside Rd.
Pencaitland Pl. G23 9 U7
Pendale Ri. G45 64 W18
Pendeen Cres. G33 39 DD13
Pendeen Pl. G33 39 DD13
Pendeen Rd. G33 39 DD13
Pendicle Cres. (Bears.) G61 7 Q6
Pendicle Rd. (Bears.) G61 7 Q6
Penicuik St. G32 37 Z13
Penilee Rd. G52 32 N12
Penilee Rd., Pais. PA1 32 N13
Penilee Ter. G52 32 N12
Peninver Dr. G51 33 R12
Penman Av. (Ruther.) G73 52 X16
Pennan Pl. G14 18 P9
Penneld Rd. G52 32 N13
Penrith Av. (Giff.) G46 62 T19
Penrith Dr. G12 20 S9
Penryn Gdns. G32 55 CC14
Penston Rd. G33 39 CC12
Pentland Av. (Linw.), Pais. PA3 28 E13
Pentland Ct. (Barr.) G78 59 L19
Pentland Cres., Pais. PA2 46 J16
Pentland Dr. (Bishop.) G64 11 Z7
Pentland Dr. (Barr.) G78 59 M19
Pentland Dr., Renf. PA4 31 L12
Pentland Pl. G40 52 X14
Pentland Rd. G43 62 T17
Pentland Rd. (Chry.) G69 26 FF8
Penzance Way (Chry.) G69 15 GG6
Peockland Gdns., John. PA5 44 E14
Peockland Pl., John. PA5 44 E14
Percy Dr. (Giff.) G46 62 T19
Percy Rd., Renf. PA4 31 L12
Percy St. G51 34 T13
Perran Gdns. (Chry.) G69 15 GG7
Perth Cres., Clyde. G81 4 J5
Perth St. G3 35 U12
Argyle St.
Peters Ct. G20 20 T8
Maryhill Rd.
Petershill Ct. G21 23 Y10
Petershill Dr. G21 23 Y10
Petershill Pl. G21 23 Y10
Petershill Rd. G21 22 X10
Peterson Dr. G13 18 N8
Peterson Gdns. G13 18 N8
Petition Pl. (Udd.) G71 69 HH17
Pettigrew St. G32 38 BB13
Peveril Av. G41 50 T15
Peveril Av. (Ruther.) G73 65 Z17
Pharonhill St. G31 38 AA13
Phoenix Business Pk., Pais. PA1 29 G13
Phoenix Pk. Ter. G4 35 V11
Corn St.
Phoenix Pl. (Elder.), John. PA5 44 F14
Phoenix Rd. G4 35 V11
Great Western Rd.
Piccadilly St. G3 35 U12
Piershill St. G32 38 AA12
Pikeman Rd. G13 19 Q9
Pilmuir Av. G44 63 U18
Pilrig St. G32 38 AA12
Pilton Rd. G15 6 P6
Pine Av. (Camb.) G72 67 DD18
Pine Cres., John. PA5 44 E15
Pine Gro. (Udd.) G71 57 HH16
Pine Pl. G5 52 W14
Pine Pl. (Cumb.) G67 71 RR2
Pine Rd. (Cumb.) G67 71 RR2
Pine Rd., Clyde. G81 4 J6
Pine St., Pais. PA2 47 L15
Pinelands (Bishop.) G64 11 Y6
Pinewood Av. (Kirk.) G66 12 BB5
Pinewood Ct. (Kirk.) G66 12 BB5
Pinewood Pl. (Kirk.) G66 12 BB5
Pinewood Sq. G15 6 N6
Pinkerton Av. (Ruther.) G73 52 X16
Pinkerton La., Renf. PA4 31 M11
Pinkston Dr. G21 36 W11
Pinkston Rd. G4 36 W11
Pinkston Rd. G21 22 W10
Pinmore Path G53 60 N17
Pinmore Pl. G53 60 N17
Pinmore St. G53 60 N17
Pinwherry Dr. G33 24 AA9
Pinwherry Pl. (Both.) G71 69 HH18
Hume Dr.
Pirn St. G40 52 X14
Pitcairn St. G31 54 AA14
Pitcaple Dr. G43 62 S17
Pitlochry Dr. G52 48 P14
Pitmedden Rd. (Bishop.) G64 11 Z7
Pitmilly Rd. G15 7 Q6
Pitreavie Pl. G33 39 CC11
Pitt St. G2 35 V12
Pladda Rd., Renf. PA4 31 M11
Plaintrees Ct., Pais. PA2 46 K15
Carriagehill Dr.
Planetree Pl., John. PA5 44 E15
Planetree Rd., Clyde. G81 5 L5
Planetrees Av., Pais. PA2 46 K15
Carriagehill Dr.
Plant St. G31 37 Z13
Plantation Pk. Gdns. G51 34 T13
Plantation Pl. G51 35 U13
Govan Rd.
Plantation Sq. G51 35 U13
Playfair St. G40 53 Y14
Pleaknowe Cres. (Chry.) G69 15 GG7
Pleamuir Pl. (Cumb.) G68 70 MM3
Plean St. G14 18 P9
Pleasance La. G43 50 T16
Pleasance St. G43 50 T16
Plover Pl., John. PA5 43 C16
Pointhouse Rd. G3 35 U12
Finnieston St.
Pollock Dr. (Bishop.) G64 10 X7
Pollock Rd. (Bears.) G61 8 S6
Pollok Av. G43 50 T16
Pollokshaws Rd.
Pollokshaws Rd. G41 51 U15
Pollokshaws Rd. G43 50 S16
Pollokshields Sq. G41 51 U15
Polmadie Av. G5 52 W15
Polmadie Rd. G5 52 W15
Polmadie Rd. G42 52 W15
Polmadie St. G42 52 W15
Polnoon Av. G13 18 P9
Polquhap Ct. G53 48 P16
Polquhap Gdns. G53 48 P16
Polquhap Pl. G53 48 P16
Polquhap Rd. G53 48 P16
Polson Cres., Pais. PA2 46 J15
Polson Dr., John. PA5 43 D15
Polsons Cres., Pais. PA2 46 J15
Polwarth Gdns. G12 20 S10
Novar Dr.
Polwarth La. G12 20 S10
Novar Dr.
Polwarth St. G12 20 S10
Poplar Av. G11 19 R10
Poplar Av., John. PA5 43 D15
Poplar Cotts. G14 18 N9
Dumbarton Rd.
Poplar Dr. (Kirk.) G66 12 BB5
Poplar Dr., Clyde. G81 4 K5
Poplar Pl. (Blan.) G72 68 FF19
Poplar Rd. G41 34 S13
Urrdale Rd.
Poplar Way (Camb.) G72 67 DD18
Poplin St. G40 52 X14
Porchester St. G33 39 CC11
Port Dundas Pl. G2 36 W12
Port Dundas Rd. G4 36 W11
Port St. G3 35 U12
Portal Rd. G13 19 Q8
Porterfield Rd., Renf. PA4 31 L11
Portland Rd. (Cumb.) G68 70 NN1
Portland St., Pais. PA2 47 L14
Portman Pl. G12 35 U11
Cowan St.
Portman St. G41 35 U13
Portmarnock Dr. G23 20 T8
Portreath Rd. (Chry.) G69 15 GG6
Portsoy Av. G13 18 N8
Portsoy Pl. G13 18 N8
Portugal La. G5 35 V13
Bedford St.
Portugal St. G5 35 V13
Bedford St.
Possil Cross G22 21 V10
Possil Rd. G4 21 V10
Post La., Renf. PA4 17 M10
Potassels Rd. (Muir.) G69 26 FF8
Potter Clo. G32 54 AA14
Potter Pl.
Potter Gro. G32 54 AA14
Potter Pl.
Potter Pl. G32 54 AA14
Potter St. G32 54 AA14
Potterhill Av., Pais. PA2 46 K16
Potterhill Rd. G53 48 P15
Powburn Cres. (Udd.) G71 56 FF16
Powfoot St. G31 37 Z13
Powrie St. G33 25 CC10
Prentice La. (Udd.) G71 57 HH16
Preston Pl. G42 51 V15
Preston St. G42 51 V15
Cathcart Rd.
Prestwick Ct. (Cumb.) G68 70 NN2
Prestwick St. G53 60 P17
Priesthill Av. G53 61 Q17
Priesthill Cres. G53 61 Q17
Priesthill Rd. G53 60 P17
Primrose Ct. G14 19 Q10
Primrose St. G14 19 Q10
Prince Albert Rd. G12 20 S10
Prince Edward St. G42 51 V15
Prince of Wales Gdns. G20 20 T8
Prince of Wales Ter. G12 20 T10
Byres Rd.
Prince's Dock G51 34 T12
Princes Gdns. G12 20 S10
Princes Gate (Udd.) G71 69 GG18
Princes Gate (Ruther.) G73 53 Y16
Greenbank St.
Princes Pl. G12 20 T10
Princes Sq. G1 36 W12
Princes Sq. (Barr.) G78 59 M18
Princes St. (Ruther.) G73 53 Y16
Princes Ter. G12 20 T10
Princess Cres., Pais. PA1 31 L13
Princess Dr. (Bail.) G69 41 GG13
Priory Av., Pais. PA3 31 L12
Priory Cotts. (Blan.) G72 68 FF19
Priory Dr. (Udd.) G71 56 FF16
Priory Pl. G13 19 Q8
Priory Rd. G13 19 Q8

Street	Page	Grid	Street	Page	Grid	Street	Page	Grid
Prosen St. G32	54	AA14	Queenshill St. G21	22	X10	Ravenswood Dr. G41	50	T15
Prospect Av. (Udd.) G71	57	GG16	Queensland Ct. G52	33	Q13	Ravenswood Rd. (Bail.) G69	40	FF13
Prospect Av. (Camb.) G72	66	AA17	Queensland Dr. G52	33	Q13	Rayne Pl. G15	6	P6
Prospect Rd. G43	50	T16	Queensland Gdns. G52	33	Q13	Red Rd. G21	23	Y10
Prospecthill Circ. G42	52	W15	Queensland La. E. G52	32	P13	Red Rd. Ct. G21	23	Y10
Prospecthill Cres. G42	52	X16	*Kingsland Dr.*			Redan St. G40	36	X13
Prospecthill Dr. G42	52	W16	Queensland La. W. G52	33	Q13	Redcastle Sq. G33	39	CC11
Prospecthill Pl. G42	52	X16	*Queensland Dr.*			Redford St. G33	37	Z12
Prospecthill Rd. G42	51	V16	Queenslie Ind. Est. G33	39	CC12	Redgate Pl. G14	18	P10
Prospecthill Sq. G42	52	W16	Queenslie St. G33	37	Z11	Redhill Rd. (Cumb.) G68	70	MM2
Provan Rd. G33	37	Z11	Quendale Dr. G32	54	AA14	Redhurst Cres., Pais. PA2	45	H16
Provand Hall Cres. (Bail.) G69	56	EE14	Quentin St. G41	51	U15	Redhurst La., Pais. PA2	45	H16
Provanhill St. G21	36	X11	Quinton Gdns. (Bail.) G69	40	EE13	Redhurst Way, Pais. PA2	45	H16
Provanmill Pl. G33	23	Z10				Redlands La. G12	20	T10
Provanmill Rd.			**R**			*Kirklee Rd.*		
Provanmill Rd. G33	23	Z10	Raasay Dr., Pais. PA2	46	J16	Redlands Rd. G12	20	T10
Provost Driver Ct., Renf. PA4	31	M11	Raasay Pl. G22	22	W8	Redlands Ter. G12	20	T10
King George Pk. Av.			Raasay St. G22	22	W8	Redlands Ter. La. G12	20	T10
Purdon St. G11	34	S11	Rachan St. G34	40	FF11	*Julian Av.*		
			Radnor St. G3	34	T11	Redlawood Pl. (Camb.) G72	68	EE17
Q			*Argyle St.*			*Redlawood Rd.*		
Quadrant Rd. G43	63	U17	Radnor St., Clyde. G81	5	L6	Redlawood Rd. (Camb.) G72	68	EE17
Quarrelton Rd., John. PA5	43	D15	Raeberry St. G20	21	U10	Redmoss St. G22	21	V9
Quarry Av. (Camb.) G72	67	DD18	Raeswood Dr. G53	48	N16	Rednock St. G22	22	W10
Quarry Pl. (Camb.) G72	66	AA17	Raeswood Gdns. G53	48	N16	Redpath Dr. G52	32	P13
Quarry Rd. (Barr.) G78	59	L18	Raeswood Pl. G53	48	N16	Redwood Ct. (Camb.) G72	67	DD18
Quarry Rd., Pais. PA2	46	K15	Raeswood Rd. G53	48	N16	*Redwood Cres.*		
Quarry St., John. PA5	43	D14	Rafford St. G51	34	S12	Redwood Cres. (Camb.) G72	67	DD18
Quarrybank (Mill.Pk.), John. PA10	43	C15	Raglan St. G4	35	V11	Redwood Dr. G21	23	Y10
Quarrybrae St. G31	38	AA13	Raith Av. G44	64	W18	*Foresthall Dr.*		
Quarryknowe (Ruther.) G73	52	X16	Raithburn Av. G45	64	W18	Redwood Pl. (Kirk.) G66	12	BB5
Quarryknowe St. G31	38	AA13	Raithburn Rd. G45	64	W18	Redwood Rd. (Cumb.) G67	71	QQ3
Quarrywood Av. G21	23	Z10	Ralston Av. G52	48	N14	Redwood Way (Camb.) G72	67	DD18
Quarrywood Rd. G21	23	Z10	Ralston Av., Pais. PA1	48	N14	Reelick Av. G13	18	N8
Quay Rd. (Ruther.) G73	53	Y15	Ralston Ct. G52	48	N14	Reelick Quad. G13	18	N8
Quay Rd. N. (Ruther.) G73	53	Y15	Ralston Dr. G52	48	N14	Reen Pl. (Both.) G71	69	HH18
Quebec Ho., Clyde. G81	4	J5	Ralston Path G52	48	N14	Regent Ct. (Ruther.) G73	53	Y16
Perth Cres.			*Ralston Dr.*			*King St.*		
Queen Arc. G2	35	V12	Ralston Pl. G52	48	N14	Regent Moray St. G3	34	T11
Renfrew St.			Ralston Rd. (Bears.) G61	7	R5	Regent Pk. Sq. G41	51	U15
Queen Elizabeth Av. G52	32	N12	Ralston Rd. (Barr.) G78	59	M19	Regent Pk. Ter. G41	51	U15
Queen Elizabeth Sq. G5	52	W14	Ralston St., Pais. PA1	47	L14	*Pollokshaws Rd.*		
Queen Margaret Ct. G20	21	U10	*Seedhill Rd.*			Regent Pl., Clyde. G81	4	K6
Queen Margaret Cres. G12	21	U10	Ram St. G32	38	AA13	Regent Sq. (Lenzie) G66	13	CC6
Hamilton Dr.			Rampart Av. G13	18	P8	Regent St., Clyde. G81	4	K6
Queen Margaret Dr. G12	20	T10	Ramsay Av., John. PA5	43	D15	Regent St., Pais. PA1	31	L13
Queen Margaret Dr. G20	21	U10	Ramsay Cres. (Mill.Pk.), John. PA10	42	B15	Regents Gate (Both.) G71	69	GG18
Queen Margaret Rd. G20	21	U10	Ramsay Pl., John. PA5	43	D15	Regwood St. G41	50	T16
Queen Mary Av. G42	51	V15	Ramsay St., Clyde. G81	4	K6	Reid Av. (Bears.) G61	8	S5
Queen Mary Av., Clyde. G81	5	M7	Ranald Gdns. (Ruther.) G73	65	Z18	Reid Av. (Linw.), Pais. PA3	28	E13
Queen Mary St. G40	52	X14	Randolph Av. (Clark.) G76	63	U19	Reid Pl. G40	52	X14
Queen Sq. G41	51	U15	Randolph Dr. (Clark.) G76	63	U19	Reid St. G40	52	X14
Queen St. G1	36	W12	Randolph Gdns. (Clark.) G76	63	U19	Reid St. (Ruther.) G73	53	Y16
Queen St. (Ruther.) G73	53	Y16	Randolph Rd. G11	19	R10	Reidhouse St. G21	22	X10
Queen St., Pais. PA1	46	J14	Randolph Ter. (Camb.) G72	66	BB17	*Muir St.*		
Queen St., Renf. PA4	17	M10	*Hamilton Rd.*			Reidvale St. G31	36	X13
Queen Victoria Dr. G13	19	Q10	Ranfurly Dr. (Cumb.) G68	70	NN2	Renfield St. G2	35	V12
Queen Victoria Dr. G14	19	Q10	Ranfurly Rd. G52	32	N13	Renfield St., Renf. PA4	17	M10
Queen Victoria Gate G13	19	Q9	Rankine Pl., John. PA5	43	D14	Renfrew Ct. G2	35	V12
Queens Av. (Camb.) G72	66	BB17	Rankine St., John. PA5	43	D14	*Renfrew St.*		
Queens Cres. G4	35	V11	Rankines La., Renf. PA4	17	M10	Renfrew La. G2	35	V12
Queens Cres. (Bail.) G69	41	GG13	*Manse St.*			*Renfield St.*		
Queens Cross G20	21	U10	Rannoch Av. (Bishop.) G64	11	Y7	Renfrew Rd. G51	32	P11
Queens Dr. G42	51	U15	Rannoch Dr. (Bears.) G61	8	S7	Renfrew Rd., Pais. PA3	30	K13
Queens Dr. (Cumb.) G68	70	NN1	Rannoch Dr., Renf. PA4	17	M10	Renfrew Rd., Renf. PA4	32	P11
Queens Dr. La. G42	51	V15	Rannoch Gdns. (Bishop.) G64	11	Y7	Renfrew St. G2	35	V11
Queens Gdns. G12	20	T10	Rannoch Pl., Pais. PA2	47	L14	Renfrew St. G3	35	V11
Victoria Cres. Rd.			Rannoch Rd. (Udd.) G71	57	GG15	Rennies Rd. (Inch.), Renf. PA4	16	J8
Queens Gate La. G12	20	T10	Rannoch Rd., John. PA5	43	D15	Renshaw Dr. G52	32	P13
Victoria Cres. Rd.			Rannoch St. G44	63	V17	Renshaw Rd. (Elder.), John. PA5	44	F15
Queens Pk. Av. G42	51	V15	Raploch Av. G14	18	P10	Renton St. G4	36	W11
Queens Pl. G12	20	T10	Raploch La. G14	18	P10	Renwick St. G41	35	U13
Queens Rd. (Elder.), John. PA5	44	F15	*Raploch Av.*			*Scotland St.*		
Queensbank Av. (Gart.) G69	27	GG8	Rathlin St. G51	34	S12	Resipol Rd. (Stepps) G33	25	DD9
Queensborough Gdns. G12	20	S10	Ratho Dr. G21	22	X9	Reston Dr. G52	32	P13
Queensby Av. (Bail.) G69	40	EE13	Rattray St. G32	54	AA14	Reuther Av. (Ruther.) G73	53	Y16
Queensby Rd.			Ravel Row G31	37	Z13	Revoch Dr. G13	18	P8
Queensby Dr. (Bail.) G69	40	EE13	Ravel Wynd (Udd.) G71	57	HH16	Rhannan Rd. G44	63	V17
Queensby Rd.			Ravelston Rd. (Bears.) G61	7	R7	Rhannan Ter. G44	63	V17
Queensby Pl. (Bail.) G69	40	EE13	Ravelston St. G32	37	Z13	Rhindhouse Dr. (Bail.) G69	40	EE13
Queensby Rd.			Ravens Ct. (Bishop.) G64	22	X8	Rhindhouse Pl. (Bail.) G69	40	FF13
Queensby Rd. (Bail.) G69	40	EE13	*Lennox Cres.*			Rhindhouse Rd. (Bail.) G69	40	FF13
Queensferry St. G5	52	X15	Ravenscliffe Dr. (Giff.) G46	62	S18	*Swinton Av.*		
Rosebery St.			Ravenscraig Av., Pais. PA2	46	J15	Rhindmuir Av. (Bail.) G69	40	FF13
			Ravenscraig Dr. G53	60	P17	Rhindmuir Ct. (Bail.) G69	40	FF13
			Ravenscraig Ter. G53	61	Q17	Rhindmuir Cres. (Bail.) G69	40	FF13
			Ravenshall Rd. G41	50	T16	Rhindmuir Dr. (Bail.) G69	40	FF13
			Ravenstone Dr. (Giff.) G46	62	T18	Rhindmuir Gdns. (Bail.) G69	40	FF13
			Ravenswood Av., Pais. PA2	45	G16	Rhindmuir Gro. (Bail.) G69	40	FF13
						Rhindmuir Path (Bail.) G69	40	FF13

Name	Page	Grid
Rhindmuir Pl. (Bail.) G69	40	FF13
Rhindmuir Rd. (Bail.) G69	40	FF13
Rhindmuir Vw. (Bail.) G69	40	FF13
Rhindmuir Wynd (Bail.) G69	40	FF13
Rhindmuir Cres.		
Rhinds St., Coat. ML5	57	HH14
Rhinsdale Cres. (Bail.) G69	40	FF13
Rhumhor Gdns., John. PA10	42	B15
Rhymer St. G21	36	X11
Rhymie Rd. G32	55	CC14
Rhynie Dr. G51	34	S13
Riccarton St. G42	52	W15
Riccartsbar Av., Pais. PA2	46	J14
Richard St. G2	35	V12
Cadogan St.		
Richard St., Renf. PA4	17	M10
Richmond Ct. (Ruther.) G73	53	Z16
Richmond Dr. (Bishop.) G64	11	Y6
Richmond Dr. (Camb.) G72	66	AA17
Richmond Dr. (Ruther.) G73	53	Z16
Richmond Dr. (Linw.), Pais. PA3	28	E12
Richmond Gdns. (Chry.) G69	14	EE7
Richmond Gro. (Ruther.) G73	53	Z16
Richmond Pl. (Ruther.) G73	53	Z16
Richmond St. G1	36	W12
Richmond St., Clyde. G81	5	M7
Riddell St., Clyde. G81	5	M6
Riddon Av. G13	18	N8
Riddon Av., Clyde. G81	18	N8
Riddon Pl. G13	18	N8
Riddrie Cres. G33	38	AA12
Riddrie Knowes G33	38	AA12
Riddrie Ter. G33	23	Z10
Provanmill Rd.		
Riddrievale Ct. G33	38	AA11
Riddrievale St. G33	38	AA11
Rigby St. G32	37	Z13
Rigg Pl. G33	39	DD12
Rigghead Av. (Cumb.) G67	71	PP1
Riggside Rd. G33	39	CC11
Riglands Way, Renf. PA4	17	M10
Riglaw Pl. G13	18	P8
Rigmuir Rd. G51	33	Q13
Rimsdale St. G40	37	Y13
Ringford St. G21	22	X10
Ripon Dr. G12	20	S9
Risk St. G40	36	X13
Risk St., Clyde. G81	4	K6
Ristol Rd. G13	19	Q9
Anniesland Rd.		
Ritchie Cres. (Elder.), John. PA5	44	F14
Ritchie Pk., John. PA5	44	E14
Ritchie St. G5	51	V14
River Dr. (Inch.), Renf. PA4	16	J10
River Rd. G32	54	BB16
River Rd. G41	51	U16
Mansionhouse Rd.		
Riverbank St. G43	50	T16
Riverford Rd. G43	50	T16
Riverford Rd. (Ruther.) G73	53	Z15
Riversdale Cotts. G14	18	N9
Dumbarton Rd.		
Riversdale La. G14	18	P10
Ardsloy Pl.		
Riverside Ct. G44	63	V19
Riverside Pk. G44	63	V19
Linnpark Av.		
Riverside Pl. (Camb.) G72	67	DD17
Riverside Rd. G43	51	U16
Riverview Av. G5	35	V13
West St.		
Riverview Dr. G5	35	V13
Riverview Gdns. G5	35	V13
Riverview Pl. G5	35	V13
Roaden Av., Pais. PA2	45	G16
Roaden Rd., Pais. PA2	45	G16
Roadside (Cumb.) G67	71	PP1
Robb St. G21	22	X10
Rober Dr. G51	34	S12
Robert Burns Av., Clyde. G81	5	M6
Robert St. G51	34	S12
Robert Templeton Dr. (Camb.) G72	67	CC17
Roberton Av. G41	50	T15
Roberts St., Clyde. G81	4	K6
Robertson La. G2	35	V12
Robertson St.		
Robertson St. G2	35	V12
Robertson St. (Barr.) G78	59	L18
Robertson Ter. (Bail.) G69	40	FF13
Edinburgh Rd.		
Robin Way G32	55	CC16
Robroyston Av. G33	24	AA10
Robroyston Dr. G33	24	AA9
Robroyston Rd. G33	24	AA9
Robroyston Rd. (Bishop.) G64	12	AA7
Robslee Cres. (Giff.) G46	62	S18
Robslee Dr. (Giff.) G46	62	S18
Robslee Rd. (Thorn.) G46	62	S19
Robson Gro. G42	51	V15
Rock Dr. (Kilb.), John. PA10	42	B15
Rock St. G4	21	V10
Rockall Dr. G44	64	W18
Rockbank Pl. G40	37	Y13
Broad St.		
Rockbank Pl., Clyde. G81	5	L5
Glasgow Rd.		
Rockbank St. G40	37	Y13
Rockcliffe St. G40	52	X14
Rockfield Pl. G21	23	Z9
Rockfield Rd. G21	23	Z9
Rockmount Av. (Thorn.) G46	62	S18
Rockmount Av. (Barr.) G78	59	M19
Rockwell Av., Pais. PA2	46	J16
Rodger Dr. (Ruther.) G73	65	Y17
Rodger Pl. (Ruther.) G73	65	Y17
Rodil Av. G44	64	W18
Rodney St. G4	35	V11
Roebank Dr. (Barr.) G78	59	M19
Roebank St. G31	37	Y12
Roffey Pk. Rd., Pais. PA1	31	M13
Rogart St. G40	36	X13
Orr St.		
Rogerfield Rd. (Bail.) G69	40	FF12
Rokeby Ter. G12	20	T10
Great Western Rd.		
Roman Av. G15	6	P7
Roman Av. (Bears.) G61	7	R5
Roman Ct. (Bears.) G61	7	R5
Roman Dr. (Bears.) G61	7	R5
Roman Gdns. (Bears.) G61	7	R5
Roman Rd. (Bears.) G61	7	R5
Roman Rd., Clyde. G81	5	L5
Romney Av. G44	64	W17
Rona St. G21	37	Y11
Rona Ter. (Camb.) G72	66	AA18
Ronaldsay Dr. (Bishop.) G64	11	Z7
Ronaldsay Pl. (Cumb.) G67	70	MM4
Ronaldsay St. G22	22	W8
Ronay St. G22	22	W8
Rooksdell Av., Pais. PA2	46	J15
Ropework La. G1	36	W13
Clyde St.		
Rose Cotts. G13	19	R9
Crow Rd.		
Rose Dale (Bishop.) G64	23	Y8
Rose Knowe Rd. G42	52	X15
Rose St. G3	35	V12
Rosebank Av. (Blan.) G72	69	GG19
Rosebank Dr. (Camb.) G72	67	CC18
Rosebank Gdns. (Udd.) G71	56	EE15
Rosebank Pl. (Udd.) G71	56	EE15
Rosebank Ter. (Bail.) G69	57	GG14
Rosebery Pl., Clyde. G81	5	L7
Miller St.		
Rosebery St. G5	52	X15
Rosedale Av., Pais. PA2	44	F16
Rosedale Av. (Bail.) G69	56	EE14
Rosedale Gdns. G20	20	T8
Rosefield Gdns. (Udd.) G71	57	GG16
Roselea Gdns. G13	19	R8
Roselea Pl. (Blan.) G72	68	FF19
Rosemount (Cumb.) G68	70	NN1
Rosemount Cres. G21	37	Y11
Rosemount St. G21	36	X11
Rosemount Ter. G51	35	U13
Paisley Rd. W.		
Rosemount Meadows (Both.) G71	69	GG19
Roseness Pl. G33	38	BB12
Rosevale Rd. (Bears.) G61	7	R6
Rosevale St. G11	34	S11
Rosewood Av., Pais. PA2	45	H15
Rosewood St. G13	19	R8
Roslea Dr. G31	37	Y12
Roslyn Dr. (Bail.) G69	41	GG13
Rosneath St. G51	34	S12
Ross Av., Renf. PA4	31	L11
Ross Hall Pl., Renf. PA4	17	M10
Ross St. G40	36	W13
Ross St., Pais. PA1	47	L14
Rossendale Rd. G41	50	T16
Rossendale Rd. G43	50	T16
Rosshall Av., Pais. PA1	47	M14
Rosshill Av. G52	32	N13
Rosshill Rd. G52	32	N13
Rossie Cres. (Bishop.) G64	23	Z8
Rosslea Dr. (Giff.) G46	62	T19
Rosslyn Av. (Ruther.) G73	53	Y16
Rosslyn Ter. (Bears.) G61	6	P5
Rosslyn Ter. G12	20	T10
Rostan Rd. G43	62	T17
Rosyth Rd. G5	52	X15
Rosyth St. G5	52	X15
Rotherwick Dr., Pais. PA1	48	N14
Rotherwood Av. G13	7	Q7
Rotherwood Av., Pais. PA2	45	G16
Rotherwood La. G13	7	Q7
Rotherwood Av.		
Rotherwood Pl. G13	19	Q8
Rothes Dr. G23	8	T7
Rothes Pl. G23	8	T7
Rottenrow G4	36	W12
Rottenrow E. G4	36	W12
Roual Ter., Pais. PA1	31	L13
Greenlaw Av.		
Rouken Glen Pk. (Thorn.) G46	61	R19
Rouken Glen Rd. (Thorn.) G46	61	R19
Roukenburn St. (Thorn.) G46	61	R18
Roundhill Dr. (Elder.), John. PA5	45	G14
Roundknowe Rd. (Udd.) G71	56	FF15
Rowallan Gdns. G11	20	S10
Rowallan La. G11	20	S10
Churchill Dr.		
Rowallan La. E. G11	20	S10
Churchill Dr.		
Rowallan Rd. (Thorn.) G46	61	R19
Rowallan Ter. G33	24	BB10
Rowan Av., Renf. PA4	17	M10
Rowan Cres. (Lenzie) G66	13	CC5
Rowan Dr., Clyde. G81	4	K6
Rowan Gdns. G41	50	S14
Rowan Gdns. (Both.) G71	69	HH18
Rowan Gate, Pais. PA2	46	K15
Rowan Pl. (Camb.) G72	67	CC17
Elm Dr.		
Rowan Rd. G41	50	S14
Rowan Rd. (Cumb.) G67	71	QQ2
Rowan St., Pais. PA2	46	K15
Rowand Av. (Giff.) G46	62	T19
Rowandale Av. (Bail.) G69	56	EE14
Rowanlea Av., Pais. PA2	44	F16
Rowanlea Dr. (Giff.) G46	62	T18
Rowanpark Dr. (Barr.) G78	59	L17
Rowans, The (Bishop.) G64	10	X7
Rowans Gdns. (Both.) G71	69	HH18
Rowantree Av. (Ruther.) G73	65	Y17
Rowantree Gdns. (Ruther.) G73	65	Y17
Rowantree Pl., John. PA5	43	D15
Rowantree Rd.		
Rowantree Rd., John. PA5	43	D15
Rowchester St. G40	37	Y13
Rowena Av. G13	7	Q7
Roxburgh La. G12	20	T10
Saltoun St.		
Roxburgh Rd., Pais. PA2	44	F16
Roxburgh St. G12	20	T10
Roy St. G21	22	W10
Royal Bk. Pl. G1	36	W12
Buchanan St.		
Royal Cres. G3	35	U12
Royal Cres. G42	51	V15
Royal Ex. Bldgs. G1	36	W12
Royal Ex. Sq.		
Royal Ex. Ct. G1	36	W12
Queen St.		
Royal Ex. Sq. G1	36	W12
Royal Inch Cres., Renf. PA4	17	M9
Royal Ter. G3	35	U11
Royal Ter. G42	51	V14
Queens Dr.		
Royal Ter. La. G3	35	U11
North Claremont St.		
Royston Rd. G21	36	X11
Royston Rd. G33	24	AA10

Royston Sq. G21	36	X11
Roystonhill G21	36	X11
Rozelle Av. G15	6	P6
Rubislaw Dr. (Bears.) G61	7	R6
Ruby St. G40	53	Y14
Ruchazie Pl. G33	38	AA12
Ruchazie Rd. G32	38	AA13
Ruchazie Rd. G33	38	AA13
Ruchill Pl. G20	21	U9
Ruchill St. G20	21	U9
Ruel St. G44	51	V16
Rufflees Av. (Barr.) G78	59	M18
Rugby Av. G13	18	P8
Rullion Pl. G33	38	AA12
Rumford St. G40	52	X14
Rupert St. G4	35	U11
Rushyhill St. G21	23	Y10
Cockmuir St.		
Ruskin Pl. G12	20	T10
Great Western Rd.		
Ruskin Sq. (Bishop.) G64	11	Y7
Ruskin Ter. G12	21	U10
Ruskin Ter. (Ruther.) G73	53	Y15
Russell Cres. (Bail.) G69	56	FF14
Russell Dr. (Bears.) G61	7	R5
Russell Gdns. (Udd.) G71	57	HH16
Kingston Av.		
Russell St. G11	34	S11
Vine St.		
Russell St., John. PA5	44	E14
Russell St., Pais. PA3	30	J12
Rutherford Av. (Kirk.) G66	14	EE5
Chryston Rd.		
Rutherford Gra. (Kirk.) G66	13	CC5
Rutherford La. G2	35	V12
Hope St.		
Rutherglen Bri. G40	52	X14
Rutherglen Bri. G42	52	X14
Rutherglen Rd. G5	52	W14
Rutherglen Rd. (Ruther.) G73	52	W14
Ruthven Av. (Giff.) G46	62	T19
Ruthven La. G12	20	T10
Byres Rd.		
Ruthven Pl. (Bishop.) G64	23	Z8
Ruthven St. G12	20	T10
Rutland Ct. G51	35	U13
Govan Rd.		
Rutland Cres. G51	35	U13
Rutland La. G51	35	U13
Govan Rd.		
Rutland Pl. G51	35	U13
Ryan Rd. (Bishop.) G64	11	Y7
Ryan Way (Ruther.) G73	65	Z18
Rye Cres. G21	23	Z9
Rye Rd. G21	23	Z9
Rye Way, Pais. PA2	45	G15
Ryebank Rd. G21	23	Z9
Ryecroft Dr. (Bail.) G69	40	EE13
Ryedale Pl. G15	6	P6
Ryefield Av., John. PA5	43	C15
Ryefield Pl., John. PA5	43	C15
Ryefield Rd. G21	23	Y9
Ryehill Pl. G21	23	Z9
Ryehill Rd. G21	23	Z9
Ryemount Rd. G21	23	Z9
Ryeside Rd. G21	23	Y9
Ryewraes Rd. (Linw.), Pais. PA3	28	E13
Rylands Dr. G32	55	DD14
Rylands Gdns. G32	55	DD14
Rylees Cres. G52	32	N12
Rylees Pl. G52	32	N13
Rylees Rd. G52	32	N13
Ryvra Rd. G13	19	Q9

S

Sackville Av. G13	19	R9
Sackville La. G13	19	R9
Sackville Av.		
Saddell Rd. G15	6	P6
St. Abbs Dr., Pais. PA2	45	H15
St. Andrews Av. (Bishop.) G64	10	X7
St. Andrew's Av. (Both.) G71	69	HH19
St. Andrews Cres. G41	51	U14
St. Andrews Cres., Pais. PA3	30	J11
St. Andrews Cross G41	51	V14
St. Andrews Dr. G41	50	T15
St. Andrews Dr. (Abbots.), Pais. PA3	30	J12
St. Andrews Dr. W. (Abbots.), Pais. PA3	30	J11
St. Andrews La. G1	36	W13
Gallowgate		
St. Andrews Rd. G41	51	U14
St. Andrews Rd., Renf. PA4	31	M11
St. Andrews Sq. G1	36	W13
St. Andrews St. G1	36	W13
St. Annes Av., Ersk. PA8	16	J8
St. Annes Wynd, Ersk. PA8	16	J8
St. Anns Dr. (Giff.) G46	62	T19
St. Blanes Dr. (Ruther.) G73	64	X17
St. Boswell's Cres., Pais. PA2	45	H15
St. Brides Rd. G43	50	T16
St. Brides Way (Both.) G71	69	HH18
St. Catherines Rd. (Giff.) G46	62	T19
St. Clair Av. (Giff.) G46	62	T18
St. Clair St. G20	35	U11
Woodside Rd.		
St. Conval Pl. G43	50	S16
Shawbridge St.		
St. Cyrus Gdns. (Bishop.) G64	11	Z7
St. Cyrus Rd. (Bishop.) G64	11	Y7
St. Enoch Pl. G1	35	V13
Howard St.		
St. Enoch Sq. G1	35	V13
St. Enoch Wynd G2	35	V12
Argyle St.		
St. Fillans Rd. G33	25	CC9
St. Georges Cross G3	35	V11
St. Georges Pl. G20	35	V11
St. Georges Rd.		
St. Georges Rd. G3	35	V11
St. Germains (Bears.) G61	7	R6
St. Helena Cres., Clyde. G81	5	M5
St. Ives Rd. (Mood.) G69	15	GG6
St. James Av., Pais. PA3	29	H12
St. James Pl., Pais. PA3	30	K13
Love St.		
St. James Rd. G4	36	W12
St. James St., Pais. PA3	30	J13
St. Johns Ct. G41	51	U14
St. Johns Quad. G41	51	U14
St. Johns Rd. G41	51	U14
St. Johns Ter. G12	35	U11
Southpark Av.		
St. Joseph's Ct. G21	36	X11
St. Joseph's Pl. G21	36	X11
St. Josephs Pl. G40	36	X13
Abercromby St.		
St. Joseph's Vw. G21	36	X11
St. Kenneth Dr. G51	33	R12
St. Kilda Dr. G14	19	R10
St. Leonards Dr. (Giff.) G46	62	T18
St. Margarets Pl. G1	36	W13
Bridgegate		
St. Mark Gdns. G32	38	AA13
St. Mark St.		
St. Mark St. G32	38	AA13
St. Marnock St. G40	37	Y13
St. Mary's Cres. (Barr.) G78	59	M19
St. Mary's Gdns. (Barr.) G78	59	M19
Heys St.		
St. Marys La. G2	35	V12
West Nile St.		
St. Marys Rd. (Bishop.) G64	10	X7
St. Michael's Ct. G31	37	Z13
St. Michael's La. G31	37	Z13
St. Mirren St., Pais. PA1	46	K14
St. Monance St. G21	22	X9
St. Mungo Av. G4	36	W12
St. Mungo Pl. G4	36	W12
St. Mungo St. (Bishop.) G64	22	X8
St. Mungo's Rd. (Cumb.) G67	70	NN3
St. Ninian St. G5	36	W13
St. Ninian Ter. G5	36	W13
Old Rutherglen Rd.		
St. Ninians Cres., Pais. PA2	46	K15
Rowan St.		
St. Ninians Rd., Pais. PA2	46	K15
St. Peters La. G2	35	V12
Blythswood St.		
St. Peters Path G4	35	V11
Gladstone St.		
St. Peter's Path G4	35	V11
Braid St.		
St. Peters St. G4	35	V11
St. Rollox Brae G21	36	X11
St. Ronans Dr. G41	50	T15
St. Ronans Dr. (Ruther.) G73	65	Z17
St. Stephens Av. (Ruther.) G73	65	Z18
St. Stephens Cres. (Ruther.) G73	66	AA18
St. Valleyfield St. G21	22	X10
Ayr St.		
St. Vincent Cres. G3	34	T12
St. Vincent Cres. La. G3	35	U12
Corunna St.		
St. Vincent La. G2	35	V12
Hope St.		
St. Vincent Pl. G1	36	W12
St. Vincent St. G2	35	U12
St. Vincent St. G3	35	U12
St. Vincent Ter. G3	35	U12
Salamanca St. G31	37	Z13
Salasaig Ct. G33	38	BB12
Sutherness Dr.		
Salen St. G52	33	R13
Salisbury Pl. G12	20	T10
Great Western Rd.		
Salisbury Pl., Clyde. G81	4	J5
Salisbury St. G5	51	V14
Salkeld St. G5	51	V14
Salmona St. G22	21	V10
Saltaire Av. (Udd.) G71	69	HH17
Salterland Rd. G53	60	N17
Salterland Rd. (Barr.) G78	60	N17
Saltmarket G1	36	W13
Saltmarket Pl. G1	36	W13
King St.		
Saltoun Gdns. G12	20	T10
Roxburgh St.		
Saltoun La. G12	20	T10
Ruthven St.		
Saltoun St. G12	20	T10
Salvia St. (Camb.) G72	66	AA17
Sanda St. G20	21	U10
Sandaig Rd. G33	39	DD13
Sandbank Av. G20	20	T9
Sandbank Dr. G20	20	T8
Sandbank St. G20	20	T9
Sandbank Ter. G20	20	T8
Sandend Rd. G53	48	P16
Sanderling Pl., John. PA5	43	C16
Sanderling Rd., Pais. PA3	30	J12
Sandfield St. G20	21	U9
Maryhill Rd.		
Sandford Gdns. (Bail.) G69	56	EE14
Scott St.		
Sandgate Av. G32	55	CC14
Sandhaven Rd. G53	48	P16
Sandholes, Pais. PA1	46	J14
Sandholm Pl. G14	18	N9
Sandholm Ter. G14	18	N9
Sandielands Av., Ersk. PA8	16	J8
Sandilands St. G32	38	BB13
Sandmill St. G21	37	Y11
Sandra Rd. (Bishop.) G64	11	Z7
Sandringham Dr. (Elder.), John. PA5	44	E15
Glamis Av.		
Sandringham La. G12	20	T10
Kersland St.		
Sandwood Cres. G52	32	P13
Sandwood Rd.		
Sandwood Rd. G52	32	P13
Sandy La. G11	34	S11
Crawford St.		
Sandy Rd. G11	34	S11
Sandy Rd., Renf. PA4	31	M11
Sandyfaulds Sq. G5	52	W14
Sandyford Pl. G3	35	U12
Sandyford Pl. La. G3	35	U11
Elderslie St.		
Sandyford Rd., Pais. PA3	31	L12
Sandyford St. G3	34	T12
Sandyhills Cres. G32	54	BB14
Sandyhills Dr. G32	54	BB14
Sandyhills Gro. G32	55	CC15
Hamilton Rd.		
Sandyhills Pl. G32	54	BB14
Sandyhills Rd. G32	54	BB14
Sandyknowes Rd. (Cumb.) G67	71	PP4
Sannox Gdns. G31	37	Y12
Sanquhar Dr. G53	48	P16
Sanquhar Gdns. G53	48	P16
Sanquhar Gdns. (Blan.) G72	68	EE19
Sanquhar Pl. G53	48	P16

Name	Page	Grid
Sanquhar Rd. G53	48	P16
Saracen Gdns. G22	22	W9
Saracen Head La. G1	36	W13
Gallowgate		
Saracen St. G22	22	W10
Sardinia La. G12	20	T10
Great George St.		
Sardinia Ter. G12	20	T10
Cecil St.		
Saucel, Pais. PA1	46	K14
Saucel St., Pais. PA1	46	K14
Saucelhill Ter., Pais. PA2	46	K14
Sauchenhall Rd. (Kirk.) G66	15	GG5
Sauchiehall La. G2	35	V12
Sauchiehall St.		
Sauchiehall St. G2	35	U12
Sauchiehall St. G3	35	U12
Saughs Av. G33	24	AA9
Saughs Dr. G33	24	AA9
Saughs Gate G33	24	AA9
Saughs Pl. G33	24	AA9
Saughs Av.		
Saughs Rd. G33	24	AA9
Saughton St. G32	38	AA12
Saunders Ct. (Barr.) G78	59	L18
John St.		
Savoy Arc. G40	52	X14
Main St.		
Savoy St. G40	52	X14
Sawfield Pl. G4	35	V11
Garscube Rd.		
Sawmill Rd. G11	33	R11
South St.		
Sawmillfield St. G4	35	V11
Saxon Rd. G13	19	Q8
Scadlock Rd., Pais. PA3	29	H13
Scalpay Pl. G22	22	W8
Scalpay St. G22	22	W8
Scapa St. G23	21	U8
Scapa St. G40	53	Y14
Springfield Rd.		
Scaraway Dr. G22	22	W8
Scaraway Pl. G22	22	W8
Scaraway St. G22	22	W8
Scaraway Ter. G22	22	W8
Scarba Dr. G43	62	S17
Scarrel Dr. G45	65	Y18
Scarrel Gdns. G45	65	Y18
Scarrel Rd. G45	65	Y18
Scarrel Ter. G45	65	Y18
Schaw Ct. (Bears.) G61	7	Q5
Schaw Dr. (Bears.) G61	7	R5
Schaw Rd., Pais. PA3	31	L13
Schipka Pas. G1	36	W13
Gallowgate		
School Av. (Camb.) G72	66	BB17
School Rd. (Stepps) G33	25	DD9
School Rd., Pais. PA1	32	N13
School Wynd, Pais. PA1	30	K13
Scioncroft Av. (Ruther.) G73	53	Z16
Scone St. G21	22	W10
Sconser St. G23	9	U7
Scorton Gdns. (Bail.) G69	55	DD14
Scotland St. G5	35	U13
Scotland St. W. G41	34	T13
Scotsblair Av. (Kirk.) G66	13	CC5
Scotsburn Rd. G21	23	Z10
Scotstoun Mill Rd. G11	34	T11
Partick Bri. St.		
Scotstoun Pl. G14	19	Q10
Scotstoun St.		
Scotstoun St. G14	19	Q10
Scott Av., John. PA5	43	D16
Scott Dr. (Bears.) G61	7	Q5
Scott Rd. G52	32	N12
Scott St. G3	35	V11
Scott St. (Bail.) G69	56	EE14
Scott St., Clyde. G81	4	K6
Scotts Rd., Pais. PA2	47	M14
Seafar Rd. (Cumb.) G67	70	NN4
Seafield Dr. (Ruther.) G73	65	Z18
Seaforth Cres. (Barr.) G78	59	L18
Seaforth La. (Chry.) G69	15	HH7
Burnbrae Av.		
Seaforth Rd. G52	32	P12
Seaforth Rd., Clyde. G81	5	L7
Seaforth Rd. N. G52	32	P12
Seaforth Rd. S. G52	32	P12
Seagrove St. G32	37	Z13
Seamill Path G53	60	N17
Seamill Pl. G53	60	N17
Seamill St. G53	60	N17
Seamore St. G20	35	U11
Seath Rd. (Ruther.) G73	53	Y15
Seath St. G42	52	W15
Seaward La. G41	35	U13
Seaward St.		
Seaward Pl. G41	35	U13
Seaward St. G41	35	U13
Second Av. (Stepps) G33	24	BB9
Second Av. G44	63	V17
Second Av. (Bears.) G61	8	S6
Second Av. (Kirk.) G66	13	CC7
Second Av. (Udd.) G71	57	GG15
Second Av., Clyde. G81	5	L6
Second Av., Renf. PA4	31	M11
Second Gdns. G41	50	S14
Second St. (Udd.) G71	57	GG16
Seedhill, Pais. PA1	46	K14
Seedhill Rd., Pais. PA1	46	K14
Seggielea La. G13	19	Q9
Helensburgh Dr.		
Seggielea Rd. G13	19	Q9
Seil Dr. G44	64	W18
Selborne Pl. G13	19	R9
Selborne Rd.		
Selborne Pl. La. G13	19	R9
Selborne Rd.		
Selborne Rd. G13	19	R9
Selby Gdns. G32	39	DD13
Selkirk Av. G52	49	Q14
Selkirk Av., Pais. PA2	45	H15
Selkirk Dr. (Ruther.) G73	53	Z16
Sella Rd. (Bishop.) G64	11	Z6
Selvieland Rd. G52	32	N13
Semple Pl. (Linw.), Pais. PA3	28	E12
Seton Ter. G31	36	X12
Settle Gdns. (Bail.) G69	55	DD14
Seven Sisters (Kirk.) G66	13	DD5
Seventh Av. (Udd.) G71	57	GG16
Seyton Av. (Giff.) G46	62	T19
Shaftesbury St. G3	35	U12
Shaftesbury St., Clyde. G81	4	K7
Shafton Pl. G13	19	R8
Shafton Rd. G13	19	R8
Shakespeare Av., Clyde. G81	4	K6
Shakespeare St. G20	21	U9
Shamrock Cotts. G13	19	R9
Crow Rd.		
Shamrock St. G4	35	V11
Shandon St. G51	34	T12
Govan Rd.		
Shandwick St. G34	40	EE12
Shanks Av. (Barr.) G78	59	M19
Shanks Cres., John. PA5	43	C15
Shanks St. G20	21	U9
Shannon St. G20	21	U9
Shapinsay St. G22	22	W8
Sharrocks St. G51	34	T13
Clifford St.		
Shaw Pl. (Linw.), Pais. PA3	28	E13
Shaw St. G51	34	S12
Shawbridge St. G43	50	S16
Shawfield Dr. G5	52	X15
Shawfield Rd. G5	52	X15
Shawhill Rd. G41	50	T16
Shawhill Rd. G43	50	T16
Shawholm Cres. G43	50	S16
Shawlands Arc. G41	51	U16
Shawlands Sq. G41	51	U16
Shawmoss Rd. G41	50	T15
Shawpark St. G20	21	U9
Shearer La. G5	35	U13
Shearer Pl. G51	35	U13
Sheddens Pl. G32	38	AA13
Sheepburn Rd. (Udd.) G71	57	GG16
Sheila St. G33	24	AA10
Sheldrake Pl., John. PA5	43	C16
Shelley Ct. G12	20	S9
Shelley Rd.		
Shelley Dr. (Both.) G71	69	HH18
Shelley Dr., Clyde. G81	5	L6
Shelley Rd. G12	19	R9
Sheppard St. G21	22	X10
Cowlairs Rd.		
Sherbrooke Av. G41	50	T14
Sherbrooke Dr. G41	50	T14
Sherbrooke Gdns. G41	50	T14
Sherburn Gdns. (Bail.) G69	55	DD14
Sheriff Pk. Av. (Ruther.) G73	53	Y16
Sherwood Av. (Udd.) G71	69	HH17
Sherwood Av., Pais. PA1	31	L13
Sherwood Dr. (Thorn.) G46	62	S18
Sherwood Pl. G15	6	P6
Shetland Dr. G44	64	W18
Shettleston Rd. G31	37	Z13
Shettleston Rd. G32	38	AA13
Shettleston Sheddings G31	38	AA13
Shettleston Rd.		
Shiel Ct. (Barr.) G78	59	L17
Shiel Rd. (Bishop.) G64	11	Y7
Shieldaig Dr. (Ruther.) G73	65	Y18
Shieldaig Rd. G22	21	V8
Shieldbridge Gdns. G23	9	U7
Shieldburn Rd. G51	33	Q12
Shieldhall Gdns. G51	33	Q12
Shieldhall Rd. G51	32	P12
Shields Rd. G41	35	U13
Shilford Av. G13	18	P8
Shillay St. G22	22	X8
Shilton Dr. G53	60	P17
Shinwell Av., Clyde. G81	5	M7
Clyde St.		
Shipbank La. G1	36	W13
Clyde St.		
Shiskine Dr. G20	20	T8
Shiskine Pl. G20	20	T8
Shiskine St.		
Shiskine St. G20	20	T8
Shore St. G40	52	X15
Shortridge St. G20	21	U9
Shanks St.		
Shortroods Av., Pais. PA3	30	J12
Shortroods Cres., Pais. PA3	30	J12
Shortroods Rd., Pais. PA3	30	J12
Shotts St. G33	39	CC12
Shuna Pl. G20	21	U9
Shuna St. G20	21	U9
Shuttle La. G1	36	W12
George St.		
Shuttle St. G1	36	W12
Shuttle St. (Kilb.), John. PA10	42	A14
Shuttle St., Pais. PA1	46	K14
Sidland Rd. G21	23	Z9
Sidlaw Av. (Barr.) G78	59	M19
Ochil Dr.		
Sidlaw Rd. (Bears.) G61	6	P5
Sielga Pl. G34	40	EE12
Siemens Pl. G21	37	Y11
Siemens St. G21	37	Y11
Sievewright St. (Ruther.) G73	53	Z15
Hunter Rd.		
Silk St., Pais. PA1	30	K13
Silkin Av., Clyde. G81	5	M7
Silverburn St. G33	38	AA12
Silverdale St. G31	53	Z14
Silverfir Pl. G5	52	W14
Silverfir St. G5	52	W14
Silvergrove St. G40	36	X13
Silverwells (Both.) G71	69	HH19
Silverwells Cres. (Both.) G71	69	HH19
Simons Cres., Renf. PA4	17	M9
Simpson Ct. (Udd.) G71	69	GG17
Simpson Ct., Clyde. G81	5	L7
Simpson Gdns. (Barr.) G78	59	L19
Simpson St. G20	21	U10
Simshill Rd. G44	63	V18
Sinclair Av. (Bears.) G61	7	R5
Sinclair Dr. G42	51	U16
Sinclair Gdns. (Bishop.) G64	23	Y8
Sinclair St., Clyde. G81	17	M8
Singer Rd., Clyde. G81	4	K6
Singer St., Clyde. G81	5	L6
Sir Michael Pl., Pais. PA1	46	J14
Sixth Av., Renf. PA4	31	M11
Sixth St. (Udd.) G71	57	GG15
Skaethorn Rd. G20	20	S8
Skaterig La. G13	19	R9
Skaterigg Dr. G13	19	R9
Skaterigg Gdns. G13	19	R9
Skaterigg Rd. G13	19	R9
Crow Rd.		
Skelbo Path G34	40	FF11
Auchingill Rd.		
Skelbo Pl. G34	40	FF11
Skene Rd. G51	34	S13
Skerray Quad. G22	22	W8
Skerray St. G22	22	W8
Skerryvore Pl. G33	38	BB12

Skerryvore Rd. G33	38	BB12
Skibo Dr. (Thorn.) G46	61	R18
Skibo La. (Thorn.) G46	61	R18
Skipness Dr. G51	33	R12
Skirsa Ct. G23	21	V8
Skirsa Pl. G23	21	U8
Skirsa Sq. G23	21	U8
Skirsa St. G23	21	U8
Skirving St. G41	51	U16
Skye Av., Renf. PA4	31	M11
Skye Ct. (Cumb.) G67	70	MM4
Skye Cres. (Old Kil.) G60	4	J5
Skye Cres., Pais. PA2	46	J16
Skye Dr. (Old Kil.) G60	4	J5
Skye Dr. (Cumb.) G67	70	MM4
Skye Gdns. (Bears.) G61	6	P5
Skye Pl. (Cumb.) G67	70	MM4
Skye Rd. (Cumb.) G67	70	MM4
Skye Rd. (Ruther.) G73	65	Z18
Skye St. G20	20	T8
Bantaskin St.		
Slakiewood Av. (Gart.) G69	27	GG8
Slatefield St. G31	37	Y13
Sleads St. G41	35	U13
Sloy St. G22	22	W10
Smeaton Dr. (Bishop.) G64	11	Y6
Smeaton St. G20	21	U9
Smith Cres., Clyde. G81	5	L5
Smith St. G14	33	R11
Smith Ter. (Ruther.) G73	53	Y15
Smithhills St., Pais. PA1	30	K13
Smiths La., Pais. PA3	30	K13
Smithycroft Rd. G33	38	AA11
Smithyends (Cumb.) G67	71	PP1
Snaefell Av. (Ruther.) G73	65	Z18
Snaefell Cres. (Ruther.) G73	65	Z17
Snuff Mill Rd. G44	63	V17
Society St. G31	37	Y13
Soho St. G40	37	Y13
Sollas Pl. G13	18	N8
Solway Pl. (Chry.) G69	26	FF8
Solway Rd. (Bishop.) G64	11	Z7
Solway St. G40	52	X15
Somerford Rd. (Bears.) G61	7	R7
Somerled Av., Pais. PA3	30	K11
Somerset Dr. G3	35	U11
Somerset Pl. Ms. G3	35	U11
Elderslie St.		
Somervell St. (Camb.) G72	66	AA17
Somerville Dr. G42	51	V16
Somerville St., Clyde. G81	5	L7
Sorby St. G31	37	Z13
Sorn St. G40	53	Y14
South Annandale St. G42	51	V15
South Av., Clyde. G81	5	L7
South Av., Pais. PA2	46	K16
South Av., Renf. PA4	17	M10
South Bk. St., Clyde. G81	17	M8
South Brook St., Clyde. G81	4	K6
South Campbell St., Pais. PA2	46	K14
South Carbrain Rd. (Cumb.) G67	71	PP4
South Chester St. G32	38	BB13
South Cotts. G14	33	R11
Curle St.		
South Cft. St., Pais. PA1	30	K13
Lawn St.		
South Crosshill Rd. (Bishop.) G64	11	Y7
South Dean Pk. Av. (Both.) G71	69	HH19
South Douglas St., Clyde. G81	17	M8
South Dr. (Linw.), Pais. PA3	28	E13
South Elgin Pl., Clyde. G81	17	M8
South Elgin St.		
South Elgin St., Clyde. G81	17	M8
South Erskine Pk. (Bears.) G61	7	Q5
South Ex. Ct. G1	36	W12
Queen St.		
South Frederick St. G1	36	W12
South Moraine La. G15	7	Q7
Moraine Av.		
South Muirhead Rd. (Cumb.) G67	71	PP3
South Pk. Av. (Barr.) G78	59	M19
South Pk. Dr., Pais. PA2	46	K15
South Portland St. G5	35	V13
South Scott St. (Bail.) G69	56	EE14
South Spiers Wf. G4	35	V11
South St. G11	33	Q11
South St. G14	18	P10
South Vesalius St. G32	38	BB13
South Vw. (Kirk.) G66	13	CC7
Gadloch Av.		
South Vw. (Blan.) G72	68	FF19
South Vw., Clyde. G81	4	K6
South Wardpark Ct. (Cumb.) G67	71	QQ1
South Wardpark Pl. (Cumb.) G67	71	QQ1
South William St., John. PA5	43	D15
South Woodside Rd. G4	35	U11
South Woodside Rd. G20	21	U10
Southampton Dr. G12	20	S9
Southbank St. G31	37	Z13
Sorby St.		
Southbar Av. G13	18	P8
Southbrae Dr. G13	19	Q9
Southbrae La. G13	19	R9
Milner Rd.		
Southcroft Rd. (Ruther.) G73	52	X15
Southcroft St. G51	34	S12
Southdeen Av. G15	6	P6
Southdeen Rd. G15	6	P6
Southend Rd., Clyde. G81	5	L5
Southern Av. (Ruther.) G73	65	Y17
Southerness Dr. (Cumb.) G68	71	PP1
Dornoch Way		
Southesk Av. (Bishop.) G64	10	X7
Southesk Gdns. (Bishop.) G64	10	X6
Southfield Av., Pais. PA2	46	K16
Southfield Cres. G53	49	Q16
Southfield Rd. (Cumb.) G68	70	MM3
Southhill Av. (Ruther.) G73	65	Z17
Southinch Av. G14	18	N9
Southinch La. G14	18	N9
Tweedvale Av.		
Southlea Av. (Thorn.) G46	62	S18
Southloch St. G21	22	X10
Southmuir Pl. G20	20	T9
Southpark Av. G12	34	T11
Southpark Av. G12	21	U10
Glasgow St.		
Southpark Ter. G12	35	U11
Southpark Av.		
Southview Ct. (Bishop.) G64	22	X8
Southview Dr. (Bears.) G61	7	Q5
Southview Pl. (Gart.) G69	27	GG9
Southview Ter. (Bishop.) G64	22	X8
Southwold Rd., Pais. PA1	32	N13
Southwood Dr. G44	64	W17
Spateston Rd., John. PA5	43	C16
Spean St. G44	51	V16
Speirs Rd., John. PA5	44	E14
Speirshall Clo. G14	18	N9
Speirshall Ter. G14	18	N9
Spence St. G20	20	T8
Spencer Dr., Pais. PA2	44	F16
Spencer St. G13	19	R8
Spencer St., Clyde. G81	5	L6
Spey Av., Pais. PA2	45	G15
Spey Dr., Renf. PA4	32	N11
Almond Av.		
Spey Pl., John. PA5	43	C16
Spey Rd. (Bears.) G61	7	Q7
Spey St. G33	38	AA12
Spiers Gro. (Thorn.) G46	61	R18
Spiers Pl. (Linw.), Pais. PA3	28	E12
Spiers Rd. (Bears.) G61	8	S6
Spiersbridge Av. (Thorn.) G46	61	R18
Spiersbridge La. (Thorn.) G46	61	R18
Spiersbridge Rd. (Thorn.) G46	61	R19
Spiersbridge Ter. (Thorn.) G46	61	R18
Spiersfield Gdns., Pais. PA2	46	J14
Spindlehowe Rd. (Udd.) G71	69	GG17
Spinners Gdns., Pais. PA2	45	H14
Spinners Row, John. PA5	43	C15
Spittal Rd. (Ruther.) G73	64	X18
Spittal Ter. (Camb.) G72	68	EE19
Spoolers Rd., Pais. PA1	46	J14
Spoutmouth G1	36	W13
Spring La. G5	52	W14
Lawmoor St.		
Springbank Rd., Pais. PA3	30	J12
Springbank St. G20	21	U10
Springbank Ter., Pais. PA3	30	J12
Springboig Av. G32	39	CC13
Springboig Rd. G32	39	CC12
Springburn Rd. G21	22	X9
Springburn Rd. (Bishop.) G64	22	X9
Springburn Way G21	22	X10
Springcroft Av. (Bail.) G69	40	EE13
Springcroft Cres. (Bail.) G69	40	EE13
Springcroft Gdns. (Bail.) G69	40	FF13
Springcroft Gro. (Bail.) G69	40	EE13
Springcroft Rd. (Bail.) G69	40	FF13
Springcroft Wynd (Bail.) G69	40	EE13
Springdale Dr., Pais. PA2	45	G15
Springfield Av. (Bishop.) G64	23	Y8
Springfield Av. (Udd.) G71	69	GG17
Springfield Av., Pais. PA1	47	M14
Springfield Ct. G1	36	W12
Buchanan St.		
Springfield Cres. (Bishop.) G64	23	Y8
Springfield Cres. (Udd.) G71	69	GG17
Springfield Dr. (Barr.) G78	60	N19
Springfield Gro. (Barr.) G78	59	M19
Springfield Pk., John. PA5	44	E15
Springfield Pk. Rd. (Ruther.) G73	65	Z17
Springfield Quay G5	35	U13
Springfield Rd. G31	53	Z14
Springfield Rd. G40	53	Y14
Springfield Rd. (Bishop.) G64	11	Y7
Springfield Rd. (Cumb.) G67	71	PP2
Springfield Sq. (Bishop.) G64	23	Y8
Springhill Dr. N. (Bail.) G69	40	EE12
Springhill Dr. S. (Bail.) G69	40	EE12
Springhill Fm. Gro. (Bail.) G69	40	EE13
Springhill Fm. Pl. (Bail.) G69	40	EE13
Springhill Fm. Rd. (Bail.) G69	40	EE13
Springhill Fm. Way (Bail.) G69	40	EE13
Springhill Gdns. G41	51	U15
Springhill Parkway (Bail.) G69	40	EE13
Springhill Rd. (Bail.) G69	39	DD13
Springhill Rd. (Barr.) G78	59	L19
Springkell Av. G41	50	T14
Springkell Dr. G41	50	S14
Springkell Gdns. G41	50	T15
Springkell Gate G41	50	T15
Springside Pl. G15	6	P6
Springvale Ter. G21	22	X10
Hillkirk Pl.		
Spruce Av., John. PA5	44	E15
Spruce Dr. (Kirk.) G66	12	BB5
Spruce Dr. (Camb.) G72	67	DD18
Spruce Rd. (Cumb.) G67	71	QQ2
Spruce St. G22	22	W9
Spruce Way (Camb.) G72	67	DD18
Spynie Pl. (Bishop.) G64	11	Z7
Squire St. G14	33	R11
Stable Gro., Pais. PA1	45	H14
Staffa Av., Renf. PA4	31	M11
Staffa Dr., Pais. PA2	46	K16
Staffa Rd. (Camb.) G72	66	AA18
Staffa St. G31	37	Y13
Staffa Ter. (Camb.) G72	66	AA18
Staffin Dr. G23	8	T7
Staffin St. G23	9	U7
Stafford St. G4	36	W11
Stag St. G51	34	T12
Stair St. G20	21	U10
Stamford St. G31	37	Y13
Stamford St. G40	37	Y13
Stampernald Gdns. (Clark.) G76	63	U19
Stanalane St. (Thorn.) G46	61	R18
Standburn Rd. G21	23	Z8
Stanely Av., Pais. PA2	45	H15
Stanely Ct., Pais. PA2	45	H16
Stanely Cres., Pais. PA2	45	H16
Stanely Dr., Pais. PA2	46	J15
Stanely Rd., Pais. PA2	46	J15
Stanford St., Clyde. G81	5	M7
Stanhope Dr. (Ruther.) G73	65	Z17
Stanley Dr. (Bishop.) G64	11	Y6
Stanley Pl. (Blan.) G72	68	FF19
Stanley St. G41	35	U13

Street	Page	Grid
Tiree Gdns. (Bears.) G61	6	P5
Tiree Pl. (Old Kil.) G60	4	J5
Tiree Rd. (Cumb.) G67	70	MM4
Tiree St. G21	37	Z11
Tirry Way, Renf. PA4	32	N11
Morriston Cres.		
Titwood Rd. G41	50	T15
Tiverton Av. G32	55	CC14
Tobago Pl. G40	36	X13
Tobago St. G40	36	X13
Tobermory Rd. (Ruther.) G73	65	Z18
Todburn Dr., Pais. PA2	46	K16
Todd St. G31	37	Z12
Todholm Rd., Pais. PA2	47	L15
Todholm Ter., Pais. PA2	47	L15
Tofthill Av. (Bishop.) G64	10	X7
Tofthill Gdns. (Bishop.) G64	10	X7
Toll La. G51	34	T13
Paisley Rd. W.		
Tollcross Pk. Gdns. G32	54	AA14
Tollcross Rd.		
Tollcross Pk. Vw. G32	54	AA14
Tollcross Rd. G31	37	Z13
Tollcross Rd. G32	37	Z13
Tolsta St. G23	9	U7
Tontine La. G1	36	W13
Bell St.		
Tontine Pl. (Ruther.) G73	66	AA18
Toppersfield (Mill.Pk.), John. PA10	43	C15
Torbreck St. G52	33	R13
Torbrex Rd. (Cumb.) G67	71	PP3
Torburn Av. (Giff.) G46	62	S18
Tordene Path (Cumb.) G68	70	MM2
Torgyle St. G23	8	T7
Tormore St. G51	33	Q13
Tormusk Dr. G45	65	Y18
Tormusk Gdns. G45	65	Y18
Tormusk Gro. G45	65	Y18
Tormusk Rd. G45	65	Y18
Torness St. G11	34	T11
Torogay Pl. G22	22	X8
Torogay St. G22	22	W8
Torogay Ter. G22	22	W8
Toronto Wk. G32	55	CC16
Torphin Cres. G32	38	BB13
Torphin Wk. G32	38	BB13
Torr Rd. (Bishop.) G64	11	Z7
Torr St. G22	22	W10
Torran Dr., Ersk. PA8	16	K8
Torran Rd. G33	39	DD12
Torrance St. (Torrance) G64	11	Z5
Torrance St. G21	22	X10
Springburn Way		
Torridon Av. G41	50	S14
Torrin Rd. G23	8	T7
Torrington Av. (Giff.) G46	62	S19
Torrington Cres. G32	55	CC14
Torrisdale St. G42	51	U15
Torryburn Rd. G21	23	Z10
Torwood La. (Chry.) G69	15	HH7
Burnbrae Av.		
Toryglen Rd. (Ruther.) G73	52	X16
Toryglen St. G5	52	W15
Toward Ct. (Blan.) G72	69	GG19
Toward Rd. G33	39	CC12
Tower Av. (Barr.) G78	59	M18
Tower Cres., Renf. PA4	31	L11
Tower Dr., Renf. PA4	31	L11
Tower Pl. G20	20	T9
Glenfinnan Dr.		
Tower Pl., John. PA5	43	D15
Tower Rd., John. PA5	43	D15
Tower St. G41	35	U13
Tower Ter., Pais. PA1	46	J14
Towerhill Rd. G13	7	Q7
Towerhill Ter. G21	23	Y10
Broomfield Rd.		
Towerside Cres. G53	48	P15
Towerside Rd. G53	48	P15
Towie Pl. (Udd.) G71	69	GG17
Townhead Rd. (Gart.) G69	41	HH11
Townhead Ter., Pais. PA1	46	J14
Townmill Rd. G31	36	X12
Townsend St. G4	36	W11
Tradeston St. G5	35	V13
Trafalgar St. G40	52	X14
Trafalgar St., Clyde. G81	4	K6
Trainard Av. G32	54	AA14
Tranent Pl. G33	38	AA12
Traquair Av., Pais. PA2	45	G16
Traquair Dr. G52	48	P14
Treeburn Av. (Giff.) G46	62	S18
Trees Pk. Av. (Barr.) G78	59	L18
Trefoil Av. G41	50	T16
Tresta Rd. G23	21	V8
Trident Way, Renf. PA4	31	M11
Newmains Rd.		
Trinity Av. G52	49	Q14
Trinity Dr. (Camb.) G72	67	CC18
Trinley Brae G13	7	Q7
Trinley Rd. G13	7	Q7
Trondra Path G34	39	DD12
Trondra Pl. G34	39	DD12
Trondra Rd. G34	39	DD12
Trongate G1	36	W13
Troon Gdns. (Cumb.) G68	71	PP1
Troon St. G40	53	Y14
Trossachs Ct. G20	21	V10
Trossachs St.		
Trossachs Rd. (Ruther.) G73	65	Z19
Trossachs St. G20	21	V10
Troubridge Av. (Mill.Pk.), John. PA10	42	B15
Troubridge Cres. (Mill.Pk.), John. PA10	42	B15
Truce Rd. G13	18	P8
Truro Av. (Chry.) G69	15	GG6
Tryst Rd. (Cumb.) G67	70	NN3
Tudor La. S. G14	19	Q10
Orleans Av.		
Tudor Rd. G14	19	R10
Tudor St. (Bail.) G69	55	DD14
Tullis Ct. G40	52	X14
Tullis St. G40	52	X14
Tulloch St. G44	63	V17
Tullochard Pl. (Ruther.) G73	65	Z18
Tummel St. G33	38	AA11
Tummel Way, Pais. PA2	45	G15
Tunnel St. G3	35	U12
Finnieston St.		
Turnberry Av. G11	20	S10
Turnberry Dr. (Ruther.) G73	64	X17
Turnberry Gdns. (Cumb.) G68	70	NN1
Turnberry Pl. (Ruther.) G73	64	X17
Turnberry Rd. G11	20	S10
Turnberry Wynd (Both.) G71	69	GG18
Turnbull St. G1	36	W13
Turner Rd. G21	36	X11
Turner Rd., Pais. PA3	30	K12
Turners Av., Pais. PA1	45	H14
Turnlaw Rd. (Camb.) G72	66	BB19
Turnlaw St. G5	52	W14
Turret Cres. G13	19	Q8
Turret Rd. G13	19	Q8
Turriff St. G5	51	V14
Tweed Av., Pais. PA2	45	G15
Tweed Cres. G33	38	AA11
Tweed Cres., Renf. PA4	18	N10
Tweed Dr. (Bears.) G61	7	Q6
Tweed Pl., John. PA5	43	C16
Tweedsmuir (Bishop.) G64	11	Z7
Tweedsmuir Rd. G52	48	P14
Tweedvale Av. G14	18	N9
Tweedvale Pl. G14	18	N9
Twinlaw St. G34	40	FF11
Tylney Rd., Pais. PA1	31	M13
Tyndrum Rd. (Bears.) G61	8	S5
Tyndrum St. G4	36	W11
Tyne St. G14	33	Q11
Tynecastle Cres. G32	38	BB12
Tynecastle Pl. G32	38	BB12
Tynecastle St. G32	38	BB12
Tynwald Av. (Ruther.) G73	65	Z18

U

Street	Page	Grid
Uddingston Rd. (Both.) G71	69	HH18
Uig Pl. G33	39	DD13
Uist Cres. (Stepps) G33	25	DD10
Uist St. G51	33	R12
Ulundi Rd., John. PA5	43	C15
Ulva St. G52	33	R13
Unden Pl. G13	19	R8
Underwood La., Pais. PA1	30	J13
Underwood Rd. (Ruther.) G73	65	Z17
Underwood Rd., Pais. PA3	30	J13
Underwood St. G41	51	U16
Tantallon Rd.		
Union Pl. G1	35	V12
Gordon St.		
Union St. G1	35	V12
Union St., Clyde. G81	17	M8
Union St., Pais. PA2	46	K15
Unity Pl. G4	35	V11
St. Peters St.		
University Av. G12	34	T11
University Gdns. G12	34	T11
University of Glasgow G12	34	T11
University Pl. G12	34	T11
University Av.		
Unsted Pl., Pais. PA1	46	K14
Uphall Pl. G33	38	AA12
Upland Rd. G14	19	Q10
Upper Bourtree Ct. (Ruther.) G73	65	Z18
Upper Bourtree Dr.		
Upper Bourtree Dr. (Ruther.) G73	65	Y18
Upper Glenburn Rd. (Bears.) G61	7	Q5
Ure Pl. G4	36	W12
Montrose St.		
Urquhart Cres., Renf. PA4	31	M11
Urrdale Rd. G41	34	S13
Usmore Pl. G33	39	DD13

V

Street	Page	Grid
Vaila Pl. G23	21	U8
Vaila St.		
Vaila St. G23	21	U8
Vale Wk. (Bishop.) G64	23	Z8
Valetta Pl., Clyde. G81	4	J6
Valeview Ter. G42	51	V16
Vallantine Cres. (Udd.) G71	57	HH16
Vallay St. G22	22	W8
Valley Vw. (Camb.) G72	67	CC17
Birch Dr.		
Valleyfield St. G21	22	X10
Ayr St.		
Van St. G31	37	Z13
Vancouver La. G14	19	Q10
Vancouver Rd.		
Vancouver Pl., Clyde. G81	4	J6
Vancouver Rd. G14	19	Q10
Vanguard St., Clyde. G81	5	M7
Vanguard Way, Renf. PA4	31	M11
Varna La. G14	19	R10
Varna Rd. G14	19	R10
Vasart Pl. G20	21	U10
Caithness St.		
Veitches Ct., Clyde. G81	5	L5
Veitch's Ct., Clyde. G81	4	K5
Dumbarton Rd.		
Vennacher Rd., Renf. PA4	17	L10
Vennard Gdns. G41	51	U15
Vere St. G22	22	W10
Vermont Av. (Ruther.) G73	53	Y16
Vermont St. G41	35	U13
Vernon Dr. (Linw.), Pais. PA3	28	E13
Verona Av. G14	19	Q10
Verona Gdns. G14	19	Q10
Verona La. G14	19	Q10
Verona Av.		
Vesalius St. G32	38	BB13
Vicarfield Pl. G51	34	S12
Vicarfield St.		
Vicarfield St. G51	34	S12
Vicarland Pl. (Camb.) G72	66	BB18
Vicarland Rd. (Camb.) G72	66	BB17
Vicars Wk. (Camb.) G72	66	BB17
Victoria Av. (Barr.) G78	59	L18
Victoria Bri. G1	36	W13
Victoria Bri. G5	36	W13
Victoria Circ. G12	20	T10
Victoria Cres. G12	20	T10
Dowanside Rd.		
Victoria Cres. (Barr.) G78	59	L18
Victoria Cres. La. G12	20	T10
Victoria Cres. Rd.		
Victoria Cres. Pl. G12	20	T10
Bowmont Ter.		
Victoria Cres. Rd. G12	20	T10
Victoria Cross G42	51	V15
Victoria Rd.		
Victoria Dr. (Barr.) G78	59	M18
Victoria Dr., Renf. PA4	17	L10

Victoria Dr. E., Renf. PA4   31   M11
Victoria Gdns. (Barr.)   59   L18
  G78
Victoria Gdns., Pais. PA2   46   J15
Victoria Gro. (Barr.) G78   59   L18
Victoria Pk. Cor. G14   19   Q10
Victoria Pk. Dr. N. G14   19   R10
Victoria Pk. Dr. S. G14   19   Q10
Victoria Pk. Gdns. N. G11   19   R10
Victoria Pk. Gdns. S. G11   19   R10
Victoria Pk. La. N. G14   19   Q10
Victoria Pk. La. S. G14   19   Q10
  Westland Dr.
Victoria Pk. St. G14   19   Q10
Victoria Pl. (Ruther.) G73   53   Y16
  Greenbank St.
Victoria Pl. (Barr.) G78   59   M18
Victoria Rd. (Stepps) G33   25   CC9
Victoria Rd. G42   51   V15
Victoria Rd. (Lenzie) G66   13   CC6
Victoria Rd. (Ruther.) G73   65   Y17
Victoria Rd. (Barr.) G78   59   L18
Victoria Rd., Pais. PA2   46   J15
Victoria St. (Ruther.) G73   53   Y16
Victory Dr. (Kilb.), John.   42   B14
  PA10
  Glentyan Av.
Viewbank (Thorn.) G46   62   S18
Viewfield Av. (Bishop.) G64   22   X8
Viewfield Av. (Lenzie) G66   13   CC5
Viewfield Av. (Bail.) G69   39   DD13
Viewfield Av. (Blan.) G72   69   GG19
Viewfield Dr. (Bishop.) G64   22   X8
Viewfield Dr. (Bail.) G69   39   DD13
Viewfield La. G12   35   U11
  Gibson St.
Viewfield Rd. (Bishop.) G64   22   X8
Viewfield Rd., Coat. ML5   57   HH14
Viewfield Ter. G12   35   U11
  Southpark Av.
Viewglen Ct. G45   64   W19
Viewmount Dr. G20   20   T8
Viewpark Av. G31   37   Y12
Viewpark Dr. (Ruther.) G73   65   Y17
Viewpark Gdns., Renf. PA4   31   L11
Viewpoint Pl. G21   22   X9
Viewpoint Rd. G21   22   X9
Viking Rd. (Thorn.) G46   61   R18
Viking Way, Renf. PA4   31   M11
  Vanguard Way
Villafield Av. (Bishop.) G64   11   Y6
Villafield Dr. (Bishop.) G64   11   Y6
Villafield Ln. (Bishop.) G64   11   Y6
Village Gdns. (Blan.) G72   69   GG19
Village Rd. (Camb.) G72   67   DD17
Villiers Ct. G31   36   X13
  Sword St.
Vine St. G31   34   S11
Vinicombe La. G12   20   T10
  Vinicombe St.
Vinicombe St. G12   20   T10
Vintner St. G4   36   W11
Violet St., Pais. PA1   47   L14
Virginia Bldgs. G1   36   W12
  Virginia St.
Virginia Ct. G1   36   W12
  Virginia St.
Virginia Pl. G1   36   W12
Virginia St. G1   36   W12
Viscount Av., Renf. PA4   31   M11
Viscount Gate (Both.) G71   69   GG17
Voil Dr. G44   63   V18
Vorlich Ct. (Barr.) G78   59   M19
Vulcan St. G21   22   X10
  Ayr St.

W

Waddell Ct. G5   36   W13
Waddell St. G5   52   W14
Waldemar Rd. G13   19   Q8
Waldo St. G13   19   R8
Walker Ct. G11   34   S11
  Walker St.
Walker Dr. (Elder.), John.   44   E15
  PA5
Walker Path (Udd.) G71   57   HH16
Walker Sq. G20   20   T8
  Bantaskin St.
Walker St. G11   34   S11
Walker St., Pais. PA1   46   J14
Walkerburn Rd. G52   48   P14

Walkinshaw Cres., Pais. PA3   29   H13
  Ferguslie Pk. Av.
Walkinshaw Rd., Renf. PA4   16   J10
Walkinshaw St. G40   53   Y14
Walkinshaw St., John. PA5   43   D14
Walkinshaw Way, Pais. PA3   30   J12
  Broomdyke Way
Wallace Av. (Elder.), John.   44   F14
  PA5
Wallace Pl. (Blan.) G72   69   GG19
Wallace Rd., Renf. PA4   31   L11
Wallace St. G5   35   V13
Wallace St. (Ruther.) G73   53   Y16
Wallace St., Clyde. G81   17   L8
Wallace St., Pais. PA3   30   K13
Wallacewell Cres. G21   23   Y9
Wallacewell Pl. G21   23   Y9
Wallacewell Quad. G21   23   Z9
Wallacewell Rd. G21   23   Y9
Wallbrae Rd. (Cumb.) G67   71   PP4
Wallneuk, Pais. PA1   30   K13
  Incle St.
Wallneuk Rd., Pais. PA3   30   K13
Walls St. G1   36   W12
Walmer Cres. G51   34   T13
Walmer Ter. G51   34   T13
  Paisley Rd. W.
Walnut Cres. G22   22   W9
Walnut Cres., John. PA5   44   E15
Walnut Dr. (Kirk.) G66   12   BB5
Walnut Pl. G22   22   W9
Walnut Rd. G22   22   W9
Walter St. G31   37   Z12
Walton Ct. (Giff.) G46   62   T19
Walton St. G41   51   U16
Walton St. (Barr.) G78   59   M18
Wamba Av. G13   19   R8
Wamba Pl. G13   19   R8
  Wamba Av.
Wandilla Av., Clyde. G81   5   M7
Wanlock St. G51   34   S12
Warden Rd. G13   19   Q8
Wardhill Rd. G21   23   Y9
Wardhouse Rd., Pais. PA2   46   J16
Wardie Path G33   39   DD12
Wardie Pl. G33   40   EE12
Wardie Rd. G33   40   EE12
Wardie Rd. G34   40   EE12
Wardlaw Av. (Ruther.) G73   53   Y16
Wardlaw Dr. (Ruther.) G73   53   Y16
Wardlaw Rd. (Bears.) G61   7   R7
Wardpark Rd. (Cumb.) G67   71   QQ1
Wardrop St. G51   34   S12
Wardrop St., Pais. PA1   46   K14
Ware Path G34   40   EE12
Ware Rd. G34   39   DD12
Warilda Av., Clyde. G81   5   M7
Warnock St. G31   36   X12
  Wishart St.
Warp La. G3   35   U12
  Argyle St.
Warren St. G42   51   V15
Warriston Cres. G33   37   Z12
Warriston Pl. G32   38   BB12
Warriston St. G33   37   Z12
Warroch St. G3   35   U12
Washington Rd., Pais. PA3   30   K12
Washington St. G3   35   V13
Water Brae, Pais. PA1   46   K14
  Forbes Pl.
Water Rd. (Barr.) G78   59   M18
Water Row G51   34   S12
Waterfoot Av. G53   49   Q16
Waterford Rd. (Giff.) G46   62   S18
Waterloo La. G2   35   V12
  Waterloo St.
Waterloo St. G2   35   V12
Watermill Av. (Lenzie) G66   13   CC6
Waterside Gdns. (Camb.)   67   DD18
  G72
Waterside La. (Mill.Pk.),   43   C15
  John. PA10
Waterside St. G5   52   W14
Waterside Ter. (Mill.Pk.),   43   C15
  John. PA10
  Kilbarchan Rd.
Watling St. (Udd.) G71   57   GG16
Watson Av. (Ruther.) G73   52   X16
Watson Av. (Linw.), Pais.   28   E13
  PA3
Watson St. G1   36   W13
Watson St. (Udd.) G71   69   GG17

Watt Low Av. (Ruther.) G73   64   X17
Watt Rd. G52   32   N12
Watt St. G5   35   U13
Waukglen Av. G53   60   P19
Waukglen Cres. G53   61   Q18
Waukglen Dr. G53   60   P18
Waukglen Gdns. G53   60   P19
Waukglen Path G53   60   P18
  Waukglen Dr.
Waukglen Rd. G53   60   P18
Waulkmill Av. (Barr.) G78   59   M18
Waulkmill St. (Thorn.)   61   R18
  G46
Waverley, Clyde. G81   5   M7
  Onslow Rd.
Waverley Ct. (Both.) G71   69   HH19
Waverley Cres. (Cumb.) G67   70   MM4
Waverley Dr. (Ruther.) G73   53   Z16
Waverley Gdns. G41   51   U15
Waverley Gdns. (Elder.),   44   F15
  John. PA5
Waverley Rd., Pais. PA2   45   G16
Waverley St. G41   51   U15
Waverley Ter. G31   37   Y13
  Whitevale St.
Waverley Way, Pais. PA2   45   G16
  Waverley Rd.
Weardale La. G33   39   CC12
Weardale St. G33   39   CC12
Weaver La. (Kilb.), John.   42   B14
  PA10
  Glentyan Av.
Weaver St. G4   36   W12
Weaver Ter., Pais. PA2   47   L14
Weavers Av., Pais. PA2   45   H14
Weavers Gate, Pais. PA1   45   H14
Weavers Rd., Pais. PA2   45   H14
Webster St. G40   53   Y14
Webster St., Clyde. G81   18   N8
Wedderlea Dr. G52   32   P13
Weensmoor Pl. G53   60   P18
Weensmoor Rd. G53   60   P17
Weeple Dr. (Linw.), Pais.   28   E13
  PA3
Weighhouse Clo., Pais. PA1   46   K14
Weir Av. (Barr.) G78   59   M19
Weir St., Pais. PA3   30   K13
Weirwood Av. (Bail.) G69   55   DD14
Weirwood Gdns. (Bail.) G69   55   DD14
Welbeck Rd. G53   60   P17
Welfare Av. (Camb.) G72   67   CC18
Well Grn. G43   50   T16
Well Rd. (Kilb.), John. PA10   42   B14
Well St. G40   36   X13
Well St., Pais. PA1   30   J13
Wellbank Pl. (Udd.) G71   69   GG17
  Church St.
Wellbrae Ter. (Chry.) G69   15   GG7
Wellcroft Pl. G5   51   V14
Wellfield Av. (Giff.) G46   62   S18
Wellfield St. G21   22   X10
Wellhouse Cres. G33   39   DD12
Wellhouse Gdns. G33   39   DD12
Wellhouse Path G34   39   DD12
Wellhouse Rd. G33   39   DD12
Wellington La. G2   35   V12
  West Campbell St.
Wellington Pl., Clyde. G81   4   J6
Wellington Rd. (Bishop.)   11   Z6
  G64
Wellington St. G2   35   V12
Wellington St., Pais. PA3   30   J13
  Caledonia St.
Wellington Way, Renf. PA4   31   M11
  Tiree Av.
Wellmeadow Rd. G43   62   S17
Wellmeadow St., Pais. PA1   46   J14
Wellpark St. G31   36   X12
Wells St., Clyde. G81   4   K6
Wellshot Dr. (Camb.) G72   66   AA17
Wellshot Rd. G32   54   AA14
Wellside Dr. (Camb.) G72   67   CC18
Wemyss Gdns. (Bail.) G69   56   EE14
Wendur Way, Pais. PA3   30   J12
  Abbotsburn Way
Wenlock Rd., Pais. PA2   46   K15
Wentworth Dr. G23   9   U7
West Av. (Stepps) G33   25   CC9
West Av. (Udd.) G71   69   HH17
West Av., Renf. PA4   17   M10
West Brae, Pais. PA1   46   J14
West Campbell St. G2   35   V12

Name	Page	Ref
West Campbell St., Pais. PA1	45	H14
West Chapelton Av. (Bears.) G61	7	R6
West Chapelton Cres. (Bears.) G61	7	R6
West Chapelton Dr. (Bears.) G61	7	R6
West Chapelton La. (Bears.) G61	7	R6
West Chapelton Av.		
West Coats Rd. (Camb.) G72	66	AA18
West Cotts. (Gart.) G69	26	EE10
West Ct., Clyde. G81	4	K6
Littleholm		
West End Pk. St. G3	35	V12
West George La. G2	35	V12
West Campbell St.		
West George St. G2	35	V12
West Graham St. G4	35	V11
West Greenhill Pl. G3	35	U12
West La., Pais. PA1	45	H14
West Lo. Rd., Renf. PA4	17	L10
West Nile St. G1	35	V12
West Princes St. G4	35	U11
West Regent La. G2	35	V12
Renfield St.		
West Regent St. G2	35	V12
West Rd. (Kilb.), John. PA10	42	B14
West St. G5	51	V14
West St., Clyde. G81	18	N8
West St., Pais. PA1	46	J14
West Thomson St., Clyde. G81	5	L6
West Whitby St. G31	53	Z14
Westbank Ct. G12	35	U11
Gibson St.		
Westbank La. G12	35	U11
Gibson St.		
Westbank Quad. G12	35	U11
Gibson St.		
Westbank Ter. G12	35	U11
Gibson St.		
Westbourne Cres. (Bears.) G61	7	Q5
Westbourne Dr. (Bears.) G61	7	Q5
Westbourne Gdns. La. G12	20	T10
Lorraine Rd.		
Westbourne Gdns. N. G12	20	T10
Westbourne Gdns. S. G12	20	T10
Westbourne Gdns. W. G12	20	T10
Westbourne Rd. G12	20	S10
Westbourne Ter. La. G12	20	S10
Westbourne Dr.		
Westbrae Dr. G14	19	R10
Westburn Av. (Camb.) G72	67	CC17
Westburn Av., Pais. PA3	29	H13
Westburn Cres. (Ruther.) G73	52	X16
Westburn Dr. (Camb.) G72	66	BB17
Westburn Fm. Rd. (Camb.) G72	66	BB17
Westburn Rd. (Camb.) G72	66	BB18
Westburn Way, Pais. PA3	29	H13
Westburn Av.		
Westcastle Ct. G45	64	W18
Westcastle Cres. G45	64	W18
Westcastle Gdns. G45	64	W18
Westcastle Gro. G45	64	W18
Westclyffe St. G41	51	U15
Westend (Bears.) G61	8	S7
Maryhill Rd.		
Wester Cleddens Rd. (Bishop.) G64	11	Y7
Wester Common Dr. G22	21	V10
Wester Common Rd. G22	21	V10
Wester Common Ter. G22	21	V10
Wester Rd. G32	55	CC14
Westerburn St. G32	38	AA13
Westercraigs G31	36	X12
Westergreens Av. (Kirk.) G66	13	CC5
Parkburn Av.		
Westerhill Rd. (Bishop.) G64	11	Y6
Westerhill St. G22	22	W10
Westerhouse Rd. G34	40	EE11
Westerkirk Dr. G23	9	U7
Westerlands G12	20	S9
Ascot Av.		
Western Av. (Ruther.) G73	52	X16
Western Isles Rd. (Old Kil.) G60	4	J5
Western Rd. (Camb.) G72	66	AA18
Westerton Av. (Bears.) G61	19	R8
Westfield Av. (Ruther.) G73	52	X16
Westfield Cres. (Bears.) G61	7	R7
Westfield Dr. G52	32	P13
Westfield Dr. (Bears.) G61	7	R7
Westfield Rd. (Thorn.) G46	61	R19
Westfield Vills. (Ruther.) G73	52	X16
Westfields (Bishop.) G64	10	X6
Westhorn Dr. G32	54	BB15
Westhouse Av. (Ruther.) G73	52	X16
Westhouse Gdns. (Ruther.) G73	52	X16
Westknowe Gdns. (Ruther.) G73	65	Y17
Westland Dr. G14	19	Q10
Westland Dr. La. G14	19	Q10
Westland Dr.		
Westlands (Bishop.) G64	10	X6
Westlands Gdns., Pais. PA2	46	J15
Westminster Gdns. G12	20	T10
Kersland St.		
Westminster Ter. G3	35	U12
North Claremont St.		
Westmoreland St. G42	51	V15
Westmuir Pl. (Ruther.) G73	52	X16
Westmuir St. G31	37	Z13
Westpark Dr., Pais. PA3	29	H13
Westray Circ. G22	22	W9
Westray Ct. (Cumb.) G67	70	NN4
Westray Pl. G22	22	W8
Westray Pl. (Bishop.) G64	11	Z7
Ronaldsay Dr.		
Westray Rd. (Cumb.) G67	70	MM4
Westray Sq. G22	22	W8
Westray St. G22	22	W8
Westside Gdns. G11	34	S11
Partickhill Rd.		
Westwood Av. (Giff.) G46	62	S18
Westwood Gdns., Pais. PA3	29	H13
Westwood Quad., Clyde. G81	5	M7
Westwood Rd. G43	62	S17
Weymouth Dr. G12	20	S9
Whamflet Av. (Bail.) G69	40	FF12
Wheatfield Rd. (Bears.) G61	7	Q7
Wheatlands Dr. (Kilb.), John. PA10	42	B14
Wheatlands Fm. Rd. (Kilb.), John. PA10	42	B14
Wheatley Ct. G32	38	BB13
Wheatley Dr. G32	38	BB13
Wheatley Pl. G32	38	BB13
Wheatley Rd. G32	38	BB13
Whin Av. (Barr.) G78	59	L18
Whin St., Clyde. G81	5	L6
Whinfield Av. (Camb.) G72	54	AA16
Whinfield Path G53	60	P18
Whinfield Rd. G53	60	P18
Whinhill Rd. G53	48	P14
Whinhill Rd., Pais. PA2	47	L15
Whins Rd. G41	50	T15
Whirlow Gdns. (Bail.) G69	40	EE13
Whirlow Rd. (Bail.) G69	40	EE13
Whistlefield Ct. (Bears.) G61	7	R6
Whitacres Path G53	60	P18
Whitacres Pl. G53	60	P18
Whitacres Rd. G53	60	P18
Whitburn St. G32	38	AA12
White St. G11	34	S11
White St., Clyde. G81	17	M8
Whitecraigs Pl. G23	21	U9
Whitefield Av. (Camb.) G72	66	BB18
Whitefield Rd. G51	34	T13
Whiteford Rd., Pais. PA2	47	L15
Whitehall Ct. G3	35	U12
Whitehall St. G3	35	U12
Whitehaugh Av., Pais. PA1	31	L13
Whitehaugh Cres. G53	60	P18
Whitehaugh Dr., Pais. PA1	31	L13
Whitehaugh Path G53	60	P18
Whitehaugh Rd. G53	60	P18
Whitehill Av. (Stepps) G33	25	CC9
Whitehill Av. (Cumb.) G68	70	MM3
Whitehill Fm. Rd. (Stepps) G33	25	CC9
Whitehill Gdns. G31	37	Y12
Garthland Dr.		
Whitehill La. (Bears.) G61	7	Q6
Whitehill Rd.		
Whitehill Rd. (Stepps) G33	25	CC8
Whitehill Rd. (Bears.) G61	7	Q5
Whitehill Rd. (Kirk.) G66	25	CC8
Whitehill St. G31	37	Y12
Whitehurst (Bears.) G61	7	Q5
Whitehurst Pk. (Bears.) G61	7	Q5
Whitekirk Pl. G15	6	P7
Whitelaw St. G20	20	T8
Whiteloans (Both.) G71	69	HH18
Wordsworth Way		
Whitemoss Av. G44	63	U18
Whitesbridge Av., Pais. PA3	45	G14
Whitesbridge Clo., Pais. PA3	45	G14
Whitestone Av. (Cumb.) G68	70	MM2
Dungoil Av.		
Whitevale St. G31	37	Y13
Whithope Rd. G53	60	N18
Whithope Ter. G53	60	N18
Whithorn Cres. (Mood.) G69	15	GG6
Whitlawburn Av. (Camb.) G72	66	AA18
Whitlawburn Rd. (Camb.) G72	66	AA18
Whitlawburn Ter. (Camb.) G72	66	AA18
Whitriggs Rd. G53	60	N17
Whitslade St. G34	40	EE11
Whittingehame Dr. G12	19	R9
Whittingehame Dr. G12	19	R9
Whittingehame Gdns. G12	20	S9
Whittingehame La. G13	19	R9
Whittingehame Dr.		
Whittliemuir Av. G44	63	U18
Whitton Dr. (Giff.) G46	62	T18
Whitton St. G20	20	T8
Whitworth Dr., Clyde. G81	5	L7
Whitworth St. G20	21	V9
Whyte Av. (Camb.) G72	66	AA17
Wickets, The, Pais. PA1	47	L14
Wigton St. G4	21	V10
Wigtoun Pl. (Cumb.) G67	71	PP2
Wilderness Brae (Cumb.) G67	71	PP2
Wilfred Av. G13	19	Q8
Wilkie Rd. (Udd.) G71	69	HH18
William St. G2	35	V12
William St. G3	35	U12
William St., Clyde. G81	5	L5
William St., John. PA5	43	D14
William St., Pais. PA1	46	J14
William Ure Pl. (Bishop.) G64	11	Y5
Williamson Pl., John. PA5	44	E15
Williamson St. G31	53	Z14
Williamson St., Clyde. G81	5	L6
Williamwood Dr. G44	63	U19
Williamwood Pk. G44	63	U19
Williamwood Pk. W. G44	63	U19
Willock Pl. G20	21	U8
Willoughby Dr. G13	19	R9
Willoughby La. G13	19	R9
Willoughby Dr.		
Willow Av. (Bishop.) G64	23	Y8
Willow Av. (Lenzie) G66	13	CC5
Willow Av. (Elder.), John. PA5	44	F15
Hillview Rd.		
Willow Dr., John. PA5	43	D15
Willow La. G32	54	BB15
Willow Pl., John. PA5	44	E15
Willow St. G13	19	R8
Willowbank Cres. G3	35	U11
Willowbank St. G3	35	U11
Willowdale Cres. (Bail.) G69	56	EE14
Willowdale Gdns. (Bail.) G69	56	EE14
Willowford Rd. G53	60	N18
Wilmot Rd. G13	19	Q9
Wilson Av. (Linw.), Pais. PA3	28	E13
Wilson St. G1	36	W12
Wilson St., Pais. PA1	46	J14
William St.		
Wilson St., Renf. PA4	17	M10

Name	Page	Grid
Wilsons Pl., Pais. PA1	46	K14
Seedhill		
Wilton Cres. G20	21	U10
Wilton Cres. La. G20	21	U10
Wilton Cres.		
Wilton Dr. G20	21	U10
Wilton Gdns. G20	21	U10
Wilton Mans. G20	21	U10
Wilton St.		
Wilton St. G20	21	U10
Wiltonburn Path G53	60	P18
Wiltonburn Rd. G53	60	P18
Wilverton Rd. G13	19	R8
Winchester Dr. G12	20	S9
Windhill Pl. G43	62	T17
Windhill Rd.		
Windhill Rd. G43	62	S17
Windlaw Ct. G45	64	W19
Windlaw Gdns. G44	63	U18
Windlaw Pk. Gdns. G44	63	U18
Windlaw Rd. G45	64	W19
Windlaw Rd. (Clark.) G76	64	W19
Windmill Cres. G43	62	S17
Windmill Pl. G43	62	T17
Windhill Rd.		
Windsor Cres., Clyde. G81	5	L6
Windsor Cres. (Elder.), John. PA5	44	E15
Windsor Cres., Pais. PA1	31	L13
Windsor Path (Bail.) G69	41	GG13
Park Rd.		
Windsor Rd., Renf. PA4	31	M11
Windsor St. G20	35	V11
Windsor St. G32	39	CC13
Windsor Ter. G20	35	V11
Windsor Wk. (Udd.) G71	57	HH16
Windyedge Cres. G13	19	Q9
Windyedge Pl. G13	19	Q9
Wingfield Gdns. (Both.) G71	69	HH19
Blairston Av.		
Winifred St. G33	23	Z10
Winning Ct. (Blan.) G72	69	GG19
Ness Dr.		
Winning Row G31	38	AA13
Winton Av. (Giff.) G46	62	T19
Winton Dr. G12	20	T9
Winton Gdns. (Udd.) G71	57	GG16
Winton La. G12	20	T9
Wirran Pl. G13	18	N8
Wishart St. G31	36	X12
Wisner Ct. (Thorn.) G46	61	R18
Wiston St. (Camb.) G72	67	DD17
Woddrop St. G40	53	Y15
Wolseley St. G5	52	W14
Wood Fm. Rd. (Thorn.) G46	62	S19
Wood La. (Bishop.) G64	23	Y8
Wood Quad., Clyde. G81	18	N8
Wood St. G31	37	Y12
Wood St., Pais. PA2	47	L14
Woodbank Cres., John. PA5	43	D15
Woodburn Rd. G43	62	T17
Woodburn Way (Cumb.) G68	70	MM3
Woodcroft Av. G11	19	R10
Woodcroft Ter. G11	19	R10
Crow Rd.		
Woodend (Giff.) G46	62	S19
Milverton Rd.		
Woodend Ct. G32	55	DD15
Woodend Dr. G13	19	R9
Woodend Dr., Pais. PA1	47	M14
Woodend Gdns. G32	55	DD15
Woodend La. G13	19	R9
Woodend Dr.		
Woodend Pl. (Elder.), John. PA5	44	E15
Malloch Cres.		
Woodend Rd. G32	55	CC15
Woodend Rd. (Ruther.) G73	65	Y18
Woodfield Av. (Bishop.) G64	11	Y7
Woodfoot Path G53	60	P18
Woodfoot Pl. G53	60	P18
Woodfoot Quad. G53	60	P18
Woodfoot Rd. G53	60	P18
Woodford Pl. (Linw.), Pais. PA3	28	E13
Woodford St. G41	51	U16
Woodgreen Av. G44	64	W17
Woodhall St. G40	53	Y15
Woodhead Av. (Both.) G71	69	HH19
Old Bothwell Rd.		
Woodhead Cres. (Udd.) G71	57	GG16
Woodhead Path G53	60	P17
Woodhead Rd. G53	60	N17
Woodhead Rd. (Chry.) G69	26	EE9
Woodhead Ter. (Chry.) G69	26	EE8
Woodhill Gro. (Bishop.) G64	23	Z8
Woodhill Rd.		
Woodhill Rd. G21	23	Y9
Woodhill Rd. (Bishop.) G64	11	Y7
Woodholm Av. G44	64	W17
Woodhouse St. G13	19	R8
Woodilee Cotts. (Kirk.) G66	13	DD5
Woodilee Rd. (Kirk.) G66	13	DD5
Woodland Av., Pais. PA2	46	K16
Woodland Cres. (Camb.) G72	66	BB18
Woodland Vw. (Cumb.) G67	71	PP2
Braehead Rd.		
Woodland Way (Cumb.) G67	71	PP2
Woodlands Av. (Gart.) G69	27	GG8
Woodlands Av. (Both.) G71	69	HH18
Woodlands Ct. (Thorn.) G46	61	R19
Woodlands Rd.		
Woodlands Cres. (Thorn.) G46	61	R18
Woodlands Cres. (Both.) G71	69	HH18
Woodlands Cres., John. PA5	43	D15
Woodlands Dr. G4	35	U11
Woodlands Gdns. (Both.) G71	69	GG18
Woodlands Gate G3	35	U11
Woodlands Gate (Thorn.) G46	61	R18
Woodlands Pk. (Thorn.) G46	61	R19
Woodlands Rd. G3	35	U11
Woodlands Rd. (Thorn.) G46	61	R19
Woodlands Ter. G3	35	U11
Woodlands Ter. (Both.) G71	69	HH18
Woodlea Dr. (Giff.) G46	62	T18
Woodlinn Av. G44	63	V17
Woodneuk Rd. G53	60	P17
Woodneuk Rd. (Gart.) G69	27	GG9
Woodneuk Rd. (Gart.) G69	27	GG9
Woodrow Circ. G41	50	T14
Woodrow Pl. G41	50	T14
Maxwell St.		
Woodrow Rd. G41	50	T14
Woods La., Renf. PA4	17	M10
Woodside Av. (Thorn.) G46	62	S18
Woodside Av. (Lenzie) G66	13	CC5
Woodside Av. (Ruther.) G73	53	Z16
Woodside Cres. G3	35	U11
Woodside Cres. (Barr.) G78	59	M19
Woodside Cres., Pais. PA1	46	J14
William St.		
Woodside Gro. (Ruther.) G73	53	Z16
Woodside Pl. G3	35	U11
Woodside Pl. La. G3	35	U11
Elderslie St.		
Woodside Rd. G20	21	U10
Woodside Ter. G3	35	U11
Woodside Ter. (Bishop.) G64	10	W6
Woodside Ter. La. G3	35	U11
Woodlands Rd.		
Woodstock Av. G41	50	T15
Woodstock Av., Pais. PA2	45	G16
Woodvale Av. (Bears.) G61	8	S7
Woodvale Dr., Pais. PA3	29	H13
Woodville Pk. G51	34	S13
Woodville St.		
Woodville St. G51	34	S13
Wordsworth Way (Both.) G71	69	HH18
Works Av. (Camb.) G72	67	DD17
Wraes Av. (Barr.) G78	59	M18
Wraes Vw. (Barr.) G78	58	K19
Wren Pl., John. PA5	43	C16
Wright Av. (Barr.) G78	59	L19
Wright St., Renf. PA4	31	L11
Wrightlands Cres., Ersk. PA8	16	K8
Wykeham Pl. G13	19	Q9
Wykeham Rd. G13	19	Q9
Wynd, The (Cumb.) G67	71	PP1
Wyndford Dr. G20	20	T9
Wyndford Pl. G20	20	T9
Wyndford Rd.		
Wyndford Rd. G20	20	T9
Wyndham Ct. G12	20	T10
Wyndham St.		
Wyndham St. G12	20	T10
Wynford Ter. (Udd.) G71	57	HH16
Myrtle Rd.		
Wyper Pl. G40	37	Y13
Gallowgate		
Wyvil Av. G13	7	R7
Wyvis Av. G13	18	N8
Wyvis Pl. G13	18	N8
Wyvis Quad. G13	18	N8

Y

Name	Page	Grid
Yair Dr. G52	32	P13
Yarrow Ct. (Camb.) G72	67	DD17
Yarrow Gdns. G20	21	U10
Yarrow Gdns. La. G20	21	U10
Yarrow Gdns.		
Yarrow Rd. (Bishop.) G64	11	Y6
Yate St. G31	37	Y13
Yetholm St. G14	18	N9
Yew Dr. G21	23	Y10
Foresthall Dr.		
Yew Pl., John. PA5	44	E15
Yoker Ferry Rd. G14	18	N9
Yoker Mill Gdns. G13	18	N8
Yoker Mill Rd. G13	18	N8
Yokerburn Pl. G13	18	N8
Yoker Mill Gdns.		
Yokerburn Ter., Clyde. G81	17	M8
York Dr. (Ruther.) G73	65	Z17
York La. G2	35	V12
York St.		
York St. G2	35	V13
York St., Clyde. G81	5	M7
York Way, Renf. PA4	31	M11
Yorkhill La. G3	34	T12
Yorkhill St.		
Yorkhill Par. G3	34	T11
Yorkhill Quay G3	34	S12
Yorkhill St. G3	34	T12
Young Pl. (Udd.) G71	57	HH16
Young St., Clyde. G81	5	L6
Young Ter. G21	23	Y10

Z

Name	Page	Grid
Zambesi Dr. (Blan.) G72	68	FF19
Zena Cres. G33	23	Z10
Zena Pl. G33	23	Z10
Zena St. G33	23	Z10
Zetland Rd. G52	32	N12